CW01020346

THE CONSTITUTIO
COMMONWEAᴌᴛᴛ ᴄᴀᴋɪᴅᴅᴇᴀɴ

The Commonwealth Caribbean comprises a group of countries (mainly islands) lying in an arc between Florida in the north and Venezuela in the south. Varying widely in terms of their size, population, ethnic composition and economic wealth, these countries are, nevertheless, linked by their shared experience of colonial rule under the British Empire and their decision, upon attaining independence, to adopt a constitutional system of government based on the so-called 'Westminster model'.

Since independence these countries have, in the main, enjoyed a sustained period of relative political stability, which is in marked contrast to the experience of former British colonies in Africa and Asia. This book seeks to explore how much of this is due to their constitutional arrangements by examining the constitutional systems of these countries in their context and questioning how well the Westminster model of democracy has successfully adapted to its transplantation to the Commonwealth Caribbean.

While taking due account of the region's colonial past and its imprint on postcolonial constitutionalism, the book also considers notable developments that have occurred since independence. These include the transformation of Guyana from a parliamentary democracy to a Cooperative Republic with an executive president; the creation of a Caribbean Single Market and Economy and its implications for national sovereignty; and the replacement of the Judicial Committee of the Privy Council by the Caribbean Court of Justice as the final court of appeal for a number of countries in the region. The book also addresses the resurgence of interest in constitutional reform across the region in the last two decades, which has culminated in demands for radical reforms of the Westminster model of government and the severance of all remaining links with colonial rule.

Constitutional Systems of the World
General Editors: Peter Leyland and Andrew Harding
Associate Editors: Benjamin L Berger and Grégoire Webber

In the era of globalisation, issues of constitutional law and good governance are being seen increasingly as vital issues in all types of society. Since the end of the Cold War, there have been dramatic developments in democratic and legal reform, and post-conflict societies are also in the throes of reconstructing their governance systems. Even societies already firmly based on constitutional governance and the rule of law have undergone constitutional change and experimentation with new forms of governance; and their constitutional systems are increasingly subjected to comparative analysis and transplantation. Constitutional texts for practically every country in the world are now easily available on the internet. However, texts which enable one to understand the true context, purposes, interpretation and incidents of a constitutional system are much harder to locate, and are often extremely detailed and descriptive. This series seeks to provide scholars and students with accessible introductions to the constitutional systems of the world, supplying both a road map for the novice and, at the same time, a deeper understanding of the key historical, political and legal events which have shaped the constitutional landscape of each country. Each book in this series deals with a single country, or a group of countries with a common constitutional history, and each author is an expert in their field.

Published volumes

The Constitution of the United Kingdom; The Constitution of the United States; The Constitution of Vietnam; The Constitution of South Africa; The Constitution of Japan; The Constitution of Germany; The Constitution of Finland; The Constitution of Australia; The Constitution of the Republic of Austria; The Constitution of the Russian Federation; The Constitutional System of Thailand; The Constitution of Malaysia; The Constitution of China; The Constitution of Indonesia; The Constitution of France; The Constitution of Spain; The Constitution of Mexico

Link to series website
http://www.hartpub.co.uk/series/csw

The Constitutional Systems of the Commonwealth Caribbean

A Contextual Analysis

Derek O'Brien

·HART·
PUBLISHING
OXFORD AND PORTLAND, OREGON
2014

Published in the United Kingdom by Hart Publishing Ltd
16C Worcester Place, Oxford, OX1 2JW
Telephone: +44 (0)1865 517530
Fax: +44 (0)1865 510710
E-mail: mail@hartpub.co.uk
Website: http://www.hartpub.co.uk

Published in North America (US and Canada) by
Hart Publishing
c/o International Specialized Book Services
920 NE 58th Avenue, Suite 300
Portland, OR 97213-3786
USA
Tel: +1 503 287 3093 or toll-free: (1) 800 944 6190
Fax: +1 503 280 8832
E-mail: orders@isbs.com
Website: http://www.isbs.com

© Derek O'Brien 2014

Derek O'Brien has asserted his right under the Copyright, Designs and
Patents Act 1988, to be identified as the author of this work.

Hart Publishing is an imprint of Bloomsbury Publishing plc.

All rights reserved. No part of this publication may be reproduced, stored in a
retrieval system, or transmitted, in any form or by any means, without the
prior permission of Hart Publishing, or as expressly permitted by law or
under the terms agreed with the appropriate reprographic rights
organisation. Enquiries concerning reproduction which may
not be covered by the above should be addressed to
Hart Publishing Ltd at the address above.

British Library Cataloguing in Publication Data
Data Available

ISBN: 978-1-84946-152-8

Typeset by Compuscript Ltd, Shannon
Printed and bound in Great Britain by
CPI Group UK (Ltd), CR0 4YY

Preface

Thanks are owed to a number of people who helped, either directly or indirectly, with the writing of this book. First, to the series editors, Andrew Harding and Peter Leyland, without whose support and encouragement the book would never have got out of the starting blocks. Their keen but always constructive criticism of the early chapters was immensely valuable to me. Second, to the associate editor of the series, Ben Berger, who made a number of very helpful comments on the final draft. Third, to my colleagues at the School of Law at Oxford Brookes University—Professor Peter Edge, Professor Meryll Dean and Professor Lucy Vickers—all of whom were immensely supportive of this project. Fourth, to those who read and commented on various draft chapters along the way, including my friend and colleague since my days at the Cayman Islands Law School, Simon Cooper, who commented on chapter one; Alecia Johns, who commented on chapter five; Nadia Bernaz, who commented on chapter six; David Berry, who commented on chapter seven; and finally, Se-shauna Wheatle, with whom I worked on the article on the Jamaica Charter of Rights and Freedoms on which I have drawn in chapter eight.

Though they did not read or comment on any of the chapters, I also owe an enormous debt of gratitude to a number of Caribbean scholars on whose work I have drawn in writing this book. They include in no particular order: Selwyn Ryan, Trevor Munroe, Lloyd Barnett, Hamid Ghany, Rose-Marie Antoine, Cynthia Barrow-Giles and Simeon McIntosh who was the original source of inspiration for this book, but who sadly passed away prior to its publication.

The last word of thanks must, however, go to my long suffering wife, Lesley, and my lovely daughter, Beth, both of whom are completely oblivious to Commonwealth Caribbean constitutional law and so allowed me always to keep a proper sense of perspective when writing this book.

Contents

7. THE CONSTITUIONAL IMPLICATIONS
OF REGIONAL INTEGRATION 241

Table of Cases

Table of Legislation

Commonwealth Caribbean (West Indies)

xxviii   *Table of Legislation*

Introduction

———»·•·«———

THE INDEPENDENT COUNTRIES of the Commonwealth Caribbean comprise a group of islands and archipelagos— Antigua and Barbuda (henceforth abbreviated for reasons of space to Antigua), the Bahamas, Belize, Dominica, Grenada, Jamaica, Saint Christopher and Nevis (henceforth St Kitts), Saint Lucia (henceforth St Lucia), Saint Vincent and the Grenadines (henceforth St Vincent) and Trinidad and Tobago (henceforth Trinidad)—which form a wide arc between Florida in the north and Venezuela in the south.[1] To this group must be added the mainland countries of Belize in Central America and Guyana in South America. These countries vary enormously in terms of their size, their populations, their ethnic composition and their economic wealth. In terms of sheer land mass, Guyana is by far the largest country in the region, with a land area of 214,970 square kilometres, which places it eighty-third in the world. The next largest is Belize, with a land area of 22,966 square kilometres. These countries apart, the remaining countries in the region are among the smallest in the world, many with land areas of less than 500 square kilometres—Barbados, Grenada, St Kitts and St Vincent. Land area does not, however, in all cases equate either to population or wealth. Thus, the most populous country in the region by far is Jamaica with a population of 2,706,000, which is more than double that of the second most populous, Trinidad, which has a population of 1,324,699, though some of the smaller islands—Antigua, Dominica, Grenada, St Kitts and St Vincent—do have correspondingly small populations, which hover around 100,000 or less. Measured in terms of Gross Domestic Product (GDP) per capita the Bahamas, which is by no means the

---

[1] There are also a number of British Overseas Territories located in the Caribbean—Virgin Islands, Turks and Caicos, Cayman Islands, Montserrat and Anguilla—but they are not the subject of this book.

largest country in the region, is by far the wealthiest, with a GDP per capita figure of nearly US$22,000, which is comparable to that of a number of European countries.[2] On the other hand, Belize, Guyana and Jamaica, with GDP per capita figures of US$4218, US$2920 and US$4969 respectively, are among some of the poorest countries in the Western hemisphere. Though most of the countries are racially very homogenous, there is a small but significant Chinese community in Jamaica, and both Guyana and Trinidad are ethnically very divided with large Afro-Caribbean and Indo-Caribbean populations.[3]

Their diversity notwithstanding, what links these countries, what distinguishes them from their neighbours in the wider Caribbean region and what makes a book like this possible at all, is their shared experience of colonial rule under the British Empire. Not only are their legal systems based predominantly on the English common law, but upon attaining independence in the 1960s, 1970s and 1980s[4] each country also adopted a constitution (henceforth referred to as the 'Independence Constitution') which incorporated the so-called 'Westminster model' of government, albeit within a context in which the Constitution is supreme and in which certain fundamental rights and freedoms are guaranteed by the Constitution. These Independence Constitutions, which form the core of the subject-matter of this book, have been much criticised by Commonwealth Caribbean scholars for being neither original, in the sense that they replicate to a large extent the system of government introduced by the former colonial power prior to independence; nor autochthonous, in the sense that they came into existence, not as the result of an act of a local constituent assembly established for the purpose of ratifying a new constitution, but by virtue of an Act of the imperial Parliament in Westminster.[5]

---

[2] Such as Greece, Portugal and Slovenia. Figures produced by the World Bank.

[3] See S Ryan, *Race and Nationalism in Trinidad and Tobago: A Study of Decolonisation in a Multi-Racial Society* (Toronto, University of Toronto Press, 1973).

[4] Jamaica and Trinidad and Tobago attained independence in 1962. They were followed by Barbados and Guyana in 1966; the Bahamas in 1973; Grenada in 1974; Dominica in 1978; St Lucia and St Vincent and the Grenadines in 1979; Belize and Antigua and Barbuda in 1981; and finally St Kitts and Nevis in 1983.

[5] Eg, Jamaica Independence Act 1962. See further S McIntosh, *Caribbean Constitutional Reform: Rethinking the West Indian Polity* (Kingston, Jamaica, Caribbean Law Publishing Company, 2002) 294.

Undoubtedly, there is some force in these criticisms and the influence of the particularly British version of the Westminster model of government incorporated within the Independence Constitutions can be seen on a number of different levels. It is there, for example, in the office of the Governor General, serving as the Queen's representative, and exercising similar prerogative powers, in all the countries in the region which embarked upon independence as constitutional monarchies; the exception being Dominica, which embarked upon independence as a republic. It is there in the decision by all the countries in the region, with the exception of Guyana (for reasons considered in chapter three), to continue with a 'first past the post' electoral system even though this was, arguably, unsuited to countries with very small populations, or to a country such as Trinidad where politics is divided along racial lines. The British influence is also there in those countries which retained a bicameral legislature, which included a nominated second chamber—a much criticised feature of the old colonial legislatures. And, finally, it is there, albeit indirectly, in the decisions of all countries in the region to vest ultimate legal sovereignty in the Judicial Committee of the Privy Council (JCPC) based in London which, until relatively recently, has served as the final court of appeal for all the independent countries in the region, with the exception of Guyana, which abolished the right of appeal to the JCPC when it became a republic in 1970.

Set against this, however, it could be argued that the lack of originality of the Independence Constitutions was not due to any lack of vision or imagination on the part of the region's political leaders at the time of independence, but was instead the result of pure political pragmatism. As Norman Manley, Premier of Jamaica at the time its Independence Constitution was being negotiated explained:

> I make no apology for the fact that we did not attempt to embark upon any original or novel exercise for constitution-building. We had a system which we understood; we had been operating it for many years with sense. It's a system which has endured in other countries for generations successfully. It is a system which is consistent with the sort of ideals we have in this country, and it was not difficult to decide that we would follow that familiar system with those modifications which we thought the circumstances of Independence deserved.[6]

[6] Quoted by LG Barnett, *The Constitutional Law of Jamaica* (Oxford, Oxford University Press, 1977) 25.

It could also be argued that if the definition of autochthony is extended to include a constitution which is based on the informed choice of the people exercised through their elected representatives, then the Independence Constitutions largely satisfy such a definition. They may also have acquired autochthonous status by virtue of the sheer force of their longevity, having now endured in some cases for more than 50 years. During this period, the fundamental institutions and principles of the Westminster model—parliamentary democracy, Cabinet government, an independent public service, the rule of law and separation of powers, all of which are embodied in the Independence Constitutions—have come to be widely accepted across the region, with the exception of Guyana, which remains very much a special case. Some scholars even argue that the decision to cleave to the Westminster model of government has done much to underpin the relative political stability which the region has enjoyed since independence.[7] Certainly, if measured in terms of the holding of regular free and fair elections, resulting in the peaceful transition of power from one government to another, Britain's former colonies in the Caribbean could be said to have exhibited a capacity to sustain liberal democracy which is far superior to that exhibited by former British colonies in Africa and Asia, for example, and to that of the former colonies of other major powers.[8]

It would be wrong, however, to characterise the Commonwealth Caribbean as a paragon of postcolonial political stability, for it is possible—even if we exclude Guyana during its experiment with socialism under Forbes Burnham—to point to several instances where liberal democratic government has been threatened, and even one instance where it has been completely overthrown. In Trinidad, for example, the government came perilously close to being overthrown by the Black Power Revolution of 1970;[9] and, in 1990, there was a further attempted coup when members of the Jamaat al Muslimeen—a sect of Afro-Trinidadian Muslims—seized, and held hostage at gunpoint, the

---

[7] A Payne, 'Westminster Adapted: The Political Order of the Commonwealth Caribbean' in JI Dominguez, RA Pastor and D Worrell (eds), *Democracy in the Caribbean* (Baltimore, John Hopkins University Press, 1993) 57.

[8] JI Dominguez, 'The Caribbean Question: Why has Liberal Democracy (Surprisingly) Flourished?' in Dominguez, Pastor and Worrell (eds), *Democracy in the Caribbean*, above (n 7).

[9] S Ryan, *The Black Power Revolution of 1970: A Retrospective* (St Augustine, Trinidad, ISER, University of the West Indies Press, 1995).

Prime Minister, six other Cabinet ministers and several other MPs in the country's Parliament building. This rebellion was only brought to an end after the Acting President granted an amnesty to the rebels pursuant to section 87(1) of the Constitution.[10] In Dominica, too, democratic government has come under threat when, following independence in 1978, there was an almost immediate breakdown of law and order, as exemplified by the disarmament of the Dominica Defence Force on the discovery that its weapons were being exchanged with members of the local Rastafarian community, known as the 'Dreads', in return for marijuana. As a result of this disorder, both the President and the first Prime Minister, Patrick John, were obliged to flee the country. In 1981, the new Prime Minister, Eugenia Charles, announced that she had received information of a plot to overthrow her government and it later emerged that the plot involved Ku Klux Klan activists and a group of mercenaries from the United States who were to be paid a large sum of money in return for restoring the former Prime Minister, Patrick John, to office.[11] Elections in a number of countries, including Guyana, Trinidad and Jamaica have also been marred by serious violence: in Jamaica alone there were 800 murders attributed to political violence in 1980, the year of the general election. But without doubt the most serious and sustained threat to democratic government was the revolution in Grenada, in 1979, when the New Jewel Movement, led by Maurice Bishop, used the Prime Minister's temporary absence from the island to seize power and establish a People's Revolutionary Government (PRG), which survived until 1983 when its leader was executed by members of the People's Revolutionary Army (PRA) and a Revolutionary Military Council, led by General Austin, the head of the PRA, succeeded to power. The latter's period in power was, however, to be very short lived: within a matter of days it was, in its turn, overthrown by an invasion force led by US marines, supported by members of the armed forces of Jamaica and Barbados, and democratic government was eventually restored to the island.[12]

---

[10] F Phillips, *Commonwealth Caribbean Constitutional Law* (London, Cavendish Publishing, 2002) 173.

[11] Ibid, 199–206.

[12] A Payne, P Sutton and T Thorndike, *Grenada: Revolution and Invasion* (New York, St Martin's Press, 1984).

Though it could be argued that these are rather extreme and somewhat isolated examples that do not ultimately undermine the long term political stability in the region that is associated with the Westminster model, there has nevertheless been a pervasive undercurrent of dissatisfaction with the Westminster model throughout the region, which is regarded by many Commonwealth Caribbean scholars as being entirely unsuited to the task of promoting representative and responsible government. Thus, it is argued that the tendency of the Westminster model to concentrate power in the executive and, within the executive, in the office of the Prime Minister, has led to an autocratic style of government. It is further argued that local legislatures, because they are relatively small and dominated by government ministers, are weak and ineffectual, unable to provide the check upon executive power that is, in theory at least, such a crucial element of the Westminster model. Finally, it is argued that the first past the post electoral system which, with the exception of Guyana is the electoral system of choice across the region, has encouraged a 'winner takes all' political culture, and this has led in turn to the corruption of public life in general and the emergence of 'clientilism' in a number of countries.[13]

This book seeks to contribute to this ongoing discourse by offering a contextual approach to the study of the constitutional systems of the Commonwealth Caribbean. This will not only entail taking due account of the region's colonial past and the disfiguring effect of slavery upon its constitutional development, but will also entail recognising the challenges to post-independence constitutionalism that the region has faced; in particular, the small size of many countries in the region, their relative poverty, their economic vulnerability and the ethnic tensions that continue to pervade countries such as Guyana and Trinidad.

I will begin, in chapter one, by providing an overview of the region's constitutional history; charting the effect of the sugar industry and the slave trade upon the transition from the original 'representative system' of government, established when the first islands were settled by the British in the mid-seventeenth century, to the system of 'Crown Colony rule' government under which most of the countries in the region were

---

[13] S Ryan, *Winner Takes All: The Westminster Experience in the Caribbean* (St Augustine, Trinidad, ISER, University of the West Indies Press, 1999) 317.

governed during the twentieth century, up until independence in the 1960s, 1970s and 1980s.

In the chapters that follow I will explore the constitutional framework embodied in the Independence Constitutions. Thus, in chapter two, I will examine the constitutional role and functions of the head of state who, in most countries, is a Governor General, appointed by the reigning British monarch to serve as their representative in the country concerned. I will also examine the debate that continues to rage across the region about replacing the British monarch with a president appointed locally, and consider the constitutional impact that has occurred in countries such as Dominica and Trinidad, which have abandoned constitutional monarchy in favour of republicanism.

In chapter three, I will examine the constitutional framework that surrounds the management, conduct and financing of elections. I will also examine the operation of the first fast the post electoral system, which is the electoral system of choice for all the countries in the region, with the exception of Guyana, but which has been associated with a number of problems, not the least of which is its tendency to exaggerate the popularity of the winning party, resulting in what have been characterised as 'elective dictatorships' which encourage clientilism.

In chapter four, I will examine the constitutional framework within which Cabinet government functions and the mechanisms that exist for ensuring that the government is held politically accountable. I will also look at the constitutional framework surrounding the relationship between the government and the public service, and reflect upon how this relationship has been affected by the region's changing political, social and economic environment.

In chapter five, I will examine the structure and internal characteristics of the region's parliaments and the ways in which the former determine the latter's relationship with the other key components of the Westminster model of governance: the executive and the judiciary. This examination will encompass the rules governing qualification for membership of Parliament; the roles played by the Leader of the Opposition and the Speaker; the privileges and immunities afforded to MPs; and the regulation of members' financial interests.

In chapter six, I will examine the role of the courts in upholding the principle of constitutionalism by ensuring that the executive and the legislature do not exceed the limitations imposed upon each by the Constitution. This will necessarily entail an examination of the institutional arrangements in place at the national and sub-regional levels for securing judicial independence and the extent to which these institutional arrangements have been undermined by the wider political culture in the region. I will also examine the efforts of the region's political leaders to reclaim ultimate legal sovereignty by substituting the Caribbean Court of Justice (CCJ) in place of the JCPC as the final appellate court for the region. I will then proceed to consider the juridical basis for the courts' powers of constitutional review and the principles of constitutional interpretation that have been developed by the courts and how these have been shaped by a final appellate court—the JCPC—which is geographically and culturally remote from the region.

In chapter seven, I will examine regional efforts through organisations such as the Caribbean Community and Common Market (CARICOM) and the Organisation of Eastern Caribbean States (OECS) to respond to the pressures of globalisation and the erosion of trade preferences for the region's exports by establishing a Caribbean Single Market and Economy (CSME) and an Eastern Caribbean Single Market and Economy (ECSME) respectively. I will be concerned, in particular, to explore the constitutional implications for national sovereignty that arise from the vesting of the CCJ and the Eastern Caribbean Court of Appeal (ECCA) with a supervisory jurisdiction over the interpretation and application of the treaties governing the CSME and ECSME respectively, which are similar in many ways to those that had to be confronted by Britain upon its accession to the European Community (as it was then known).

In conclusion, I will explore the debate surrounding post-independence constitutional reform in the region and examine the reasons why, despite its manifest deficiencies, there have been, Guyana apart, relatively few tangible reforms to the Westminster model of government in the 50 years since independence.

1

Constitutional History

————⟫•◦⟪————

Background – Colonial Government – Independence – Conclusion

PART I: BACKGROUND

CONSTITUTIONAL DEVELOPMENT DOES not take place in a vacuum, but is shaped by the surrounding economic, social and political environment. The Commonwealth Caribbean is no exception in this regard and no attempt to provide an account of its constitutional history would be complete without reference to the impact of the sugar industry and the system of slavery upon which that industry depended. Together, these had a profound impact in shaping the region's constitutional destiny as the switch from tobacco and cotton to the production of sugar in the mid-seventeenth century—initially in Barbados, but subsequently extending to most, though not all the other colonies in the region—transformed both the region's economic fortunes and its demographics.[1] By the end of the eighteenth century, the region had become the 'hub of the Empire', with four-fifths of the income derived from Britain's overseas colonies emanating from these so-called 'sugar colonies'.[2] At the same time, the sugar industry, with its demands for large plantations and a constant supply of fresh slaves, had radically altered the composition of the local population, which at the

---

[1] See, G Heuman, 'From Slavery to Freedom' in PD Morgan and S Hawkins (eds), *Black Experience and the Empire* (Oxford, Oxford University Press, 2004) 142.

[2] See HMcD Beckles, 'The "Hub of Empire": The Caribbean and Britain in the Seventeenth Century' in N Canny (ed), *The Origins of Empire* (Oxford, Oxford University Press, 1998) 218.

outset was mainly Anglo-Saxon, made up of the original settlers from England, and indentured labourers recruited from England, Scotland and Ireland, to make up for the absence of an indigenous population that could be put to work, living on small farms and engaged in a mixed agricultural economy.[3] Following the introduction of sugar in the mid-seventeenth century, however, the composition of this population changed completely as large parts of the region were given over to a system of large sugar plantations, worked by very large numbers of slaves, transported mainly from West Africa, under the direction of a few white men. By 1823, the ratio of blacks to whites in British Guiana, for example, was 20:1, while in Jamaica it was 10:1.[4] This pattern was repeated across the region and in some cases the imbalance was even greater.[5] This demographic was altered still further with the emancipation of slaves in 1834, as the subsequent shortage of labour resulted in large numbers of indentured workers being imported, mainly from India, in the second half of the nineteenth century. During this period over 500,000 indentured labourers arrived in the Caribbean from India. Of this number 239,000 went to British Guiana (now Guyana) and some 150,000 to Trinidad, thus permanently altering the racial structure of two of the largest colonies in the region.[6]

As we will see, this bifurcation of society between rich white planters, on the one hand, and slaves, and later indentured labourers, on the other, brought about by the growth of the sugar industry, is important in explaining why the 'representative system' of government—which was originally established in the settled colonies of St Kitts, Barbados, Nevis, Antigua, the Bahamas and Jamaica, before being extended to the ceded colonies of Grenada, Dominica, St Vincent and Tobago—failed to evolve into 'responsible' government, as occurred in the so-called 'white' Dominions of Australia, South Africa and Canada. As will be demonstrated later, this bifurcation is also important in explaining why the representative system of government was eventually abandoned in all these colonies, with the exception of Barbados and the Bahamas, and replaced by 'Crown Colony rule' in the latter part of the nineteenth century.

[3] Ibid, 222.
[4] Heuman, above (n 1) 141.
[5] See C Harris, 'The Constitutional History of the Windwards' (1960) 6(2) and 6(3) *Caribbean Quarterly* (special issue: The Federal Principle) 160, 163.
[6] Heuman, above (n 1) 157.

PART II: COLONIAL GOVERNMENT

A. THE 'REPRESENTATIVE SYSTEM'

The 'representative system' of government was composed of three branches: a Governor, representing the Crown, a Council, and a legislative Assembly (the Assembly). The head of this system was the Governor who had the power of granting or withholding their assent to any Bills which might be passed by the Assembly. The Council, which varied in size with the size of the colony, ranging from half a dozen in the small islands to 18 or 20 in the larger islands, was composed of 'the most substantial men in the colony',[7] appointed by the King on the recommendation of the Governor. The chief qualifications for member ship were the possession of a good estate and freedom from debt. Being under the control of the Governor, the Council could usually be relied upon to support the Governor against the Assembly. The latter, as a result of the property qualifications for both members and voters, was comprised almost exclusively of white freeholders, all of them elected by white freeholders: white servants, those of mixed race and slaves being excluded from the franchise.[8]

Though it was originally intended that the Assembly would play a minor part in government, being kept under control by the Governor and Council and with no right to meddle in executive matters, the reality was somewhat different. Since no proposal for the expenditure of public money could be made except in the Assembly, the latter possessed a powerful weapon which it was not afraid to use against the former whenever the Governor sought to implement a policy which was deemed not to be compatible with the interests of its members. This placed the Governor in a very difficult situation, particularly where sources of Crown revenue other than tax (such as quit rents, land sales, forfeitures and escheats) were limited. As the representative of the Crown and head of the local executive Governors were continually required to choose between ignoring instructions from the Colonial Office or risk falling out with the Assembly, the support of

---

[7] H Wrong, *Government of the West Indies* (Oxford, Clarendon Press, 1923) 40.

[8] GK Lewis, *The Growth of the Modern West Indies* (Kingston, Jamaica, Ian Randle Publishers, 2004) 102.

which Governors depended upon for the supply of the funds necessary for carrying out their instructions.[9] The difficulty of their situation was made even worse by the fact that there was no system for resolving the frequent conflicts that arose between the Governor and the Assembly, since the Governor was not responsible to the Assembly and neither could control the other. As a result, Assemblies rarely lasted for a full term.[10] In Jamaica, for example, the tensions between the Governor and the Assembly resulted in the latter continually being dissolved for disobedience, and it was not until 1816 that any Jamaican Assembly lasted its full term of seven years.[11] Though the tensions between the Governor and the Assembly may not have been quite as great in the other islands, everywhere 'the machinery of government groaned and grated, and deadlock succeeded deadlock'.[12] It was, however, the issue of slavery that finally demonstrated that the representative system of government was untenable.

The abolition of slavery in 1834 meant that 700,000 former slaves could no longer be regarded as 'property' since they were now 'free' citizens. As a consequence, it was no longer possible to defend the representative system by arguing that colonial Assemblies were 'representative' of the local community, the slave being represented by their master, or that they served as the guardians of the rights of the local community against the interests of the imperial power enforced by the Governor and their Council.[13] The Assemblies had always been representative only of the white planter class, and the powers that they possessed were exercised by and on behalf of a small and self-interested minority of the citizens of each colony.[14] In Jamaica, for example, out of a population of some 450,000 there were only 1457 actual voters; in St Kitts, there were 25 members to be returned and only 166 names

---

[9] Up until 1768 the Governor would have received his instructions from the Board of Trade and Plantations. After 1768, responsibility for the colonies was transferred to the War Office, which was subsequently renamed the War and Colonial Office.

[10] E Wallace, *The British Caribbean: From the Decline of Colonialism to the End of Federation* (Toronto, University of Toronto Press, 1977) 10.

[11] Wrong, above (n 7) 44.

[12] Ibid.

[13] GK Lewis, 'British Colonialism in the West Indies: The Political Legacy' (1967) 7(1) *Caribbean Studies* 3–22.

[14] Wrong above (n 7) 56.

on the electoral register, of whom only 47 actually voted in 1856; and in Tobago, in 1662, two members were elected to the Assembly by the vote of a single illiterate.[15] Unsurprisingly, the members of local Assemblies were, as a result, often completely unsuited to the functions they were required to perform. Describing the situation in St Vincent, in 1854, the Lieutenant Governor at the time observed that, 'there are hardly any persons of education and ability who are able or willing to devote their time to the public service without remuneration'.[16] Whatever their original claims to legitimacy based on their 'representativeness', emancipation meant that the Assemblies, as then constituted, had become an anachronism.[17]

Their parochialism and their record of resistance to and obstruction of any and all proposals for the amelioration of the conditions of the slaves both before and after emancipation did not pass unnoticed in England where a growing body of opinion began to emerge in the course of the nineteenth century, which strongly disapproved of the continued existence of these local Assemblies.[18] This culminated in a devastating critique of these local Assemblies prepared by Henry Taylor of the Colonial Office for the Cabinet, following yet another refusal by the Jamaican Assembly to pass any of the legislation necessary to remove the many anomalies in the status of newly emancipated slaves:

> The West Indian legislatures have neither the will nor the skill to make such laws as you want made; and they cannot be converted on the point of willingness, and they will not be instructed ... [T]he obvious truth is that attempts at a representative system ... must result in an oligarchy. Such the Assembly of Jamaica always has been, now is, and will inevitably continue to be, until the mass of the population shall have been educated and raised in the scale of society.[19]

The Cabinet was not, however, prepared to act on Taylor's conclusion that Assemblies should be abolished by Parliament in all the West Indian colonies, as colonial policy had long been based on the principle that the imperial power would not withdraw representative institutions once granted. Instead, the end of the representative system came

---

[15] Ibid, 70.
[16] Cited by Wrong, above (n 7).
[17] See Harris, above (n 5) 163.
[18] Ibid, 164.
[19] Wrong, above (n 7) 57.

about by the voluntary action of the Jamaican Assembly following the Morant Bay rebellion in Jamaica in 1865. The rebellion, which resulted in the deaths of the Chief Magistrate and 17 other occupants of the court house in Morant Bay, was met by an extremely harsh and violent response by the Governor of Jamaica, George Eyre, during the course of which 586 were put to death, some by sentences of courts martial, and others shot without trial. In addition, 1005 houses were burned and large numbers, including some women, were flogged. Those put to death included Paul Bogle, a Baptist deacon and friend of fellow Baptist, George William Gordon, who served as the chief spokesman in the Assembly for a group of squatters who had settled on Crown land or abandoned estates and who were angered by the requirement that they should pay rent. Gordon was subsequently arrested in Kingston, illegally taken on the Governor's orders to Morant Bay, where he was tried by court martial and hanged on entirely insufficient evidence.[20]

Before he stepped down as Governor, Eyre had succeeded in passing an Act of Indemnity, which indemnified him as Governor of Jamaica and all others acting under his authority in respect of all acts done in order to put an end to the rebellion.[21] However, the rebellion was to have two important and lasting consequences. First, it convinced the British Government of the need for urgent constitutional reform in Jamaica. Second, it alarmed the Jamaican Assembly to such an extent that its members were persuaded to entrust the task of constitutional reform to the British Government. As a result, in June 1866, Crown Colony rule was established in Jamaica by an Order in Council issued by the British Government, and the Assembly was replaced by a nominated Legislative Council, composed of the Governor, six officials who held their seats ex officio and an unspecified number of unofficial members, of whom three were at first appointed. Thus, the Assembly of Jamaica which for the previous two centuries had clung so tenaciously to its rights and privileges ultimately became the author of its own demise.[22]

---

[20] For a detailed account of the 'Jamaica Rebellion' and its aftermath, see *The Cambridge History of the British Empire: Volume II The Growth of the New Empire 1783–1870* (London, Cambridge University Press, 1940) 735–37.

[21] The validity of this indemnity was unsuccessfully challenged in *Phillips v Eyre* (1870–71) LR 6 QB 1.

[22] Wrong, above (n 7) 77.

The example of Jamaica was soon followed in the other settled and ceded colonies, beginning with Antigua, St Kitts and Nevis (which at the time was a separate colony) in 1886, before being extended to Grenada and St Vincent in 1879 and Dominica in 1898. This brought the settled and ceded colonies into line with the conquered colonies of Trinidad, which had been acquired from the Spanish in 1797, and St Lucia, which had finally been captured from the French in 1803, both of which had by this time been governed under Crown Colony rule for almost a century. This had been because unlike the settled colonies, where the principle was applied that that an Englishman carried with him English law and liberties (which included a representative legislature) into any unoccupied country in which he settled, the constitutions of conquered colonies, such as Trinidad and St Lucia, were regarded as being in the gift of the Crown.[23] Though there had, initially, been calls in both countries, upon their surrender to the British, for the establishment of a representative system of government, these had been firmly rejected by the British Government which, based on its experience in the ceded colonies of Grenada, Dominica, St Vincent and Tobago, had concluded that the representative system was unsuited to colonies in which a majority of the voters were not British because of the danger that legislative power could be seized by an alien majority.[24] Furthermore, after its experience of dealing with hostile Assemblies in both the settled and ceded colonies, the British Government wanted to make sure that these newly acquired slave-owning colonies were under the immediate control of the Crown so that it could enforce the 1807 Act abolishing the slave trade.[25] The net result of this was that by the end of the nineteenth century, Jamaica and all the Windward and Leeward islands were governed under the system of Crown Colony rule.

The mainland territories of British Guiana (now Guyana) and British Honduras (now Belize) were also eventually to succumb to Crown Colony rule, though these two colonies had developed along a quite different constitutional path from Britain's other colonies in the region. Thus, in British Guiana, a 'semi-representative' system of government had been inherited from the Dutch when the colony was surrendered to

---

[23] H Jenkyns, *British Rule and Jurisdiction beyond the Seas* (Oxford, Clarendon Press, 1902). Available at: HeinOnline.org.
[24] *The Cambridge History of the British Empire*, above (n 20).
[25] Ibid, 154.

the British in 1803, which remained in place, albeit modified somewhat in the course of the nineteenth century, up until as late as 1928 when it was finally replaced by Crown Colony rule. By contrast, British Honduras had been administered under what has been described as a system of 'Public Meeting Government', since it had been settled in approximately 1728 by a small community bearing allegiance to the British Crown in the midst of territories over which Spanish sovereignty was undisputed.[26] This was a relatively simple system of government, based on a public meeting of the free inhabitants of the settlement together with an elected magistracy of about seven members to administer justice and control finance. This system remained in place, albeit again modified somewhat in the course of the nineteenth century, until Crown Colony rule was finally established in 1880.

As a result of the above changes, virtually the entire region—with the exception of the Bahamas and Barbados which retained representative Assemblies—was governed under a system of Crown Colony rule for the first half of the twentieth century.

B. 'CROWN COLONY RULE'

'Crown Colony rule' was intended to cure the central defect of the old representative system—the failure to locate power as between the executive and the legislature—by ensuring that the executive could always prevail over legislative opposition. Ultimately, however, 'the remedy proved to be as undemocratic as the disease it was supposed to cure'.[27]

Though the component parts differed in different colonies, the common elements of the system were a Governor, an Executive Council and a Legislative Council. The final say on matters affecting the colony always lay with the Governor who was neither accountable nor responsible to the people over whom they governed, but was instead responsible to the Secretary of State for the Colonies. The Governor sat as chairman of the Legislative Council, which was in most cases composed of an equal number of official members (senior civil servants

---

[26] Ibid.
[27] Lewis, *The Growth of the Modern West Indies*, above (n 8) 98.

appointed by the Secretary of State for the Colonies) and nominated unofficial members who were selected by the Governor from among the colonists to represent the interests of the community. In theory this should have made the Legislative Council more representative; in practice Governors tended to select only representatives of the dominant groups in each colony, the planter or merchant class. Moreover, the official members, being British civil servants, were required to support the Crown in the Legislative Council, thereby ensuring that any potential local opposition was neutralised by the official majority. In any event, the Governor could always carry or veto any measure upon which the votes were evenly divided since the Governor had the casting vote. The Governor also presided over the Executive Council, which had a purely advisory role, and was usually comprised of three ex officio members—the Colonial Secretary, the Financial Secretary and the Attorney General, all appointed by the British Government—and two or more non-officials nominated by the Governor and appointed by the Crown. Within the limits of their instructions from London, Governors were, in effect, virtual autocrats.[28]

One of the principal justifications for the introduction of Crown Colony rule was that it offered a better and fairer system of government for the black majority than had been provided by the representative system of government which operated more or less exclusively in the interests of a wealthy white oligarchy. The timing of the introduction of Crown Colony rule into the settled colonies was, however, unfortunate because it came just as a black and brown middle class was beginning to emerge following the abolition of slavery. With the gradual extension of the franchise this group might have had some hope of a voice in government had this not been taken away from them by the closure of the Assemblies.[29] The fact therefore that the Assemblies themselves had voted for Crown Colony rule in order to curtail such a possibility, made the system even less palatable.[30] Almost immediately there were protests in Jamaica, which led to the restoration of nine elected members to the Legislative Council in 1884 (the number was increased from nine to 14 in 1895). In addition, provision was made for six out of the nine elected members to veto any financial proposition, and for

[28] Ibid.
[29] Wallace, above (n 10).
[30] Ibid, 16.

the nine elected members, acting unanimously, to veto any proposition whatever; though in such a case the Governor could always declare a question to be 'of paramount importance to the public interest' thereby overriding the votes of the elected members. Hostility towards Crown Colony rule was not, however, confined to Jamaica and by the end of the nineteenth century it was prevalent across the region; especially in a country such as Trinidad, which had not had a single elected representative in its Legislative Council since it was established in 1831.[31]

Discontent with Crown Colony rule continued to grow throughout the region during the first quarter of the twentieth century with the emergence of figures such as TA Marryshow in Grenada who, in 1914, formed a Representative Government Association, which petitioned the Secretary of State for the Colonies to introduce a small elected element into the island's Legislative Council. Inspired by Marryshow's example, similar Associations were formed in a number of the smaller islands, such as St Vincent and Dominica, which called for an increase in the number of elected members in the Legislative Councils. In Trinidad, Captain Arthur Andrew Cipriani became the President of the Trinidad Workingman's Association, which attacked Crown Colony rule as 'a façade of autocracy' and argued that the British West Indies were just as entitled to dominion status as Canada or Australia. In Jamaica, the People's Political Party, founded by Marcus Garvey, campaigned for self-government; while in Barbados the Democratic League, founded in 1924 by Charles Duncan O'Neale, argued that Barbados deserved 'free institutions and the full flower of democratic development'.[32]

In response to this groundswell of discontent the Under Secretary of State for the Colonies, the Honourable EFL Wood, visited the region for three months between December 1921 and February 1922. While he did not consider that the region was yet ready for full responsible government he did acknowledge that the demand for at least some local representation in government was irresistible. As a result of his report,[33] a small number of elected members were introduced into the Legislative Councils of Dominica, Grenada, St Lucia and St Vincent in 1923 and 1924, and in Trinidad in 1925 seven elected members were

[31] Ibid, 17.
[32] Ibid, 24.
[33] *Report by the Hon EFL Wood, MP, on His Visit to the West Indies and British Guiana, December 1921 to February 1922* (Cmd 1679, 1922).

for the first time introduced as unofficial members into its Legislative Council. Elsewhere in the region, constitutional reforms in Antigua and St Kitts, following the Report of the Closer Union Commission in 1933,[34] provided for the introduction of elected unofficial members of the Legislative Council; and in British Honduras, in 1935, a new constitution provided for five of the seven unofficial members of the Legislative Council to be elected.

These reforms were not, however, sufficient to quell the demand for fully representative government which continued to be voiced throughout the 1930s. At the same time, strikes, some of them marked by serious violence, erupted across the region in response to the reduction in wages and increase in unemployment brought about by over-production and low prices for sugar, which continued to be the region's principal export. This wave of political and industrial unrest led eventually, in 1938, to the appointment of a Royal Commission chaired by Lord Moyne (the Moyne Commission), with a remit to investigate economic and social conditions in the British Caribbean and to make appropriate recommendations. Though the Commission did make some recommendations for constitutional reform—such as a wider franchise and lower qualifications for candidates in order to increase West Indian participation in government—its main recommendation was the establishment of a West Indian welfare fund to be used to help small farmers and to improve education, health and housing. As a result, the Commission was not prepared to recommend immediate self-government for the region since this would have made it impossible to exert financial control over the substantial monetary aid that it had recommended should be provided by the United Kingdom.[35]

The progressive forces unleashed globally by the Second World War, however, heralded a change in British policy towards its colonies in the West Indies, and in the two decades which followed the publication of the Moyne Commission's report in 1940, the system of Crown Colony rule was slowly dismantled, as the foundations for responsible government began to be laid. Though these developments took place at different times in different colonies, the broad outline of the process was similar in each. First, universal adult suffrage was introduced as the

[34] *Report of the Closer Union Commission (Leeward Islands, Windward Islands, Trinidad and Tobago)* (Cmd 4383, 1933).
[35] *Report of the West Indian Royal Commission 1938–39* (Cmd 6607, 1945).

property and income qualifications were replaced by a simple literacy test, which itself was eventually abandoned. Second, the number of elected members in the Legislative Councils was incrementally increased, while the number of ex officio and nominated unofficial members was correspondingly decreased. In some cases, such as Jamaica and Trinidad, the Legislative Council was replaced by a bicameral parliament modelled on the British Parliament, with a wholly elected lower house (the House of Representatives) and a nominated upper house (the Senate), which had a power to suspend legislation for up to one year. Third, the Executive Council, formerly a purely advisory body, became the principal policy-making body. At the same time, the number of members drawn from the elected element of the Legislative Council steadily increased until it reached the point when the elected members formed a majority on the Executive Council. Fourth, the semblance of Cabinet government began to emerge as one of the elected members of the Executive Council was appointed as Chief Minister with the approval of the House of Representatives, which also had the power to dismiss the Chief Minister by majority vote, and the Governor assigned portfolios to the other elected members of the Executive Council on the Chief Minister's recommendation. In this way the autocratic rule of the Governor under a system of Crown Colony rule was gradually displaced by a system of collective, democratic self-government.[36]

With the benefit of hindsight it is tempting to see each of these developments as a natural progression, leading inexorably to independence for each of these colonies. However, that was certainly not the official view at the time, which held that Britain's colonies in the region were too small and too isolated to be capable of being fully self-governing. Instead, it was presumed that independence could only be granted to these colonies if they were united in a federation, which would increase their effective size to the point at which the region would become eligible for self-government as a single cohesive unit.[37]

---

[36] K Meighoo and P Jamadar, *Democracy and Constitution Reform in Trinidad and Tobago* (Kingston, Jamaica, Ian Randle Publishers, 2008).
[37] See *Memorandum on the Closer Association of the British West Indian Colonies* (Cmnd 7120, 1947).

C. FEDERATION

Though the idea of a federation of Britain's Caribbean colonies had first been tentatively proposed in the nineteenth century it did not really begin to take firm shape until after the end of the Second World War. This was because up until this point the view of the British authorities had been that 'anything approaching a general federal system' in the region was both 'inopportune and impracticable'.[38] Indeed, as late as 1939 the Moyne Commission still doubted 'whether the time [was] yet ripe for the introduction of a large measure of federation'.[39] While it is true that, locally, support for the idea of a British Caribbean federation first began to be voiced soon after the end of the First World War, with the radicalisation of West Indians returning from abroad who were determined to put an end to a system of Crown Colony rule that denied them an effective voice in the government of their own countries,[40] the idea of federation still did not enjoy unanimous support across the region. As Eric Williams, the Prime Minister of Trinidad and one of the champions of regional unity observed, the development of these territories as plantation economies had 'engendered and nurtured an inter-colonial rivalry, an isolationist outlook, a provincialism that is almost a disease'.[41] Thus, the smaller and poorer territories were afraid of being dominated by the larger and more prosperous ones, while the latter feared that they might have to contribute to the support of the former. The less densely populated territories had visions of being flooded by immigrants from the overcrowded islands, while the mainland territories of British Guiana and British Honduras were afraid that federation would prejudice the development of their relations with other continental countries. Moreover, certain groups within various territories felt that their own economic positions might be adversely affected by federation. The 'East Indians' in Trinidad and British Guiana, for example, objected to entering what would be a predominantly 'Negro' political unit. A number of the big business and planting interests were also

---

[38] See *Report of the Closer Union Commission*, above (n 34).

[39] See *Report of the West Indian Royal Commission 1938–39*, above (n 35).

[40] H Springer, 'Federation in the Caribbean: An Attempt That Failed' (1962) 16(4) *International Organization* 758–75.

[41] E Williams, *From Columbus to Castro: The History of the Caribbean 1492–1969* (London, Andre Deutsch Ltd, 1970) 116.

unenthusiastic because they feared that with the growth of the labour movement the federal Government might well be a socialist one.[42]

The dynamics of the debate about federation were, however, changed fundamentally by the outbreak of the Second World War, which contributed to the development of air travel in the region, the absence of which had previously been regarded as a major obstacle. This, together with the achievements of regional institutions, such as the West Indian Court of Appeal and the Imperial College of Tropical Agriculture, and the cooperation of a number of wartime agencies which contributed substantially to the administrative integration of the region, brought about a shift in the Colonial Office's previously cautious approach towards federation and led directly to an invitation by the Colonial Secretary of State, in 1945, to the representatives of the various territories to a conference to discuss the possibility of federation.[43] The conference, which took place in Jamaica in 1947, marked a decisive step on the path towards closer political union; not only accepting the principle of federation, but also establishing a Standing Closer Association Committee (SCAC), which was charged with preparing a draft federal Constitution for consideration by the respective national legislatures.[44] The report of the SCAC which was approved in principle by all the colonial legislatures—with the exception of British Guiana and British Honduras which had withdrawn from the process at an early stage—was reviewed at a conference in London in April 1953. Out of this conference emerged a revised plan for a West Indies Federation (WIF) which was finally approved at a further conference in London in February 1956, following which the British Caribbean Act 1956 (BCA) was enacted.

The BCA provided for a federal system of government with a bicameral Parliament (a House of Representatives and a Senate), Cabinet government and the Queen, represented by her appointee, the Governor General, as the head of state. This had the advantage of familiarity since it was similar to the system of government that was gradually

---

[42] JH Proctor, 'The Functional Approach to Political Union, Lessons from the Effort to Federate the British Caribbean Territories' (1956) 10(1) *International Organization* 43.

[43] See Springer, above (n 40).

[44] *Report of the Conference on the Closer Association of the British West Indian Colonies, Montego Bay, Jamaica, 11–19 September 1947* (Cmd 7291, 1948).

being introduced into each of the various territories, but it was soon apparent that there were a number of inherent problems in replicating this system in a federal context. The first was the very extensive powers that were vested in the Governor General. These included: the power to appoint all the senators, the Justices of the Federal Supreme Court and members of the Public Service Commission; to refuse assent to any Bill approved by the federal Parliament or reserve it for review by the British Government; and to decide any urgent matter however important, on their own, if time did not permit them to consult their Cabinet. These powers, which were greater even than the powers traditionally vested in colonial Governors, were a far cry from the ideal of self-government which the WIF was supposed to promise and, as Lewis observed, 'relied on a tradition of gubernatorial paternalism which no longer fitted with the democratic temper of the age'.[45] The second problem was a provision that prohibited legislators from occupying federal and territorial positions at one and the same time, which meant that the federal Government was deprived of the services of many of the most eminent political leaders in the region, including the national leaders of the two federal parties who chose to remain in their own national legislatures deciding, presumably, rather like Milton's Satan, that it was better to reign in Hell than to serve in Heaven.[46] The third problem was in the composition of the Lower House, which was not initially, at least, based on population, but rather upon a number of factors, such as economic development and productivity and financial stability. The result was that Jamaica was allocated only 38 per cent of the seats, considerably less than the 52 per cent it would have been entitled to on a population basis. Trinidad too was significantly under-represented, while Barbados and the smaller units were over-represented to a greater or lesser degree.[47]

The division of powers between the federal Government and the governments of each of the territories proved to be equally problematic. The main difficulty for those drafting the federal Constitution

[45] See GK Lewis, 'West Indian Federation: The Constitutional Aspects' (1957) 6(2) *Social and Economic Studies* 215–46, 234.

[46] Ibid, 224.

[47] DG Anglin, 'The Political Development of the West Indies' in D Lowenthal (ed), *The West Indies Federation: Perspectives on a New Nation* (New York, Columbia University Press, 1961) 54.

was how to reconcile effective federal control with the degree of decentralisation demanded by the sheer distance between the territories. The solution adopted by designers of the federal Constitution was to have an Exclusive and a Concurrent List. Those matters contained in the Exclusive List were, as the name suggests, exclusively assigned to the federal Government. The geography of the region, however, required that many important and extensive functions of government had to be shared with the territories, for example, public order, agriculture and education and these, therefore, appeared in the Concurrent List. The result of this division of powers was very limited legislative authority for the federal Government which, in Eric Williams' characteristically dismissive phrase, amounted to 'just a lot of federal Ministers running about Port-of-Spain (the location of the WIF's capital), spreading joy'.[48] To make matters worse, the federal Government had no powers of taxation and a mere pittance to spend, derived exclusively from receipts from the customs and excise duties on gasoline, cigarettes and alcohol. This led the first Finance Minister to describe himself as 'the only Minister of Finance without funds'.[49] As the financial situation worsened and the federal Government became increasingly desperate the federal Prime Minister, Grantley Adams, even went so far as to threaten to impose retrospective income tax when the federal Constitution was revised in 1963. This proved, however, to be a fatal mistake since it contributed to the decision by the Jamaican Premier, Norman Manley—once one of the WIF's most vocal champions, but now faced with widespread opposition to the WIF in Jamaica—to hold a referendum on the issue of whether or not Jamaica should remain in the WIF. The outcome of the referendum, which was held in September 1961, was a vote of 46 per cent in favour and 54 per cent against remaining in the WIF.

With Jamaica having voted to withdraw, the focus turned to Trinidad, whose 850,000 people would now provide half the population and over half the wealth of a much-diminished WIF. Trinidad's Premier, Eric Williams, had however already indicated that if Jamaica withdrew Trinidad would follow suit, fearing that Trinidad alone could not bear the cost of funding the WIF or supporting the poorer eastern Caribbean islands. As Williams pithily observed, 'one from ten leaves

---

[48] E Williams, 'Speech to PNM Special Convention, 27 January 1962' (1962) 4(19) *The Nation.*
[49] Quoted by Anglin, above (n 47) 58.

nought'.[50] Thus, five weeks after the general election in Trinidad, in 1962, Williams' People's National Movement (PNM) Government announced Trinidad's intention to join Jamaica in withdrawing from the WIF, and the British Government formally dissolved the WIF shortly thereafter, in March 1962.

The reasons for the collapse of the WIF were many and complex. As we have seen, the colonial aspects of the federal Constitution, such as the extensive powers vested in the Governor General, antagonised local politicians, while the division of powers between the federal Government and national governments meant that the former lacked money, power and prestige. The uneven economic development of the constituent territories also meant that the larger islands, such as Trinidad and Jamaica, were alarmed at the prospect of having to support the smaller islands. Between 1947, when the idea of a British Caribbean Federation was first proposed, and the establishment of the WIF in 1958, the economies of both Jamaica and Trinidad had been transformed by dramatic increases in the production of bauxite and petroleum respectively.[51] In 1947, all the participating territories had hoped to gain an economic advantage from the WIF, but by 1958 only the smaller islands could reasonably have expected to benefit economically from federation. The principal reason for the collapse of the WIF was, however, that it had outlived its original purpose, which was to serve as a vehicle for independence. A number of Britain's other colonies— Ghana, Sierra Leone and Nigeria—had by 1960 already been granted independence, and in 1960 the United Nations had passed its historic resolution supporting independence for colonial territories.[52] Once Jamaica and Trinidad realised that they could achieve independence in their own right, their political leaders no longer saw any significant benefit to be gained from remaining in the WIF; on the contrary, they feared the financial obligations which it demanded of them, amounting to more than three-quarters of the WIF's budget.[53] Federation had been

---

[50] Quoted by CA Palmer, *Eric Williams and the Making of the Modern Caribbean* (North Carolina, The University of Carolina Press, 2006) 179.

[51] A Payne, *The Political History of CARICOM* (Kingston, Jamaica, Ian Randle Publishers, 2008) xxvii.

[52] Declaration on the Granting of Independence to Colonial Countries and Peoples, adopted by General Assembly Resolution 1514 (XV) of 14 December 1960.

[53] See Z Elkins and T Ginsburg, 'Constitutional Reform in the English-Speaking Caribbean: Challenges and Prospects' (2011) 16. Available at: www.agrora-parl.org.

born out of opposition to colonial rule and a wish for independence. Once the latter had been achieved by two of the largest territories in the region, the fragile nature of regional unity upon which the WIF depended was irreversibly shattered.

PART III: INDEPENDENCE

A. THE DECOLONISATION PROCESS

Immediately following the referendum in Jamaica, Norman Manley contacted the Secretary of State for the Colonies to request a prompt discussion of Jamaica's secession from the WIF and to fix a date for Jamaica's independence. Within a month the British Government had announced not only that it accepted the result of the referendum, but that it would in due course be introducing legislation providing for Jamaica's independence. A date was, accordingly, fixed for an Independence Conference to take place in London in January or February of the following year. In the meantime, in Jamaica, a Joint Select Committee, composed of members of both the House of Representatives and the Senate, was promptly appointed to draft an Independence Constitution. This draft was subsequently approved at the Independence Conference, which took place in London between 1 and 9 February 1962, attended by representatives of the Colonial Office and delegations from the two main political parties—the People's National Party (PNP) and the Jamaica Labour Party (JLP). It was further agreed that Jamaica would become independent on 6 August 1962 and that this would be achieved by means of an Order-in-Council, to which the Independence Constitution would be annexed, under the authority of section 5 of the West Indies Act 1962.[54]

At the same time, Trinidad, following its decision to withdraw from the WIF, was also busily preparing for independence. A draft Independence Constitution drawn up by the PNM Government was widely distributed on 20 February 1962, and the general public and private organisations were invited to submit written comments by no later than 31 March. Between the 25 and 27 April 1962 the Government

---

[54] See *Report of the Jamaica Independence Conference, 1962* (Cmnd 1638, 1962).

discussed numerous proposed changes to the draft at a conference attended by some 200 people. As an exercise in consultation, however, the conference was less than satisfactory, with the press having been excluded and members of the main opposition party walking out. Nevertheless, a revised version of the draft was approved on 11 May by a majority of 16 votes to nine on a straight party vote in the House of Representatives, and formed the basis for discussion at the Independence Conference held in London between 28 May and 8 June 1962. This was attended by representatives of the Colonial Office and delegations from the governing PNM and the opposition Democratic Labour Party (DLP), as well as teams from a number of voluntary organisations. The latter included two organisations representing the East Indian community—which then constituted one-third of the population—that were fearful about their position in an independent Trinidad, ruled by a predominantly 'black' government.

Partly as a consequence of the diversity of the range of opinions represented at the Independence Conference, and partly as a consequence of the fact that the draft Independence Constitution was not the product of an agreement between the two main political parties, negotiating the terms of the Independence Constitution was by no means a straightforward affair. As a result, a number of compromises had to be conceded by the PNM before the draft Independence Constitution was finally approved and a date could be fixed for Trinidad to become independent on 31 August 1962.[55]

The template for decolonisation and constitution-making set by Jamaica and Trinidad was followed, with minimal deviations, by Barbados and Guyana in 1966, the Bahamas in 1973 and Belize in 1981. The path to independence was, however, modified somewhat in the case of the eastern Caribbean islands which had entered into a new constitutional arrangement with Britain—Associated State status— under the West Indies Act 1967 (WIA), following the collapse of plans to establish an Eastern Caribbean Federation to replace the aborted WIF. Under the WIA, each of the Associated States was made fully self-governing in its internal affairs, though responsibility for external affairs and defence was reserved to Britain with the necessary legislative and executive powers to discharge this responsibility. The essence of the arrangement was that, within the limits of the powers bestowed upon

---

[55] See Wallace, above (n 10) 212–14.

them, the Associated States were as independent of Britain as were the Dominions after the Statute of Westminster. The association was intended to be free and voluntary and was terminable by either party at any time. The procedure for termination of association, however, differed depending upon whether it was initiated by the Associated State or by the British Government. In the case of the former, the procedure prescribed by section 10(1) WIA was highly complex, requiring an interval of not less than 90 days between the introduction of the Bill providing for termination of the association and its second reading, followed by the support of not less than two-thirds of all the elected members of the legislature and, assuming that it received such support, no less than two-thirds of the votes cast in a referendum. All this was in marked contrast to the procedure to be followed if it was the British Government which wished to initiate termination of the association. In the latter case, the procedure set out in section 10(2) WIA was much simpler: all that was required of the British Government was to give the Associated State concerned six months' notice of its intention to terminate the status of association, followed by an Order-in-Council approved by a resolution of each House of Parliament.

Unsurprisingly, it was the simpler procedure provided by section 10(2) WIA that was used to effect termination of the status of association in the majority of cases, but the decision to proceed in this way proved to be highly contentious in the case of Grenada, which was the first of the six Associated States to seek independence. Here, the general election, which had been held in February 1972, had been won by the Grenada United Labour Party (GULP), which had secured 13 out of the 15 seats in the House of Representatives, having previously made it clear that the first item on its agenda following the election was to seek independence. However, once elected the leader of the GULP, Eric Gairy, announced that rather than proceed by way of section 10(1) WIA he was going to ask the British Government to grant independence under the procedure laid down in section 10(2) WIA, thereby avoiding the need to hold a local referendum in accordance with section 10(1) WIA, which was being demanded by the Leader of the Opposition. However, Gairy's failure to hold a referendum led to concerns being raised in the British Parliament when the resolution to terminate the status of association came to be debated: especially in light of the widely reported allegations of human rights abuses by Gairy's Government, which included the formation and use of paramilitary forces and brutal attacks upon dissidents. In response to these concerns, however, the Minister of State for Commonwealth and Foreign Affairs pointed out that the decision to terminate the status of association had already been approved by unanimous resolutions of both Houses of Parliament in Grenada. He also argued that it was better to move to independence by mutual agreement of the two governments rather than by asking Grenada, which had obtained a greater degree of internal self-government through its constitutional status as an Associated State than had ever been obtained by Britain's other colonies in the region, to take an additional step that had not been required by these other colonies on their road to independence.[56] Thus, Grenada and the majority of the other Associated States embarked upon independence by means of an Order-in-Council in exactly the same way as all the other former colonies in the region, the exception being St Vincent where a referendum was held in accordance with section 10(1).

B. THE INDEPENDENCE CONSTITUTIONS

Notwithstanding the very different constitutional histories of the countries that make up the Commonwealth Caribbean—depending upon whether they were settled, ceded or conquered colonies—by the time of their independence each of these countries had been introduced to the so-called Westminster model of government and it is this system that was incorporated in each of the Independence Constitutions.

1. The 'Westminster Model'

The 'Westminster model' is not a legal term of art and it would be wrong to talk about it as if it were a single model, but it is, nevertheless, a useful shorthand for describing the system of government incorporated in the Independence Constitutions, always recognising that we are talking about the Westminster model in both the narrow and wider sense of the term.[57]

---

[56] See Hansard, HC Deb 11 December 1973, vol 866, cols 331–61.
[57] SA De Smith, 'Westminster's Export Models: The Legal Framework of Responsible Government' (1961) 1(1) *Journal of Commonwealth Political Studies* 2–16.

In the narrow sense, the Westminster model is characterised by certain essential features. First, that the head of state is separate from the head of government. Second, that the head of government is a Prime Minister, presiding over a Cabinet composed of ministers over whose appointment the Prime Minister has at least a substantial measure of control. Third, that the effective executive branch of government is parliamentary in as much as ministers must be members of the legislature. Fourth, that ministers are collectively and individually responsible to a freely elected and representative legislature. Fifth, and finally, that there should be a two-party system: the party in government and the official Opposition. Each of these characteristics is found in the Independence Constitutions. Thus, with one exception, they all provide that the head of state should be the Queen acting through a Governor General. The exception is Dominica, which embarked upon independence, not as a constitutional monarchy, but as a republic with a ceremonial president. The Independence Constitutions also provide that executive power is vested in the Cabinet, that the head of the Cabinet is a Prime Minister appointed by the head of state, being the member of the elected House who appears to the head of state most likely to command a majority of the members of that House, and that the other ministers are selected by the Prime Minister from among the members of the legislature. This link between the executive and the legislature is further reinforced by constitutional provisions which require the Prime Minister to vacate office if they cease to be a member of the legislature, if there is a vote of no confidence in their government by the legislature, or following the dissolution of Parliament, which may occur if they refuse to resign following a vote of no confidence. Similarly, the Independence Constitutions provide that ministers are 'responsible for the administration of their departments' to Parliament, and through Parliament, to the public for acts of the executive.[58] Finally, the office of the Leader of the Opposition is enshrined in all the Independence Constitutions, which also provide that the Leader of the Opposition must be consulted by the Prime Minister when performing a number of key constitutional functions.

In the wider sense of the term, the Westminster model may be understood to comprise the other main features of the British Constitution, many of which are also to be found in the Independence Constitutions. Thus, the majority of the Independence Constitutions provide for

---

[58] See, eg, s 71(1) Constitution of Antigua and Barbuda.

a bicameral parliament composed of an elected lower House and a nominated upper House. The British electoral system based on the first past the post system is also replicated in all the Independence Constitutions, which provide for single-member constituencies, with the exception of Guyana, which adopted a proportional representation system based on party lists prior to independence. Many of the conventions that underpin the British Constitution with regard to relations between the head of state and the head of government are also to be found either expressly or by reference in the Independence Constitutions.

Notwithstanding the manifest influence of the British version of the Westminster model of government upon the Independence Constitutions, there were, however, a number of important differences between the British and the Caribbean versions as incorporated in the Independence Constitutions. These included: the establishment of an independent ombudsman, charged with investigating the actions of government departments, their ministers, officers or MPs; the transfer of responsibility for terminating a superior judge's tenure of office from a legislative to a judicial forum; and the vesting of full control over the public service and the conduct of elections in the hands of independent commissions. By far the most important difference, however, lay in the fact that the Independence Constitutions were codified in a single document, which included a Bill of Rights, and which, with exception of Trinidad, declared that the Constitution was the 'supreme law'. This was quite different from the British Constitution, which is famously 'uncodified' and which is based on the principle of parliamentary supremacy, according to which Parliament can make or unmake any law whatsoever and no person or body can override or set aside an Act of Parliament.[59] Constitutional supremacy, by contrast, meant that judges, including the Judicial Committee of the Privy Council (JCPC) in London, which was retained as the final court of appeal by all of the newly independent countries, would have an important role to play in determining whether acts of the legislature and the executive were consistent with the limitations imposed upon each by the Constitution. Moreover, the inclusion of a Bill of Rights meant that acts of the legislature or executive which infringed the rights and freedoms contained therein could be declared unlawful and struck down.

---

[59] AV Dicey, *Introduction to the Study of the Law of the Constitution*, 10th edn (London, Macmillan, 1959) 39.

2. Bills of Rights

The first two countries to embark upon independence—Jamaica and Trinidad—both included a Bill of Rights in their Independence Constitutions, but their reasons for doing so were based on quite different considerations.[60]

In the case of Jamaica, there was almost universal enthusiasm for the inclusion of a human rights instrument within the Independence Constitution. The only real issue was, therefore, between those on the government side who wanted to include it in the preamble so that it did not have the force of law and the Opposition, which wanted to include it in the body of the Constitution and to make it justiciable. Eventually, it was the Opposition which won the day as the Government was persuaded that the inclusion of an entrenched Bill of Rights, including a right to property, was necessary to maintain the confidence of investors in Jamaica post-independence. This was especially important because Jamaica was heavily reliant on foreign investment to maintain its recent economic growth, which had been driven by an upturn in the international sugar market and the discovery of vast bauxite resources. The draft Constitution that was presented to the Independence Conference in London thus included a Bill of Rights based on the model contained in the Constitution of Sierra Leone, which was itself based on the European Convention on Human Rights. This had been selected not just because it was familiar from its inclusion in the proposed Constitution for the WIF, but also because it had, in large part, been drafted by British lawyers. The Bill of Rights proposed by the Jamaican delegation at the Independence Conference in London thus comprised the so-called 'first generation' rights, ie, civil and political rights that typically take the form of negative protection against the actions of the government. At the conference in London, however, it was agreed that the reference to slavery in the text should be removed on the ground that its inclusion was inappropriate given the advanced stage of constitutional development in Jamaica. It was also agreed to make the level of compensation for property compulsorily acquired by the government subject to a criterion of fairness.

The issues surrounding the inclusion of a Bill of Rights in Trinidad's Independence Constitution were somewhat more complex for two

---

[60] See C Parkinson, *Bills of Rights and Decolonization: The Emergence of Domestic Human Rights Instruments in Britain's Overseas Territories* (Oxford, Oxford University Press, 2007) 175–214, from which the account that follows is taken.

reasons. First, there were the tensions between the African and Indian communities to be taken into account. The last general election prior to independence, in December 1961, had been a bitterly fought contest with the main parties—the PNP led by Eric Williams and the DLP led by Rudranath Capildeo—divided along racial lines, with racially motivated violence erupting in many areas. Though Williams had won a landslide victory at the election, gaining 20 out of the 30 available seats, this only served to deepen the mistrust between the two parties and their constituencies. Second, there was considerable disagreement about what form the Bill of Rights should take. Though initially opposed to the idea of the inclusion of a Bill of Rights, Williams had subsequently come round to the idea. This was partly because a Bill of Rights had recently been included in Jamaica's Independence Constitution, and partly because there was by this time an overwhelming expectation that every modern state should have one. In addition, Williams hoped that the inclusion of a Bill of Rights would pacify certain elements within Trinidad's Indian community—a Bill of Rights being believed to hold great weight in Indian constitutional thought. The question, however, remained: what form should the Bill of Rights take? Williams' own adviser, Ellis Clarke (who went on to become Governor General of Trinidad between 1972 and 1976) favoured the model of Sierra Leone, but Williams was persuaded, on the basis of representations by Hugh Wooding, on behalf of the Bar Council, to opt for a model based on the recent Canadian Declaration of Rights, presumably because the latter gave the legislature a greater latitude of action.

The DLP, however, rejected this model, arguing that the rights contained therein were so poorly drafted as to be wholly ineffectual. Indeed, the deadlock that resulted between the Government and the Opposition over this and a host of other issues threatened to derail the Independence Conference held in London in 1962, with the Opposition delegation arguing for a five-year moratorium on independence unless its demands were met by the Government. In order to break this deadlock, Williams agreed to meet the majority of the Opposition's demands. He was not, however, prepared to abandon his preference for a Bill of Rights based on the Canadian model, though he did agree to the inclusion of a number of additional provisions, including: freedom of movement; the right of the individual to respect for his private and family life; the right of an individual to equality of treatment from any public authority in the exercise of any public functions; the right to join political parties; and the right of a parent to provide a school of their own choice for their child. He also agreed that the courts would have the power to disallow laws inconsistent with the provisions in the Bill of Rights. On the basis of these concessions, the DLP withdrew their opposition to immediate independence and Trinidad thus embarked upon independence with a Bill of Rights based on the Canadian Declaration of Rights, as amended.

Following the example of Jamaica and Trinidad, the remaining territories in the region accepted the inclusion of a Bill of Rights in their Independence Constitutions with relatively little debate, each territory including a Bill of Rights based, broadly, on the Jamaican model.

CONCLUSION

Having been variously settled, ceded or conquered, the countries that make up the Commonwealth Caribbean were subjected to a number of different systems of colonial government. Over a period of three centuries, these have included at different times and in different colonies, the representative system, the semi-representative system, Public Meeting Government and Crown Colony rule. For most of this period the majority of the population were denied a voice in government under a representative system, which laid down strict rules on who could vote and who could stand for election to the local Assemblies, and which helped to perpetuate slavery and the trade by which it was sustained. The introduction of Crown Colony rule removed even this semblance of representative government and it was only following the end of the Second World War that these former colonies began for the first time to experience a meaningful measure of democratic self-government as they were gradually introduced to the Westminster model.

Thus, by the time of their independence most of these former colonies had been self-governing for little over a decade, and in some cases even less. Their Independence Constitutions, which were the product of negotiation between the main political parties and the Colonial Office, had, in some cases, been prepared in great haste and with very limited opportunity for public consultation. Such was the desire by all the parties concerned for independence to succeed, that it was simply assumed that the Westminster model, which provided the blueprint for these Independence Constitutions, could be adapted to meet the needs and demands of these post-colonies. The empirical evidence upon which this assumption was based was, however, limited, to say the least. While the region's political leaders may have been familiar with the institutions and offices of the Westminster model by the time of independence, it was still too soon to know whether those institutions and offices could be successfully replicated, for example, in some of the very small islands. Nor was it known whether the 'conventions, understanding, habits or practices'[61] upon which the Westminster model is based, and which had been evolving in Britain over a period of four centuries, would take root, let alone flourish, when transplanted to Caribbean soil. To complicate matters further, the region's political leaders would have to function within a legal framework in which both the legislature and the executive would be subject to the limits imposed upon each by the Independence Constitutions, a concept alien to the Westminster model as it had developed in Britain. In the event, as we shall see in the chapters that follow, the durability of almost every aspect of the Westminster model would come to be tested to its limits in the post-independence era.

FURTHER READING

DG Anglin, 'The Political Development of the West Indies' in D Lowenthal (ed), *The West Indies Federation* (Westport, Connecticut, Greenwood Press, 1961).

LG Barnett, *The Constitutional Law of Jamaica* (Oxford, Oxford University Press, 1977).

GK Lewis, *The Growth of the Modern West Indies* (Kingston, Jamaica, Ian Randle Publishers, 2004).

C Parkinson, *Bills of Rights and Decolonization: The Emergence of Domestic Human Rights Instruments in Britain's Overseas Territories* (Oxford, Oxford University Press, 2007).

A Payne, *The Political History of CARICOM* (Kingston, Jamaica, Ian Randle Publishers, 2008).

E Wallace, *The British Caribbean: From the Decline of Colonialism to the End of Federation* (Toronto, University of Toronto Press, 1977).

H Wrong, *Government of the West Indies* (Oxford, Clarendon Press, 1923).

[61] Dicey, above (n 59) 24.

2

The Head of State

———➤◦◄———

Background – The Crown as Head of State – The Constitutional Framework – Judicial Review of the Constitutional Functions of Presidents and Governors General – Conclusion

PART I: BACKGROUND

U PON ATTAINING INDEPENDENCE all the Commonwealth Caribbean countries adopted a *parliamentary* system of government. This was a system with which their politicians were by then familiar, following the end of 'Crown Colony rule', and was considered preferable to striking out in an entirely new direction by, for example, adopting a *presidential* system of government as favoured by their Latin American neighbours. One of the defining features of the parliamentary system is, of course, the separation of the head of government, and the head of state; the latter being either a constitutional monarch or a ceremonial president with the word 'ceremonial' here being used to indicate that political power is exercised not by the head of state, as is the case under an executive presidency, but by the head of government.[1]

Under a parliamentary system, the head of state is generally regarded as having two principal roles to play. The first, which is largely symbolic, and which encompasses a wide range of ceremonial duties, is to serve as the representative of the nation, a focus for national unity and continuity.

---

[1] See DV Verney, 'Parliamentary Government and Presidential Government' in A Lijphart (ed), *Parliamentary Versus Presidential Government* (Oxford, Oxford University Press, 1992).

The second is to perform a number of constitutional functions, such as assenting to legislation, appointing the Prime Minister and dissolving Parliament. The exercise of these functions is usually regulated by a set of rules, which are intended to ensure that the head of state acts at all times in accordance with the advice of the Prime Minister. However, the head of state may be afforded a residual discretion in the exercise of some of their most important constitutional functions; for example, when deciding whether or not to grant a Prime Minister's request for a dissolution of Parliament where that is not in the country's best interests, or whom to appoint as Prime Minister where no one party has won a clear majority in a general election. The purpose of this discretion, it is usually argued, is to enable the head of state to act as the guardian of the Constitution at times of constitutional crisis which cannot be resolved by the ordinary democratic processes.[2]

Based on the experience of the United Kingdom, which has served as the prototype for parliamentary democracies around the Commonwealth, it is often assumed that the roles of the head of state and the head of government under a parliamentary system are complementary.[3] Certainly, it is true that in the United Kingdom, where the rules that regulate relations between the Queen and her Prime Minister appear to be well understood by the actors on both sides, having evolved and been tested over the centuries, the monarch's role as head of state is generally regarded as a source of constitutional stability, underpinning and sustaining parliamentary democracy.[4] The same cannot always be said, however, of the role of head of state elsewhere in the Commonwealth. As Butler and Low have documented, in their survey of Commonwealth heads of state and their representatives in the period 1945 to 1990, there have been numerous 'constitutional episodes', involving the head of state (acting through a locally appointed Governor General) and the head of government. These have variously resulted in the premature dismissal or resignation of the Governor General; the dismissal of the head of government; the disputed 'installation' of the

---

[2] R Brazier, *Constitutional Practice* (Oxford, Clarendon Press, 1994) 190–92.

[3] TA Baylis, 'Presidents Versus Prime Ministers: Shaping Executive Authority in Eastern Europe' (1996) 48 *World Politics* 297, 301.

[4] Brazier, *Constitutional Practice*, above (n 2).

head of government; the forced dissolution of the legislature; and the refusal of dissolution of the legislature.[5]

Several of the episodes included in Butler and Low's survey are drawn from the post-independence Commonwealth Caribbean where the problematic status of the head of state has been accentuated by the interplay of a number of factors, which I seek to explore in this chapter. Thus I will begin, in part I, by considering the changes to the understanding of the region's relationship with its colonial past that have occurred since independence; why this has prompted some countries to become republics by replacing the Queen with a ceremonial president; and how it has affected opinion about the Queen's continuing role as head of state in those countries that remain constitutional monarchies. In part II, I will turn to examine the constitutional framework within which Governors General (acting as the Queen's appointed representative) and presidents are required to function under the region's independence and post-independence constitutions. I will also consider how this framework affects relations between the Governor General, or the President, as the case may be, and the head of government, the tensions that can arise as a result and how these tensions have been aggravated by the racial divisions which blight a country such as Trinidad, as well as the highly 'personalised' nature of Commonwealth Caribbean politics more generally. Finally, in part III, I will consider the role of the courts in supervising the exercise of their constitutional functions by Governors General and presidents, and the extent to which the courts are able to ensure that these office holders exercise their powers, both formal and discretionary, in accordance with the provisions of the Constitution.

PART II: THE CROWN AS HEAD OF STATE

Upon independence all the countries in the region, with the exception of Dominica (for reasons considered below), retained the Queen as their head of state. While it is true that the older Dominions—Australia,

---

[5] See D Butler and DA Low (eds), *Sovereigns and Surrogates: Constitutional Heads of State in the Commonwealth* (Oxford, Macmillan, 1991).

Canada and New Zealand—had earlier opted to become constitutional monarchies upon independence, these countries were predominantly 'white' and their experience of colonial rule was quite different from those of the former colonies in the Caribbean which might not have been expected to feel the same sense of allegiance to the 'Mother Country'. Moreover, there were by this time several examples of other former colonies—Ireland, India, Pakistan and Ghana to name but a few—that had chosen to become republics upon independence. These examples notwithstanding, in 1962, when Jamaica and Trinidad and Tobago were considering the options open to them upon independence, there was no great groundswell of opinion in either country calling for the severance of links with the former imperial power. There had been, it is true, in the case of Jamaica, a proposal by a number of those appearing before the Joint Select Committee (JSC) charged with the drafting of the Independence Constitution, for the appointment of a ceremonial president as head of state,[6] but this was summarily rejected by the JSC on the ground that the reasons which had led other colonies to prefer a republican constitution did not apply to Jamaica. The report of the Trinidad and Tobago Independence Conference, held in London in 1962, also makes it clear that there was no popular demand for a ceremonial president. In the words of the Trinidad and Tobago delegation, which was made up of more or less equal numbers of members of the Government and the Opposition, it was 'the firm wish of the people of Trinidad and Tobago to continue after independence in their allegiance to Her Majesty the Queen as Queen of Trinidad and Tobago'.[7]

Following those early days of independence, however, there was a decisive shift in opinion in the region. This can be seen even as early as 1966 when the Guyanese Government insisted on the inclusion in its Independence Constitution of a provision for Guyana to become a republic if the National Assembly should so resolve by a majority vote of all the elected members after 1 January 1969.[8] Having won an outright victory in the elections of 1968, the People's National Congress wasted no time in implementing this provision, which they considered

[6] T Munroe, *The Politics of Constitutional Decolonization: Jamaica 1944–1962* (Mona, Jamaica, Institute of Social and Economic Research, University of the West Indies, 1972).

[7] *Report of the Trinidad and Tobago Independence Conference* (Cmnd 1757, 1962).

[8] Art 73(5) Constitution of Guyana.

to be an important step in achieving meaningful decolonisation. As the Minister for Information at the time explained:

> The British Crown is the symbolic head of Great Britain and it is from that country that we have struggled so long for our independence. It may be that some, very few, among us still accord to the British Crown a position of high idealism. But I cannot recall the British Crown successfully raising its voice in a public forum against British colonialism imposed upon millions of us across the world who now struggle to make our way as independent peoples. The fact that the British Crown today does not control the decisions of the British Government hardly seems an argument in favour of our retaining allegiance, however symbolic that allegiance may be.[9]

Thus, Guyana became the first country in the region to convert to republicanism in 1970.

Subsequently, two other countries in the region followed Guyana's lead by becoming republics with a ceremonial president. The first was Trinidad, following the Report of the Constitutional Commission, in 1974, led by Chief Justice Hugh Wooding (the 'Wooding Commission'),[10] which recommended the immediate replacement of the Queen as head of state by a ceremonial president. As the Wooding Commission noted, there was by then in Trinidad just over a decade after independence, almost unanimous support for this proposal:

> It is no more than an expression of fact that independence must involve the creation of indigenous symbols of nationhood. Among young people in particular the British Sovereign has no symbolic meaning. The thrust since independence has been towards the discovery of a new identity which involves leaving behind the colonial heritage of subjection, imitation and external dependence.[11]

The second country to follow Guyana's lead was Dominica, which is also the only country in the region to have embarked upon independence as a republic with a ceremonial president, though even this represented something of a dilution of the Opposition Party's original

---

[9] Quoted in HA Lutchman, 'The Co-operative Republic of Guyana' (1970) 10 *Caribbean Studies* 97, 100.

[10] Constitution Commission of Trinidad and Tobago, *Report of the Constitution Commission* (Port of Spain, 1974). Available at: www.ttparliament.org.

[11] Ibid, [138].

demands for a decisive break with the past by having an executive president, directly elected by popular vote.[12]

While no other countries in the region have, as yet, followed the lead of Guyana, Trinidad and Dominica, the question of whether or not to retain the Queen as head of state remains very much a live issue, even if the effective head of state is, in reality, a local Governor General appointed on the Prime Minister's recommendation. The question has thus featured prominently in the deliberations of every constitutional review commission that has taken place in the region since independence, almost all of which have recommended the replacement of the Queen as head of state with a ceremonial president chosen by the local legislature.[13] The most striking exception is the Political Reform Commission of Belize, which reported in 2000,[14] and which was unable to arrive at a majority recommendation on the issue of replacing the British monarch as the head of state of Belize with a Belizean president. However, in so far as this is out of line with the general trend of constitutional review commissions in the region this can, in large part, be explained by reference to concerns about the security of Belize in relation to Guatemala's claim to Belize, and the fear that replacing the British monarch as head of state might decrease Britain's willingness to come to the aid of Belize in the event of an invasion from Guatemala.[15]

[12]   *Report of the Dominica Constitutional Conference* (Cmnd 6901, 1977) 15.

[13]   *Report of the Antigua Constitutional Review Commission* ('Antigua 2002'), available at: www.antigua-barbuda.com; The Bahamas Constitutional Review Commission, *Preliminary Report and Provisional Recommendations* (2006), available at: www.islandwooivil.tripod.com; *Report of the Barbados Constitution Review Commission* (Barbados, Government Printing Department, 1998); *Final Report of the Political Reform Commission of Belize* (2000), available at: www.ambergriscaye.com; *Report of the Dominica Constitution Review Commission* (Roseau, Commonwealth of Dominica, 1999); Grenada Constitution Review Commission (St George's, Grenada, 2006); Jamaica, *Final Report of the Joint Select Committee of the Houses of Parliament on Constitutional and Electoral Reform* (1995). St Kitts and Nevis Constitutional Review Commission, February 2002 (no report available). *Report of St Lucia Constitutional Reform Commisssion*, March 2011, available at: www.stlucia.gov.lc and St Vincent Constitution Review Commission 2002 (no report available).

[14]   Available at: www.ambergriscaye.com.

[15]   For the background to this dispute, see CH Grant, *The Making of Modern Belize: Politics, Society and British Colonialism Central America* (Cambridge, Cambridge University Press, 1976).

While the case for replacing the Queen with a ceremonial president may, therefore, generally be regarded as unanswerable, at least by those populating the region's constitutional reform commissions, it should be noted that in the only referendum in which the issue has been put to voters, in St Vincent, in November 2009, a majority of 55 per cent voted in favour of retaining the Queen as head of state.[16] This result apart, however, the continuing association with colonial rule which attaches to the Queen means that she remains a divisive figure viewed by many in the region as an anachronism; as a result, the Queen's ability to serve as the representative of the nation and as a force for national unity[17] is fatally compromised. As the Commonwealth Caribbean constitutional scholar Simeon McIntosh has observed, speaking on behalf of the citizens of those independent countries for whom the Queen remains the titular head of state, the symbolic impact of her residual presence is profound:

> We purport to define ourselves as a political community in terms of our links to the British Crown. We live, we say, in a monarchical society. And this is no simple political status, for it has all sorts of social, cultural and even psychological implications.[18]

PART III: THE CONSTITUTIONAL FRAMEWORK

A. FUNCTIONS OF THE HEAD OF STATE

In terms of the constitutional functions that they actually perform, it makes little practical difference whether the head of state is the Queen, acting through a Governor General, or a ceremonial president (with the exception of certain powers of appointment enjoyed by the President of Trinidad). Guyana, which abandoned the Westminster model of government in favour of a more 'executive-style' presidency when it

---

[16] See report at: www.antillean.org.

[17] To paraphrase V Bogdanor. See V Bogdanor, *The Monarchy and the Constitution* (Oxford, Oxford University Press, 1995).

[18] S McIntosh, *Caribbean Constitutional Reform: Rethinking the West Indian Polity* (Kingston, Jamaica, Caribbean Law Publishing Company, 2002) 112.

became a 'Cooperative Republic' in 1980 is of course different, and further discussion of the powers of the President under the Guyanese Constitution is therefore postponed to chapter four.

By far the most important of the functions allocated to Governors General and presidents under Commonwealth Caribbean constitutions are those traditionally associated with the 'reserve' powers of the British monarch: so called because they are exercised personally by the monarch in contradistinction to the other prerogative powers which are exercised on the monarch's behalf by her ministers. These comprise: the power to summon, prorogue and dissolve Parliament; the power to appoint and dismiss the Prime Minister and other ministers; and the power to assent to Bills presented by Parliament. In addition, Commonwealth Caribbean constitutions assign some or all of the following functions to the Governor General or President respectively: the appointment of senators;[19] the appointment of the Leader of the Opposition;[20] the granting of pardons;[21] the appointment of members of the judiciary;[22] the appointment of members of the Public Service Commission;[23] and the proclamation of an emergency.[24]

In the exercise of their constitutional functions Governors General and presidents are generally constrained by a number of rules embodied in each country's Constitution. First and foremost of these rules is that the Governor General or President must act in accordance with the advice of the Cabinet or a Minister acting under the general authority of the Cabinet, except when required by the Constitution or some other law to act: (a) in accordance with the advice of, or after consultation with, some person or authority other than the Cabinet or (b) in their own 'discretion' or 'deliberate judgement'.[25] This rule reflects a fundamental principle of parliamentary democracy: namely, that it is elected ministers, collectively responsible to Parliament who govern the country, not the head of state. Thus, when appointing or dismissing ministers other than the Prime Minister,[26] and when dissolving or

---

[19] See, eg, s 79(2) Constitution of Antigua and Barbuda.
[20] See, eg, s 79(1) Constitution of Antigua and Barbuda.
[21] See, eg, s 84 Constitution of Antigua and Barbuda.
[22] See, eg, s 81(2) Constitution of Barbados.
[23] See, eg, s 99(1) Constitution of Antigua and Barbuda.
[24] See, eg, s 20(1) Constitution of Antigua and Barbuda.
[25] See, eg, s 80 Constitution of Antigua and Barbuda.
[26] See, eg, ss 69 and 73 Constitution of Antigua and Barbuda.

proroguing Parliament, the head of state must act in accordance with the Prime Minister's advice.[27] However, the rule also recognises that in the exercise of certain functions it is appropriate that the Governor General or President should be required to act in accordance with the recommendation of, or after consultation with, some person or authority other than the Prime Minister or the Cabinet. Though there is not the space here to list all these functions, they typically include: the appointment of a prescribed number of senators in accordance with the advice of the Leader of the Opposition;[28] the granting of pardons upon the recommendation of a local Privy Council;[29] the appointment of judges, other than the Chief Justice, in accordance with the advice of a Judicial and Legal Services Commission;[30] and the appointment and removal of public officers upon the recommendation of the Public Services Commission.[31]

Even in those cases where the Governor General or President is not required to act upon advice or after consultation the exercise of their constitutional powers is still constrained by rules embodied in the Constitution that reflect their subordination to the will of the people as it is expressed through Parliament. Thus, for example, when appointing a Prime Minister, the Governor General or President must appoint the member of the elected House who commands the confidence of a majority of the members of that House. More or less identical provisions apply mutatis mutandis to the appointment of the Leader of the Opposition.[32] And while the Governor General or President possesses

[27] See, eg, s 60 Constitution of Antigua and Barbuda.

[28] See, eg, s 79(2) Constitution of Antigua and Barbuda.

[29] See s 84 Constitution of Antigua and Barbuda; s 78 Constitution of Barbados; s 90 Constitution of the Bahamas; s 52 Constitution of Belize; s 90(2) Constitution of Jamaica; s 74 Constitution of St Lucia; and s 65 Constitution of St Vincent and the Grenadines.

[30] See s 81(2) Constitution of Barbados; s 94 Constitution of the Bahamas; s 97 Constitution of Belize; s 98 Constitution of Jamaica; and s 104 Constitution of Trinidad and Tobago.

[31] See s 94 Constitution of Barbados; s108, Constitution of the Bahamas; s 85(2) Constitution of Grenada; s 125 Constitution of Jamaica; s 78 Constitution of St Kitts and Nevis; and s 87 Constitution of St Lucia.

[32] See s 79 Constitution of Antigua and Barbuda; s 74 Constitution of Barbados; s 82 Constitution of the Bahamas; s 47 Constitution of Belize; s 66 Constitution of Dominica; s 66 Constitution of Grenada; s 80 Constitution of Jamaica; s 58 Constitution of St Kitts and Nevis; s 67 Constitution of St Lucia; s 59 Constitution of St Vincent and the Grenadines; and s 83(2) Constitution of Trinidad and Tobago.

the constitutional power to dismiss the Prime Minister, he can only do so if a resolution of no confidence in the government is passed by Parliament (or the elected House in the case of bicameral legislatures), and the Prime Minister refuses to resign or to request the dissolution of Parliament.[33]

There are, nonetheless, a number of key functions in the exercise of which Governors General and presidents are permitted to act in their 'own discretion' or 'deliberate judgement'. Thus, for example, when appointing a Prime Minister in the event of a hung parliament, the Governor General or President is allowed to exercise their judgement in determining which of the leaders of the different political parties is 'best able',[34] or 'most likely',[35] to command the support of the majority of the members of the elected House. With the exception of Trinidad, the Governor General or President may also exercise their judgement in determining whether to dissolve Parliament if the office of the Prime Minister is vacant and there is no prospect of their being able within a reasonable time to make an appointment to that office.[36] Under the Constitutions of Belize, St Lucia and St Vincent,[37] the Governor General, when faced with a request by the Prime Minister for the dissolution of Parliament can decide whether a dissolution would be in the country's interests and whether the government of the country could

[33] s 73(1) Constitution of Antigua and Barbus; s 66(2) Constitution of Barbados; s 74(1) Constitution of the Bahamas; s 36(4) Constitution of Belize; s 59(6) Constitution of Dominica; s 58(6) Constitution of Grenada; s 71 Constitution of Jamaica; s 52(6) Constitution of St Kitts and Nevis; s 60(6) Constitution of St Lucia; s 48 Constitution of St Vincent and the Grenadines; and s 77(1) Constitution of Trinidad and Tobago.

[34] See s 65(1) Constitution of Barbados and s 70(1) Constitution of Jamaica.

[35] s 69(2) Constitution of Antigua; s 73(1)(b) Constitution of the Bahamas; s 37(2) Constitution of Belize; s 59(2) Constitution of Dominica; s 58(2) Constitution of Grenada; s 52(2) Constitution of St Kitts and Nevis; s 60(2) Constitution of St Lucia; s 51(2) Constitution of St Vincent and the Grenadines; and s 76(1)(b) Constitution of Trinidad and Tobago.

[36] s 60 Constitution of Antigua; s 62 Constitution of the Bahamas; s 61 Constitution of Barbados; s 84 Constitution of Belize; s 54 Constitution of Dominica; s 52 Constitution of Grenada; s 64 Constitution of Jamaica; s 47 Constitution of St Kitts and Nevis; s 55 Constitution of St Lucia; and s 48 Constitution of St Vincent and the Grenadines.

[37] s 84(4)(a) Constitution of Belize, s 54(4)(a) Constitution of St Lucia and s 48(5) Constitution of St Vincent and the Grenadines.

better be carried on without one.[38] The Constitutions of the Bahamas, Barbados, Grenada, Jamaica, St Kitts and Trinidad also suggest, albeit by implication, that the Governor General or President, as the case may be, could in certain circumstances refuse their assent to legislation in so far as they provide that, 'When a Bill is presented to the Governor General [President] for assent he shall signify that he assents or that he withholds assent'.[39] These Constitutions do not, however, seek to offer any guidelines as to when the Governor General or President would be justified in withholding their assent and, to date, there is no recorded example of assent being withheld.

In Trinidad, the President also enjoys a considerable measure of discretion in the appointment of a number of the most important public offices—the Chief Justice,[40] the Ombudsman[41] and the Director of Public Prosecutions.[42] While the President must consult the Prime Minister and the Leader of the Opposition, the appointment in each case, ultimately, lies within the President's discretion. The President also appoints nine out of the 31 members of the Senate.[43]

It is arguable, indeed, that Governors General and presidents under Commonwealth Caribbean constitutions in some cases have, in the exercise of a number of their constitutional functions, an even greater discretion than the British monarch in the exercise of his or her 'reserve' powers under the British Constitution.[44] This is not, however, true in all cases, but it has led on occasions to unwarranted criticism of Governors General or presidents for failing to exercise a discretion which in reality they do not actually posses. Thus, in Jamaica, following the military intervention in Grenada in 1983 in which Jamaican troops had been involved, when Prime Minister, Edward Seaga—hoping to benefit from a surge in popularity similar to that enjoyed by the British Prime

---

[38] See *Bobb and Anor v Patrick Manning* [2006] UKPC 22.

[39] s 63(4) Constitution of the Bahamas; s 58(3) Constitution of Barbados; s 45(2) Constitution of Grenada; s 60(3) Constitution of Jamaica; s 42(2) Constitution of St Kitts and Nevis; and s 61(2) Constitution of Trinidad and Tobago.

[40] s 102 Constitution of Trinidad and Tobago.

[41] s 91(2) Constitution of Trinidad and Tobago.

[42] s 90 Constitution of Trinidad and Tobago.

[43] s 40(2)(c) Constitution of Trinidad and Tobago.

[44] See, eg, R Blackburn, 'Monarchy and the Personal Prerogatives' [2004] *Public Law* 546 and R Brazier, '"Monarchy and the Personal Prerogatives": A Personal Response to Professor Blackburn' [2005] *Public Law* 45.

Minister, Margaret Thatcher following the Falklands War—requested that the Governor General, Sir Florizel Glasspole, should dissolve Parliament only half way into his term of office the latter was criticised in some quarters for acceding to the Prime Minister's request. Such criticism was not, however, based upon anything to be found in the text of the Jamaican Constitution, which made it clear that the Governor General was bound to act in accordance with the advice of the Prime Minister. Instead, it was based on the idea, inherited from the traditional view of the monarch's discretion under the British Constitution, that the Governor General would have been constitutionally justified in such circumstances in refusing the Prime Minister's request, particularly as the Opposition claimed that they had an understanding with the Government that a new voters' list would be in place prior to the holding of new elections.

B. APPOINTMENT AND REMOVAL OF GOVERNORS GENERAL AND PRESIDENTS

Different arrangements apply as between the appointment and removal of Governors General and presidents under Commonwealth Caribbean constitutions.

1. Governors General

Governors General are customarily appointed in accordance with the recommendation of the Prime Minister of the country concerned.[45] There is no requirement that in making their recommendation the Prime Minister must consult with any other person or body. No specific qualifications are required for appointment, though it may be noted that since independence only one non-national has ever been appointed as a Governor General: Solomon Hochoy, the first Governor-General of Trinidad, had however lived in Trinidad from the age of two. There is certainly no express requirement that the Governor General should be free from any political affiliations. Indeed, a number of Governors

---

[45] W Dale, *The Modern Commonwealth* (London, Butterworths, 1983) 112.

General within the region have previously held political office and many have been members of the same political party as the incumbent Prime Minister. This is true, for example, of all the Governors General in the Bahamas since independence, with the exception of Ivy Dumont. It is also true of Sir Deighton Ward in Barbados; Carlyle Glean in Grenada; Clifford Campbell, Sir Florizel Glasspole and Howard Cooke in Jamaica; and Allen Lewis, Boswell Williams and George Mallett in St Lucia. Antigua had until recently been an exception to this rule. However, the recent appointment of a Governor General, who had not only contributed to the governing party's election campaign, but had also made frequent public appearances to support that same election, proved to be particularly controversial and resulted in the Antigua Labour Party boycotting the Throne Speech in protest.[46]

The custom of appointment upon the advice of the Prime Minister is taken also to extend to the Governor General's dismissal.[47] Governors General are thus removable by Her Majesty upon a request from the Prime Minister of the country concerned and there have been several instances since independence of the premature dismissal or resignation of Governors General. This has occurred twice in Grenada. The first occasion was in 1974 when the Governor General, Dame Hilda Bynoe, pre-empted the threat of the Prime Minister, Sir Eric Gairy, to dismiss her by leaving the island before the threat could be acted upon. Subsequently, her successor, Sir Leo de Gale, endured an equally tense relationship with Gairy, and he too resigned prematurely in 1978 to go abroad.[48] There have also been three premature departures from office in St Lucia. The first occasion was in 1980, when a new government brought pressure on the incumbent Governor General, Allen Lewis, to retire. The second was in 1982, when the former government returned to power and the Queen was obliged to dismiss the new Governor General, Boswell Williams, at the request of the Prime Minister, following his refusal to retire.[49] The third occasion was—following the St Lucia Labour Party's victory over the United Workers Party (UWP)

---

[46] See report. Available at: www.caribbeannetnews.com.

[47] Dale, above (n 45) 113, though Geoffrey Marshall and Vernon Bogdanor have suggested that the Queen may retain a residual discretion to refuse a Prime Minister's request for dismissal of a Governor General. See V Bogdanor and G Marshall, 'Dismissing Governor-Generals' [1996] *Public Law* 206.

[48] Bogdanor, above (n 17) 283.

[49] Ibid.

led by John Compton in the 1997 general election—when, according to Selwyn Ryan, the majority of incoming ministers and 'job hungry party stalwarts demanded that the "Comptonites" ... be severed' and that the Governor General (who prior to his appointment had been a UWP Member of Parliament) be replaced.[50]

In the interests of balance, it should be pointed out that there have also been several instances of long-serving Governors General who have managed to remain in office following changes of government. For example, Sir Florizel Glasspole, Governor General of Jamaica from 1973 to 1991, survived the transfer of power from the People's National Party to the Jamaica Labour Party, during a period of intense political turbulence in Jamaica. In Grenada also, Sir Paul Scoon managed not only to remain in office following the seizure of power by the New Jewel Movement in 1979, but found himself assuming executive authority on the island with the aid of an Advisory Council after the overthrow of the People's Revolutionary Government four years later, following the invasion of the island by a force of US marines.

Ultimately, however, the contingent status of Governors General, which is quite unlike that of a hereditary monarch, owing both their appointment and their survival in office to the Prime Minister, makes it difficult for them to act and to be seen to act independently of the latter. As Marshall and Bogdanor have observed, 'if a Governor General can be dismissed by a Prime Minister the constitution is destabilised at its heart'.[51] In such circumstances a perception arises that the offices of head of state and head of government are inextricably linked.[52] Such a perception is only reinforced by the nature of the close-knit communities that make up so many of the small island states of the Commonwealth Caribbean, where political leaders and Governors General may have gone to the same schools, attend the same churches and have close family and social ties. This can be particularly problematic where a Governor General is called upon to exercise their 'reserve powers': for example, to decide whether or not to grant a Prime Minister's request for the dissolution of Parliament. In such cases, their indebtedness to

---

[50] S Ryan, *Winner Takes All: The Westminster Experience in the Caribbean* (St Augustine, Trinidad, ISER, University of the West Indies Press, 1999) 79–80.

[51] Bogdanor and Marshall, above (n 47) 213.

[52] DP O'Connell, cited in Cowen, 'Crown and Representative', lecture 3, p 19. Cited by Bogdanor, above (n 17) 284.

the Prime Minister for their appointment can make it extremely difficult for Governors General to discharge their constitutional responsibility, which is to reach a decision which serves the country's best interests and not the political machinations of the Prime Minister.

2. Presidents

In comparison with the absolute control exercised by Prime Ministers over the appointment of Governors General in those countries that remain constitutional monarchies, the Prime Ministers of Dominica and Trinidad have less of a direct involvement in the appointment of their respective presidents. Thus, in Trinidad, the President is chosen by a secret ballot[53] of an electoral college; a unicameral body, consisting of all the members of the House of Representatives and the Senate.[54] The candidate who is unopposed or who obtains the greatest number of votes is elected president. In Dominica, which has a unicameral legislature (the House of Assembly), the Prime Minister is required first to consult the Leader of the Opposition about the nomination of the President. If they agree upon a candidate the Speaker is informed and the Speaker, in turn, notifies the House and declares that person duly elected.[55] If they do not agree, one or more candidates may be nominated by the Prime Minister, the Leader of the Opposition or any three members of the House, and the House decides by secret ballot.[56] The process is not always, however, quite as straightforward as the foregoing summary would appear to suggest and in proceedings which were still ongoing at the time of writing, the election of President Eluid Williams (the ruling Dominica Labour Party's nominee) has been challenged by the Leader of the Opposition on the ground that he had not been consulted prior to the President's nomination by the Prime Minister.

In order to be eligible for nomination, in both Dominica and Trinidad, a candidate must be a citizen of the country concerned. There are also minimum age limits (35 or upwards in Trinidad and 40 in Dominica), and minimum periods of time that candidates must have

---

[53] s 29 Constitution of Trinidad and Tobago.
[54] s 28 Constitution of Trinidad and Tobago.
[55] s 19(2) Constitution of Dominica.
[56] ss 19(4) and 19(5) Constitution of Dominica.

been living in the country immediately preceding nomination (10 years in Trinidad and five years in Dominica).[57]

The difference in the manner of appointment of Governors General and presidents should not, however, be overstated. In the case of both Dominica and Trinidad, the Prime Minister controls a majority of the votes in the House of Assembly and electoral college respectively. To this extent, the Prime Minister therefore still has a considerable say over the President's election, though it is not always guaranteed that the President will ultimately get their choice: Noor Hassanali's election as President of Trinidad, in 1987, for example, was not supported by the Prime Minister, Arthur Robinson. The more significant difference between Governors General and presidents in the region instead lies in the much greater security of tenure enjoyed by the latter. Thus, the Presidents of Dominica and Trinidad are both appointed for a fixed term of five years and there is no obstacle to either standing for re-election for a further term.[58] Furthermore, while in office they can only be removed if they wilfully violate any provisions of the Constitution; behave in such a way as to bring their office into hatred, ridicule or contempt; behave in a way that endangers the security of the state; or, because of physical or mental incapacity, they are unable to perform the functions of their office.[59] Even then, they cannot be removed from office unless the legislature has first received a report from a tribunal consisting of the Chief Justice and four other judges appointed by the Chief Justice in the case of Trinidad,[60] and the Chief Justice and two other Supreme Court judges appointed by the Chief Justice in the case of Dominica.[61] Furthermore, the motion for the President's removal must attract the support of not less than two-thirds of the total membership of the legislature.[62] Though it is conceivable that a government with a very large majority could, nevertheless, force the removal of a president of which it disapproved, the requirement of a report from an

[57] s 23(1) Constitution of Trinidad and Tobago and s 20(1) Constitution of Dominica.

[58] s 21 Constitution of Dominica.

[59] s 24 Constitution of Dominica and s 35 Constitution of Trinidad and Tobago.

[60] s 36(1)(d) Constitution of Trinidad and Tobago.

[61] s 25(1)(b) Constitution of Dominica.

[62] s 36(1)(e) Constitution of Trinidad and Tobago and s 25(1)(c) Constitution of Dominica.

independent tribunal might, at least, cause political embarrassment to the government and persuade it to refrain from exercising its numerical advantage in the event that the President was exonerated by the tribunal's report.

The security of tenure enjoyed by the Presidents of Dominica and Trinidad means that they are better placed to resist pressure from their Prime Ministers when exercising their discretionary powers. In the case of Trinidad, however, this has proved to be something of a mixed blessing, as it has led to a number of fractious disputes between the President and the incumbent Prime Minister. The first of these occurred in 1986, following the general election, when a dispute arose between the new Prime Minister, Arthur Robinson, and the outgoing President, Sir Ellis Clarke, with regard to a number of appointments by the latter to the Public Service Commission and the Police Commission. This resulted in proceedings being brought by the Attorney General on behalf of the Prime Minister to challenge the validity of these appointments (considered in more detail below).[63] It also led to the establishment of a constitution commission, headed by Sir Isaac Hyatali (the 'Hyatali Commission'), which considered, among other proposals, changes to the method of election of the President, and the removal of the President's immunity against judicial review.[64] The report of the Hyatali Commission was, however, never properly debated by Parliament because of the national crisis which ensued following the attempted coup on 27 July 1990 by members of the Jamaat al Muslimeen and, within a decade, relations between the incumbent President and the incumbent Prime Minister had broken down again. On this occasion, the President was the same Arthur Robinson, who had been Prime Minister between 1986 and 1991, and his Prime Minister was Basdeo Panday, leader of the United National Congress (UNC), which is generally regarded as representing the interests of the Indo-Caribbean community in Trinidad. Very shortly after Robinson's election as President he became embroiled in a series of disputes with Panday, beginning with the President's refusal to act upon the Prime Minister's advice to remove a number of senators from Tobago. This was followed by the

[63] *AG v Bain*, High Court of Trinidad and Tobago No 3260 of 1987. Unreported. Available on file with the author.
[64] The Constitution Commission of Trinidad and Tobago, *Thinking Things Over* (1987) 28. Available at: www.ttparliament.org.

President's decision to reject the Prime Minister's advice to appoint
certain losing electoral candidates from the UNC as senators, and culminated in the President's decision to appoint as Prime Minister, Patrick
Manning, the leader of the People's National Movement (PNM),[65] following an unprecedented tie in the December 2001 elections.

The inability of both Robinson and Panday to impose their will upon
their respective presidents was, no doubt, a source of enormous frustration, and is in marked contrast to the position that obtains among the
constitutional monarchies in the region where the Prime Minister can
simply request the removal of a Governor General who refuses to toe
the line. It would of course be easy to trace the source of this frustration
to the tensions that existed between the Afro-Caribbean and the Indo-
Caribbean communities which the President and the Prime Minister
respectively represented, but even if racial politics could be shown to
have played some part in their relationship, the underlying problem,
which has nothing to do with racial politics, is a constitutional relationship that invests the President with significant discretionary power for
which the President is not politically accountable, and with sufficient
security of tenure to ensure that the President can afford to ignore the
Prime Minister's wishes if they so choose.

PART IV: JUDICIAL REVIEW OF THE CONSTITUTIONAL FUNCTIONS OF PRESIDENTS AND GOVERNORS GENERAL

As noted above, the exercise by Governors General and presidents of
their functions are regulated by rules embodied in the Independence
Constitutions that are intended to mirror the uncodified conventions of the British Constitution. The inclusion of these rules in the
Independence Constitutions offers a number of advantages. First, it
ensures that the rules are conveniently located within one document
and avoids the uncertainty that could arise if the rules could only be
ascertained by reference to evolving constitutional practice in Britain

---

[65] For a more detailed account of the breakdown in relations between President
Robinson and Prime Minister Panday, see K Meighoo and P Jamadar, *Democracy and
Constitution Reform in Trinidad and Tobago* (Kingston, Jamaica, Ian Randle Publishers,
2008) 72–73.

or elsewhere in the Commonwealth, which might anyway not always be apt to meet local conditions.[66] Second, it ensures that the rules are defined with some precision, thereby offering—though not always guaranteeing as we saw in the case of Jamaica—the head of state a measure of protection against the kind of controversy that can arise when the rules surrounding their exercise are uncertain. Third, it ensures that the rules enjoy the 'greater psychological sanctity' that attaches to the provisions of a written constitution.[67] Fourth, and finally, it opens the door to supervision of the exercise of these powers by the courts. It is, however, important to recognise that the role of Commonwealth Caribbean courts in supervising the exercise of these powers is subject to a number of limitations. In order to understand the nature of these limitations it is necessary to consider two distinct but related questions. The first, and logically prior, question concerns the susceptibility of Governors General and presidents, to judicial review. The second concerns the justiciability of the exercise of the head of state's reserve or discretionary powers. The answers to these questions give rise to both legal and normative considerations.

A. SUSCEPTIBILITY TO JUDICIAL REVIEW

When considering the susceptibility of Governors General and presidents within the region to judicial review *in personam*, it is necessary first to examine the position under the common law and then to see how this is affected, if at all, by the type of immunity and ouster clauses to be found in Commonwealth Caribbean constitutions.

1. Common Law

Under the British Constitution there has never been any question of the courts reviewing the exercise by the monarch of her constituional powers. The possibility of granting a parallel immunity to Governors General, as the Queen's appointed representatives, was first considered

---

[66] KJ Keith, 'The Courts and the Conventions of the Constitution' (1967) 16 *International & Comparative Law Quarterly* 542.

[67] Ibid.

by the Court of Appeal of Trinidad and Tobago in *Hochoy v NUGE*,[68] a decision which pre-dates the adoption by Trinidad of its republican Constitution in 1976. In this case, which concerned a challenge to the appointment by the Governor General of a Commission of Inquiry to look into matters relating to a trade dispute, lawyers for the Governor General sought to argue that, as the Queen's representative in Trinidad, he enjoyed the same immunity from suit in the courts of that country in respect of acts performed by him in his official capacity as would the Queen. Though the case was concerned with the exercise of a statutory power conferred upon the Governor General by the Commission of Inquiry Ordinance, judicial recognition of a general immunity from suit for Governors General for *all* acts performed in an official capacity would clearly have had profound constitutional implications.

Aware that no such immunity had ever previously been granted to colonial Governors,[69] lawyers for the Governor General initially argued that the office of a colonial Governor should be distinguished on the basis that the powers of a colonial Governor were strictly limited by the terms of their commission and instructions, whereas the Governor General, as the Queen's representative in Trinidad, held a position analogous to that held by the Queen in England and, accordingly, must be considered to be endowed with similar attributes. This submission was, however, rejected by the Court on the ground that under the common law the sovereign's immunity from suit was a strictly personal one and stemmed entirely from 'the ancient doctrine that no lord could be compelled to answer in his own court'.[70] Nor was the Court persuaded to adopt the alternative submission by the Governor General's lawyers that it should follow the suggestion of the authors of *Halsbury's Laws*—under the rubric, 'Legal Liability of Governors-General and Governors'—and 'recognize immunity from suit in respect of claims arising out of official but not private acts'.[71] In the judges' view, the recognition of such immunity would offend the rule of law; in particular,

---

[68] *Hochoy v NUGE* (1964) 7 WIR 174.

[69] See, eg, *Bhagat Singh v The King-Emperor* (1931) LR 58 IA 169 and *Beetham v Trinidad Cement Ltd* [1960] AC 132.

[70] Holdsworth *A History of English Law*, 3rd edn, vol 3 (London, Methuen and Company, 1966) 465.

[71] *Halsbury's Laws of England*, 3rd edn, vol 5 (London, Butterworths, 1953) 468 [1033].

the maxim of equality before the law, quoting Dicey to support their analysis:

> Not only that with us no man is above the law, but (what is a different thing) that here every man, whatever be his rank or condition is subject to the ordinary law of the realm and amenable to the jurisdiction of the ordinary tribunals ... With us every official, from the Prime Minister down to a constable or a collector of taxes, is under the same responsibility for every act done without legal justification as any other citizen.[72]

2. Immunity Clauses

Hochoy v NUGE is clearly an important case in so far as it upholds the principle of equality under the law against claims for a general immunity from suit for Governors General and it is therefore, to say the least, surprising that a decade later, in 1974, Trinidad's Constitution Commission, led by the same Chief Justice Wooding who had delivered the leading judgment in *Hochoy*, recommended the grant of just such an immunity to the President under the new republican Constitution of Trinidad. In the Commission's view, 'The President should not be answerable to any court for the manner in which the President exercises any of their powers or performs any of their duties as President'.[73] The grant of such immunity is not without precedent in other Commonwealth countries[74] and, possibly, it was considered that it was unbefitting for the President, as the symbol of the nation, to be liable to the ordinary processes of the court. It is also possible that the provisions for the President's removal in the event that the President wilfully violated the Constitution were thought to offer a sufficient guarantee against misuse of the President's powers. However, the Constitution of Dominica, which contains similar provisions for the removal of the President, offers no such general immunity and only exempts the President from *criminal* proceedings in respect of acts done in the President's official capacity.[75]

[72] AV Dicey, *Introduction to the Study of the Law of the Constitution*, 9th edn (London, Macmillan, 1948) 193.
[73] *Report of the Constitution Commission*, above (n 10) para 166.
[74] See Art 13(8) Constitution of Ireland.
[75] s 27 Constitution of Dominica.

Whatever the justification, the Commission's recommendation was subsequently reproduced more or less verbatim in section 38 of the 1976 Constitution of Trinidad and Tobago, which provides that the President, 'shall not be answerable to any court for the performance of the functions of his office or for any act done by him in the performance of those functions'. On the face of it, such a clause would appear to afford the President immunity from all proceedings, including judicial review, for all acts related to the performance of his functions under the Constitution. Sir Ellis Clarke, himself a former President of Trinidad and Tobago, has argued, however, that the immunity granted by section 38, 'is a personal immunity and does not preclude a challenge to the exercise by the President of any authority conferred upon him by the Constitution'.[76] Such an interpretation, however, is not supported by the few cases in which the courts have directly addressed the effect of section 38. Thus, in *AG Trinidad v Phillip and Others*,[77] in which the Judicial Committee of the Privy Council (JCPC) was asked to consider the validity of a pardon granted to the respondents by the Acting President, arising out of the attempted coup by the Jamaat Al Muslimeen in 1990, the JCPC noted that, while it was not prevented from considering the validity of the pardon, it was precluded by section 38 from reviewing the decision of the President to grant the pardon. Again, in *Jairam v AG Trinidad*,[78] in which the High Court was asked to consider the legality of the President's decision to reverse his earlier decision to commute the appellant's death sentence to one of life imprisonment, it was held that the Court was precluded by section 38 from reviewing the President's decision, even if it was mistaken; though the Court also noted that the President could, if he so wished, waive the immunity. And finally, in *Bobb and Anor v Manning*,[79] in which reference was made to the President's power to appoint the Prime Minister in the circumstances outlined in section 76(1)(b) of the Constitution, where no one party commands the support of a majority of the House of Representatives, the JCPC noted that section 38 (together with the ouster clause contained in section 80(3)(a) which I consider below) precluded any challenge to the President's decision in such a case.

---

[76] E Clarke, 'The West Indies' in Butler and Low (eds), *Sovereigns and Surrogates*, above (n 5) 181.

[77] *AG Trinidad v Phillip and Others* [1994] UKPC 33.

[78] *Jairam v AG Trinidad* TT 1997 HC 99.

[79] *Bobb and Anor v Manning* [2006] UKPC 22.

The only other Constitution in the region to grant a general immunity to its head of state is that of Guyana, which by Article 182 provides that the President 'shall not be personally answerable to any court for the performance of the functions of his office or for any act done in the performance of those functions'. Here, however, the courts have adopted a quite different approach. Thus, in *Baird (Michael) v Public Service Commission*,[80] the Guyana Court of Appeal took the opportunity to comment generally on the immunity afforded by Article 182, even though it was not strictly necessary in deciding the appellant's claim to recover certain superannuation benefits payable in respect of his time serving in the police force. In the Court's view:

> The immunities which attach personally to the President under art 182 of the Constitution are for the limited purpose of ensuring effective performance of the functions of his high office, and not for the purpose of granting immunity to the State for any official wrongdoing. The State would still be liable for the President's wrongdoing, even though the President himself would be immune from the curial processes. It is the President who is immune from curial processes, not his acts.[81]

In Guyana, at least, it would therefore seem that the immunity clause at most prohibits actions *in personam* against the President, but does not otherwise prohibit the courts from reviewing the exercise of the President's constitutional powers.

3. Ouster Clauses

While the Constitutions of Trinidad and Guyana may be the only ones in the region to purport to grant a general immunity to their head of state, all Commonwealth Caribbean constitutions include an ouster clause which impose limits on the courts' powers of review of those functions which require the President or Governor General to act on advice or after consultation. Section 124 of the Constitution of Antigua is typical of such clauses:

> Where by this Constitution the Governor General is required to perform any function in accordance with the advice of the Cabinet, the Prime Minister or any other Minister or the Leader of the Opposition or any other person,

---

[80] *Baird (Michael) v Public Service Commission* (2001) 63 WIR 134.
[81] See further *Karanathilaka v Commissioner of Elections* [1999] 4 LRC.

body or authority or after consultation with any person, body or authority, the question whether the Governor General has received or acted in accordance with such advice, or whether such consultation has taken place, shall not be enquired into in any court of law.

The aim of such ouster clauses would appear to be twofold: first, to prevent disclosure of confidential communications between the head of state and such other person as he may be required to consult; and second, to safeguard against the courts being used to adjudicate what may ultimately be a personal dispute between the Governor General and the Prime Minister about the precise nature of the advice that has been given, leaving disputes between the two to be resolved by the other processes provided for under the Constitution; ie, dismissal on the recommendation of the Prime Minister in the case of Governors General and removal upon a resolution of the legislature in the case of presidents.

Traditionally, courts throughout the Commonwealth have been very hostile to any attempt by the legislature to exclude their jurisdiction through the deployment of ouster clauses and have sought by the use of creative interpretive methods to nullify their effect.[82] In the Commonwealth Caribbean, however, the courts have been much more willing to concede the validity of ouster clauses which purport to oust their jurisdiction to enquire into the question of whether a Governor General or President has sought or acted on advice. The validity of such a clause was first tested, in a Commonwealth Caribbean context, in the case of *AG v Bain*. As noted above, this case was concerned with a dispute between the Prime Minister of Trinidad and Tobago, Arthur Robinson, and the outgoing President, Sir Ellis Clarke, with regard to the latter's appointment of the respondent to the Public Service Commission. On behalf of the Prime Minister, it was argued that the appointment was invalid because the President had not consulted the Prime Minister and the Leader of the Opposition beforehand, in accordance with section 120(2) of the Constitution. The High Court, however, concluded that, quite apart from the general immunity clause under the Constitution, it was absolutely precluded from investigating this issue by the ouster clause contained in section 80(2) of the Constitution.

---

[82] See, eg, *Anisminic Ltd v Foreign Compensation Commission* [1969] 2 AC 147.

The effect of such ouster clauses upon the courts' powers of review has subsequently been confirmed by the JCPC in *Knowles (Austin) v Superintendent of Fox Hill Prison*,[83] in which it was held that the ouster clause contained in Article 79(4) of the Constitution of the Bahamas precluded the JCPC from enquiring whether the Governor General had acted in accordance with the advice of the Prime Minister, as required by Article 76(3) of the Constitution, when appointing a temporary Minister of Foreign Affairs. It is, however, important to note that the JCPC in *Knowles* was keen to emphasise that the ouster clause did not on its face exclude *all* enquiry into the manner of the appointment and did not prevent some other aspect of the constitutionality of the appointment being reviewed by the Court.[84] As the JCPC explained, the inclusion of such ouster clauses only precluded the Court from investigating whether a Governor General or President had acted on the recommendation or advice of, or after consultation with, any person or authority; it did not preclude a court from reviewing the other constitutional provisions that surround the exercise by Governors General of their constitutional functions. Thus, in *Lewis v AG Jamaica*,[85] for example, where the JCPC was asked to review the decision of the Governor General, acting upon the advice of the Jamaican Privy Council (the body responsible under the Constitution for advising the Governor General on granting pardons or substituting less severe forms of punishments on those convicted of criminal offences) not to commute the death sentence imposed on the applicant,[86] the existence of the ouster clause in section 32(4) did not preclude the JCPC from considering whether the Jamaican Privy Council had adopted a fair procedure in dealing with the applicant's petition. Nor would it have precluded the JCPC from considering whether the Jamaican Privy Council had been properly constituted.

Another potential limitation on the reach of these ouster clauses was identified by the JCPC in *Thomas v AG Trinidad*[87] where the Board held that the ouster clause contained in section 102(4) of the Constitution which precluded judicial review of decisions of the Police Service

[83] *Knowles (Austin) v Superintendent of Fox Hill Prison* [2005] UKPC 17.
[84] Ibid, [11].
[85] *Lewis v AG Jamaica* [2001] 2 AC 50.
[86] Pursuant to s 90(2) Constitution of Jamaica.
[87] *Thomas v AG Trinidad* [1982] AC 113, 135.

Commission (PSC) would not preclude challenges to decisions of the PSC which contravened the rights guaranteed by section 2 of the Constitution and for which a special right to apply to the High Court for redress is granted by section 6 of the Constitution. Though the Board was here concerned with the effect of the ouster clause upon decisions of the PSC, there is no reason why the same principle should not apply to decisions of a Governor General which infringe the fundamental rights guaranteed by the Constitution. Such at least was the approach of the Belize Supreme Court in *Carr v AG Belize*,[88] in which it was held by the Supreme Court that the ouster clause in section 34(4) of the Constitution did not preclude the Court from reviewing whether or not the Governor General violated the applicant's right to a fair hearing when he terminated the applicant's appointment as the acting Labour Commissioner.

B. JUSTICIABILITY

As we have seen, the ouster clauses contained in Commonwealth Caribbean constitutions are concerned only with the exercise of those constitutional powers which require Governors General and presidents to act on advice or after consultation. They do not, with the exception of the Constitution of St Kitts, which we consider below, preclude courts from reviewing the exercise of those powers in which the head of state is permitted to act in their own discretion. Thus, in the absence of the type of general immunity clause found in the Constitution of Trinidad and Tobago, the exercise of these discretionary powers is potentially exposed to judicial scrutiny, which risks involving judges in addressing issues which are politically very contentious and which may not lend themselves readily to a legal remedy.

Increasingly, judges have sought to avoid this problem by applying the doctrine of justiciability which allows them to decline jurisdiction by reference to considerations of relative constitutional and institutional competence. The contours of the doctrine of justiciability are, however, notoriously imprecise and while there are a number of examples that

---

[88] *Carr v AG Belize* 1BzLR 281; BZ 1983 SC 12. Unreported. Available on file with the author.

can be drawn upon from around the Commonwealth where judges have wrestled with the application of the doctrine to review of the exercise of a head of state's discretionary powers, these cases are, unfortunately, highly context-specific, turning on their own particular facts. It is, accordingly, difficult to extract from them any firm guidelines.[89] An insight into the likely approach of Commonwealth Caribbean judges can, however, be drawn from the case of *Re Blake*.[90]

In this case, the Court of Appeal of the Eastern Caribbean Supreme Court was asked to review a decision by the Governor General of St Kitts to reappoint a Prime Minister whom, it was alleged by the appellant, led a minority government. By section 52 of the Constitution of St Kitts, the Governor General is required to appoint as Prime Minister the member of the House of Representatives 'who appears to him likely to command the support of the majority of the representatives'. In arriving at this decision the Governor General is permitted to 'act in his own deliberate judgement'. In the event, the Court decided that review of the Governor General's decision was expressly precluded by the ouster clause contained in section 116(2) of the Constitution, which goes somewhat further than the ouster clauses discussed in the previous section by including within its ambit those functions which the Governor General is permitted to perform in their own deliberate judgement. But, even in the absence of such a widely drafted ouster clause, the judges were unanimously of the view that the exercise of the Governor General's discretion in this matter was inherently nonjusticiable:

> If the decision of the Governor General to appoint a Prime Minister was made subject to judicial review, the results could be horrendous. It would mean that the Head of State might be required to divulge sensitive confidential opinions and information imparted by the Representatives and other persons and would be exposed to all the undesirable consequences of such disclosure. Public policy dictates that the Head of State should be spared those consequences.[91]

The Court's refusal to intervene in this case can readily be defended on at least two grounds. First, it is difficult to see what remedy the court

---

[89] See, eg, *Adegbenro v Akintola* [1963] AC 614, and *Mustapha v Mohammed* [1987] LRC (Const) 16.
[90] *Re Blake* (1994) 47 WIR 174.
[91] At 182.

could have offered in the event that it found that the Governor General had acted unconstitutionally. As the Court noted, to have granted the order of mandamus sought by the appellant, requiring the Governor General to remove the Prime Minister from office, would have usurped the powers granted by the Constitution to the Governor General. Second, the Constitution itself offered an alternative procedure for determining whether the Governor General's decision and the opinion on which the Governor General's decision was based were correct by providing for a motion of no confidence in the Government, the outcome of which would establish conclusively whether or not the Prime Minister appointed by the Governor General commanded the support of the majority of the House of Representatives.

Thus, in the exercise of those functions where the Governor General or President is empowered to act in their own discretion or deliberate judgement unconstrained by a requirement to consult or to act upon advice or any other rule, the courts' powers of supervision are limited by the doctrine of justiciability, based here on considerations of confidentiality, comity between the organs of government and *realpolitik*. This ensures that the legitimacy of the exercise of these functions depends ultimately upon the commitment of the actors involved to democratic values and to the democratic process, rather than enforcement by the courts.

CONCLUSION

It is now over 50 years since Jamaica and Trinidad became the first countries in the region to gain their independence, but the role of the head of state in the post-independent Commonwealth Caribbean remains problematic. In those countries that have remained constitutional monarchies there are deeply felt objections to having the Queen as their head of state with all the connotations of subordination to the former imperial power which attach to this arrangement, and this in turn calls into question the monarch's role as a force for national unity in these countries. Currently, the Governments of both Barbados and Jamaica are committed to replacing the Queen with a ceremonial president. While this will go some way to meeting local demands for a head of state who is commensurate with the independent status of these countries, the experience of Trinidad, at least, would however suggest that republicanism is at best only a partial solution and raises its own set of problems regarding the politicisation of the head of state.

Linked to this are the normative concerns that have been expressed across the wider Commonwealth, including Britain, about the extent to which the existence of the head of state's reserve or discretionary powers is compatible with contemporary conceptions of democracy.[92] Can a head of state, whether a monarch—acting through her representative, the Governor General—or a president, who has not been elected by a popular vote, ever be constitutionally justified in refusing to exercise their powers in accordance with the advice of a Prime Minister who enjoys a democratic mandate? As we have seen, however, in the Commonwealth Caribbean the concern is not only that the head of state lacks a democratic mandate, but also that Governors General and presidents are liable to be influenced not by what they consider to be the country's best interests, but rather by their own instinct for self-preservation, by party political affiliations or even, in some countries, deep-rooted racial allegiances.

While the courts clearly have an important role to play in ensuring that both Governors General and presidents keep generally within the boundaries fixed by the Constitution, the courts' supervisory jurisdiction is significantly circumscribed by the inclusion of general immunity clauses in the republican Constitutions of Trinidad and Guyana, by the ouster clauses contained in the other Independence Constitutions and, ultimately, by considerations of justiciability. This means that, in the final analysis, the democratic legitimacy of the exercise by Governors General and by presidents of some of the most important constitutional functions depends upon assurances of independence and impartiality which Commonwealth Caribbean constitutions, unfortunately, do not guarantee.

[92] See further PH Russell and L Sossin (eds), *Parliamentary Democracy in Crisis* (Toronto, University of Toronto Press, 2009).

FURTHER READING

R Blackburn, 'Monarchy and the Personal Prerogatives' [2004] *Public Law*
546.

V Bogdanor, *The Monarchy and the Constitution* (Oxford, Oxford University
Press, 1995).

D Butler and DA Low (eds), *Sovereigns and Surrogates: Constitutional Heads of
State in the Commonwealth* (Oxford, Macmillan, 1991).

W Dale, *The Modern Commonwealth* (London, Butterworths, 1983).

S McIntosh, *Caribbean Constitutional Reform: Rethinking the West Indian Polity*
(Kingston, Jamaica, Caribbean Law Publishing Company, 2002).

K Meighoo and P Jamadar, *Democracy and Constitution Reform in Trinidad
and Tobago* (Kingston, Jamaica, Ian Randle Publishers, 2008).

3

Electoral Systems

———◆◆◆———

Background – Electoral Systems – Management and Administration of Elections – Financing of Political Parties and Access to the Media – Conclusion

PART I: BACKGROUND

COMPETITIVE GENERAL ELECTIONS underpin the 'Westminster model' of democracy, enabling voters to select their government and to hold their political leaders accountable for their performance in office. General elections have thus been described as the 'sovereign political act' of the people,[1] and the integrity of the system in place for holding general elections is, accordingly, a vital ingredient in any evaluation of the quality of democracy in the region.

In this chapter I therefore wish to explore a number of factors that potentially impact on the overall integrity of the electoral process in the region. First, I will examine the two main electoral systems in place: the 'first past the post' (FPTP) system, which remains the system of choice for the majority of countries in the region, and the 'party list' system, which operates in Guyana. I will then turn, in part II, to consider the arrangements for the management and administration of elections: in particular, the role of Boundary Commissions in fixing and reviewing constituency boundaries, and the role of Electoral Management Bodies in supervising the registration of voters and the conduct of elections. Finally, in part III, I will look at the laws that govern the financing of political parties and election campaigns, as well as the regulations surrounding access to the media by political parties.

---

[1] R Blackburn, *The Electoral System in Britain* (London, Macmillan, 1995) 2.

PART II: ELECTORAL SYSTEMS

As noted in chapter one, one of the most egregious aspects of the 'Crown Colony' system, under which the majority of countries in the region were governed for the latter part of the nineteenth and the first half of the twentieth century, was the denial of an effective voice in government to the majority of the citizens of these countries. Even when an elected element was introduced into the Legislative Councils, following the reforms recommended by the Wood Commission,[2] in 1922, the elections were based on a very narrow suffrage. This was so severely restricted by reference to income and property qualifications that even as late as the 1930s only 5 per cent of the population of Jamaica was entitled to vote. In Trinidad, it was a little better at 6.5 per cent, but elsewhere across the region the proportions were even lower: 2.2 per cent in St Lucia, 2.9 per cent in British Guiana and 3.4 per cent in Barbados.[3] As Gordon Lewis has observed, 'The West Indian electoral system, as a matter of fact, was not much more advanced in 1938 than the electoral system had been in Great Britain before the Reform Bill of 1832'.[4] Indeed, it was not until after the publication of the report of the Moyne Commission, in 1940,[5] that universal adult suffrage was finally introduced in Jamaica in 1944, and then gradually extended across the region.

A. 'FIRST PAST THE POST' (FPTP)

Prior to independence elections in Commonwealth Caribbean countries had always been held under the FPTP system and in the various constitutional conferences that preceded independence there was little, if any, discussion about whether elections should continue to be based

---

[2] *Report by the Hon EFL Wood, MP, on His Visit to the West Indies and British Guiana, December 1921 to February 1922* (Cmd 1679, 1922).
[3] E Wallace, *The British Caribbean: From the Decline of Colonialism to the End of Federation* (Toronto, University of Toronto Press, 1977).
[4] GK Lewis, *The Growth of the Modern West Indies* (Kingston, Jamaica, Ian Randle Publishers, 2004) 97.
[5] *Report of the West Indian Royal Commission 1938–39* (Cmd 6607, 1945).

on the FPTP system. The most striking exceptions are Guyana, which we consider in more detail below, and Dominica. In the latter case, at the Independence Conference in London the Opposition delegation had proposed a mixed system for electing the members of the National Assembly, based on a combination of FPTP for electing 13 of the 21 members of the National Assembly, with the remaining eight members being elected by a system of proportional representation.[6] However, this proposal was not supported by the Government of Dominica because it deviated from the British version of the Westminster model to which the Government of Dominica was determined to adhere and in the absence of agreement between the parties the FPTP system was retained.[7]

Under the FPTP system (which should be distinguished from other majoritarian systems such as the majority–plurality and alternative vote systems), voting usually takes place in single-member constituencies and the candidate with the most votes is elected.[8] Supporters of the FPTP system argue that it is simple to understand and to use; produces quick results; maintains a link between the elected MP and their constituency; and results in strong and stable government. Critics of the system, however, argue that it disfavours small parties; gives a disproportionate benefit in terms of seats to the party that secures the largest share of popular votes; and encourages adversarial politics.

Certainly, the force of the first and second of the above criticisms can be seen in the results of the general elections that have been held across the region since independence. It has thus proved to be difficult for smaller parties in many countries to gain a toehold in a political landscape which has been dominated at any one time by, at most, two political parties, each of which has been able to govern in their turn with reasonably comfortable majorities. The paradigmatic example of this is Jamaica where the Jamaica Labour Party (JLP) and the People's National Party (PNP) have been competing for power ever since the country was first granted universal suffrage in 1944, but the same is

---

[6] *Report of the Dominica Constitutional Conference* (Cmnd 6901, 1977).

[7] Miscellaneous No 20 (1978) Dominica. Termination of Association (Cmnd 7279, 1977–78) para 21.

[8] The system of double-member constituencies in Barbados, which had prevailed since 1845, was finally abandoned in 1971 in favour of single-member constituencies.

also broadly true of Antigua, the Bahamas, Barbados, St Lucia and St Vincent. The main exception to this pattern is Grenada where, since the resumption of parliamentary democracy in 1984, the party political system has become increasingly fragmented, with up to five political parties contesting general elections at any one time, and where power has alternated between no less than four political parties in the last two decades. There have also been a small number of coalition governments: in Dominica, in 2000, between the conservative Dominica Freedom Party and the Dominica Labour Party; in St Kitts, in 1993, when the centrist People's Action Movement with a minority of the popular vote managed to govern in coalition with the Nevis Reform Party which had secured one seat; and in Trinidad, in 1995, when the United National Congress formed a coalition government with the National Alliance for Reconstruction, which had secured two seats. Most recently in 2010, Trinidad has been governed by The People's Partnership, a multi-ethnic political coalition between four political parties. At the time of writing it is too soon to know exactly what will become of The People's Partnership, but already it appears to be going the way of coalitions elsewhere, which have tended to be short-lived and which have been immediately followed by the resumption of the normal dominant two-party system.

The FPTP system has also resulted in an almost unbroken pattern of disproportionality in terms of the votes cast and seats won in Parliament, usually in favour of the winning party. There have thus been several examples of parties winning an outright majority of seats with something less than 50 per cent of the votes: Dominica in 1990; St Kitts in 1984 and 1989; and Trinidad in 1991.[9] Losing parties, on the other hand, have routinely received a share of the seats significantly lower than their share of the votes.[10] Perhaps the most notorious example of this phenomenon is the 1998 elections in St Vincent where the party with the majority of the popular vote, the Unity Labour Party, still failed to win the majority of seats in Parliament, leading to a period of prolonged civil unrest and, ultimately, the signing of the 'Grand Beach Accord' providing for new elections to be held two years before they

---

[9] See PA Emmanuel, *Governance and Democracy in the Commonwealth Caribbean: An Introduction* (Bridgetown, Barbados, Institute of Social and Economic Research, 1993).

[10] Ibid.

were due.[11] Though the fallout from a party with a majority of the votes failing to win a majority of the seats in Parliament has not been quite so dramatic elsewhere in the region, there are numerous other examples of losing parties receiving a share of the seats significantly below their share of the vote. Thus, between 1980 and 1991 there were three instances—Antigua (1984), St Vincent (1989) and Trinidad (1981)—where a competing party won no seats, but polled vote shares of 23 per cent, 30 per cent and 22 per cent respectively. Moreover, in Grenada, in 1984, the Grenada United Labour Party (GULP) won only one out of a possible 15 seats, having polled 36 per cent of the vote; while in Antigua, in 1989, the United National Democratic Party won only one out of a possible 17 seats with 31 per cent of the vote.[12]

It is, however, the encouragement that the 'winner takes all' nature of the FPTP system affords to the worst kind of adversarial politics that has given rise to most concern in the region. Many commentators have thus drawn a direct causal connection between the FPTP system and the culture of state patronage or 'clientilism', which is endemic in a number of countries in the region: most notably, Antigua, Jamaica and Trinidad. State patronage in this context means that supporters and favourites of the party in power are rewarded through employment in one of the public services, promotion, the award of government contracts and licences, as well as the distribution of land and other assets directly or indirectly at the disposal of the party in power. Conversely, opponents of the winning party are victimised in a variety of ways. As the Antiguan politician and journalist, Tim Hector (who, as a vocal critic of the Bird family's dynasty in that country since the 1950s, had direct personal experience of the effects of this kind of politics) has observed:

> Adversarial politics is competition between parties, not based on ideas of policy and program, but based on 'I appoint and I disappoint' in opposition, but more so in government … Adversarial politics has reached the absurdity where politicians in power use every means to deny their opponents work for years; the right to practice their progression, and even to destroy by terrorist arson their means of livelihood. There is no longer, in appearance or

---

[11] See C Grant, *Democracy and Governance in the Caribbean*, 7 May 2003. Available at: www.caricom.org/jsp/pressreleases/pres75_03.pdf.

[12] See Emmanuel, above (n 9).

in substance, parliamentary democracy here, but an idea-less struggle for naked power.[13]

In particular, in the smaller islands, such as Antigua, the Government, even if its dimensions are not significantly greater when compared with larger countries, nevertheless occupies a disproportionate space within the life of its citizens. The reach of executive power as well as the impact of political patronage and victimisation in these small microstates is, accordingly, magnified and accentuated.[14] As Selwyn Ryan notes, 'in such an environment elections function not so much as an expression of the political will of the people, but as a tool to sustain patronage'.[15]

In Jamaica, clientilism has been linked to the establishment of so-called 'garrison communities,' originally developed in the 1960s and 1970s from large-scale government housing schemes where the units were allocated to supporters of the governing party. In these garrison communities any individual/group that seeks to oppose, raise opposition to or organise against the locally dominant party could be in physical danger, thus making continued residence in the area extremely difficult, if not impossible. These communities have, accordingly, come to be associated with violent crime and widespread electoral manipulation. The impact of such garrison communities has been documented by Figueroa and Sives, who note that in the 1993 general election five of Jamaica's 60 constituencies were almost completely dominated by the 'garrison' process, while there were another six constituencies where the process was very significant.[16] In Trinidad, state patronage is largely based on racial lines as people vote according to the political party which is perceived to be representative of their race, and has

---

[13] T Hector, 'The Current Economic Crisis—Why and Wherefore?' *Outlet* (29 September 2000) 10–11.

[14] National Integrity Systems, *Transparency International Country Study Report: Caribbean Composite Study 2004*, 20. Available at: www.transparency.org.

[15] S Ryan, *Winner Takes All: The Westminster Experience in the Caribbean* (St Augustine, Trinidad, ISER, University of the West Indies Press, 1999) 317.

[16] M Figueora and A Sives, 'Homogenous Voting, Electoral Manipulation and the "Garrison" Process in Post-Independence Jamaica' (2002) 40(1) *Commonwealth & Comparative Politics* 81, 83.

contributed, it has been suggested, to the polarisation of that society along ethnic political–tribal lines.[17]

There has not, however, been any great groundswell of opinion either within these two countries or across the region more generally, calling for the introduction of an alternative voting system. Indeed, in each case that a constitutional reform commission has reviewed the issue, the recommendation has been, with two exceptions,[18] to retain the FPTP system. Though imperfect, the FPTP system has always appeared preferable to its alternatives, in particular, the party list system that has been in place in Guyana since the 1960s and which has been forever tainted by its association with the efforts of the British authorities' to remove the People's Progressive Party (PPP) from office prior to granting independence.[19]

B. GUYANA AND THE 'PARTY LIST' SYSTEM

Under the 'party list' system each political party nominates a list of candidates. The votes for each party are then calculated on a nationwide basis—rather than a constituency basis—and the parties obtain the number of seats in the legislature in direct proportion to their share of the votes in the country. One of the attractions of the party list system, in contrast to the FPTP system which is often highly disproportionate, is that it adheres to the principle of proportional representation, which requires that the composition of the legislature should reflect the proportion of votes cast for that party in the election. Almost half a century since the first countries in the region were granted independence, however, Guyana remains the only country in the region to have adopted the party list system. In order to understand how and why this has happened, it is necessary first to sketch out the events leading up to Guyana's independence.

[17] NT Duncan and D Woods, 'What About Us? The Anglo-Caribbean Democratic Experience' (2007) 45(2) *Commonwealth & Comparative Politics* 202–18, 213.
[18] See Constitution Commission of Trinidad and Tobago, *Report of the Constitution Commission* (Port of Spain, 1974). Available at: www.ttparliament.org; and St Vincent Constitution Review Commission 2002 (no report available).
[19] A Payne, 'Westminster Adapted: The Political Order of the Commonwealth Caribbean' in JI Dominguez, RA Pastor and D Worrell (eds), *Democracy in the Caribbean* (Baltimore, John Hopkins University Press, 1993) 70.

In 1953, following the introduction of universal adult suffrage, the general election was won under the FPTP system by the PPP: a popular, nationalist party, led by Dr Cheddi Jagan, and committed to a redistributive economic programme intended to reduce poverty. The PPP's plans were, however, regarded as a threat to British interests in the country[20]—in particular the interests of Bookers, a multinational company, which controlled the country's main export, sugar—and after a mere 133 days the British Government despatched warships and troops to British Guiana (as it was then still known) with the aim of countering any resistance by the PPP and its supporters as the Constitution was suspended. A state of emergency was then declared with the Governor assuming direct rule of the colony under an interim government, made up of members of the 'plantocracy', the business community and others sympathetic to British rule, until fresh elections were held in 1957.[21] To the dismay of the British Government, however, the 1957 election was again won by the PPP, though by this point the leaders of the PPP, Jagan and Forbes Burnham, had parted company and formed their own parties, with Jagan's PPP representing the Indo-Guyanese Community and Burnham's People's National Congress (PNC) representing the Afro-Guyanese Community. As a result, voting was split along racial lines. This enabled the PPP, in the 1961 elections, to win 42.6 per cent of the votes and 20 seats in the House of Assembly, while the PNC, having won 41 per cent of the votes only managed to secure 11 seats. The third party, the United Force (UF), led by Peter D'Aguiar, having won 16.4 per cent of the votes, managed to secure only four seats.

Though the British Government had by now accepted, in principle, that British Guiana should be granted independence, and the House of Assembly had passed a resolution to this effect in November 1961, it was reluctant to grant independence for as long as the PPP remained in power. At the time, the British Government was also being lobbied very strongly by the US Government, which feared that Jagan had too many communist connections, in particular with Castro's Cuba, and might even threaten nationalisation or confiscation of foreign and local

---

[20] See M Curtis, *Unpeople: Britain's Secret Human Rights Abuses* (London, Vintage, 2004) 279.

[21] RP Premdas, 'Guyana: Ethnic Politics and Erosion of Human Rights and Democratic Governance' in CJ Edie (ed), *Democracy in the Caribbean: Myths and Realities* (Westport, Connecticut, Praeger, 1994) 46.

businesses. In a letter from the US Secretary of State, Dean Rusk, to the British Foreign Secretary, Sir Alec Douglas-Home, the US position was made clear:

> The continuation of Jagan in power is leading us to disaster in terms of the colony itself, strains on Anglo-American relations and difficulties for the Inter-American system … I hope we can agree that Jagan should not accede to power again.[22]

To this end the United States, in February 1962, began a covert operation to organise and fund anti-Jagan protests, which resulted in riots (during which the British Government sent troops to restore order) and a general strike, beginning in April 1963, which lasted for 80 days. By 1964, the ethnic tensions which had followed as a result of the 1961 elections had escalated to warlike proportions, with widespread loss of life and property during six months of ethnic conflict, the outcome of which was a de facto partitioning of the country.[23]

In the meantime, the British Government was making its own plans to effect a 'constitutional coup' by introducing a new electoral system based on the principle of proportional representation, justifying its actions, in large part, on the civil and political disorder that had engulfed the country. As the report of the Independence Conference (the Report) held in London in 1963 notes:

> Unfortunately, in British Guiana, [the] electoral system, while providing clear parliamentary majorities, has not provided strong government. The fact is that the administration of the country has been largely paralysed, the Government is insolvent, and law and order can only be maintained with the help of outside troops.[24]

The Report makes no mention, however, of the involvement of the CIA in sponsoring this civil disorder. Instead, the blame is placed squarely on the racial divisions in the country and there is much discussion in the Report about the need to introduce an electoral system based on the

---

[22] US State Department to Embassy in UK, 19 February 1962, *FRUS*, 1961–63, Vol XII, USGPO, Washington 1996, Document 264. Quoted by Curtis, above (n 20) 282.
[23] D Hinds, *Ethno-Politics and Power-Sharing in Guyana: History and Discourse* (Washington, New Academia Publishing, 2011) 10.
[24] *British Guiana Independence Conference Report* (Cmd 2203, 1963).

principle of proportional representation with a view to encouraging the development of new political parties which were not racially aligned.

The reality, however, so far as the British and the US governments were concerned, was that replacing the FPTP system with a system based on proportional representation offered the best—indeed the only—hope of removing the PPP from power by constitutional means. While the PPP's traditional base in the Indo-Guyanese community may have constituted less than half of the total population, it was feared that this would always be sufficient to secure it victory in any general election based on the FPTP system. Accordingly, with the full backing of the opposition parties—the PNC and the UF—the British Government announced, at the conclusion of the 1963 conference, that prior to the grant of independence there would have to be fresh elections and that these elections would for the first time in the country's history be based on the party list system, which the British Government regarded as the 'simplest and the fairest' of the various proportional representation systems available.[25] To this end, it was provided that, henceforth, for the purpose of returning all 53 members to the House of Assembly, British Guiana would form a single electoral area.[26] At the subsequent elections, in December 1964, the PPP actually increased its share of the vote to 46 per cent and won more seats than any other single party, but under the new party list system Forbes Burnham and his coalition partner, Peter D'Aguiar of the UF, had between them won a majority of the seats, and were accordingly asked to form the government.

Despite the promise of the British authorities that an electoral system based on the principle of proportional representation offered the best hope for the formation of a coalition government of parties supported by different races, it actually proved to have quite the opposite effect. Having won the 1964 election, Burnham's main priority was to consolidate his power, using funds provided by the United States. To this end, he began by establishing a National Defence Force (NDF), which was to transform Guyana into the most militarised country in the region, and ensured that the police force was much better equipped. Members of the NDF and police force were recruited mainly from the Afro-Guyanese sector of the population. A state of emergency was also declared and detentions without trial were authorised. At the same time—knowing

[25] Ibid.
[26] Constitutional Order-in-Council, 1964.

that the PPP even under the new system of proportional representation stood a good chance of winning the next election as a result of the rapid increase in the Indo-Guyanese population—Burnham set about gaining control of the electoral machinery. The 'independent' Electoral Commission was reconstituted and the Minister for Home Affairs was put in charge of elections. Premdas recounts of this time that the central election office in Georgetown was barricaded like an impregnable fortress with high security fences, barbed wire, floodlights and armed guards, protecting its activities under the utmost secrecy. In addition, 'overseas voting' was introduced, thereby extending the domestic electorate to England and the United States.[27] This was wholly administered by the PNC's politically appointed ambassadors to Britain and the United States and supplemented the already 'padded' domestic voters list. By this means, the PNC was able to win an outright majority in the 1968 elections (securing 30 out of 53 seats).[28]

This rigging was repeated in the 1973 elections as the PNC increased its majority to 66 per cent (37 out of 53 seats). Such a result was highly improbable based on the continuing ethnic divisions within the country and was only achieved, according to some commentators, as a result of the Army hijacking the ballot boxes and transporting them to their headquarters. When PPP activists tried to prevent this happening, three of them were fatally shot by soldiers.[29] However improbable, the PNC's two-thirds majority, combined with an equally rigged referendum,[30] enabled it to reform the Independence Constitution and replace it with the socialist Constitution of 1980 which provided, inter alia, for the replacement of the Queen as head of state with an executive president and made a number of corresponding changes to the electoral system. The list of each party contesting the elections for the National Assembly now had to be headed by the party's presidential candidate who would be appointed President if that party's list received the most votes. In addition, the country was divided into 10 administrative regions, governed by Regional Democratic Councils (RDCs), with voters simultaneously electing the 53 'national' members of the National

---

[27] Premdas, above (n 21) 50.
[28] Hinds, above (n 23) 11.
[29] See ibid, 15.
[30] Review of Guyana: *Fraudulent Revolution* (London, Latin America Bureau, 1984) 75–76.

Assembly and the 10 RDCs. The RDCs then elected from among their members, according to the size of their respective populations, the parliamentary representatives for the 12 remaining 'regional' seats in the National Assembly.

These change, notwithstanding, the PNC continued to retain its grip on power, winning comfortable majorities in the general election of 1980, when it won 41 of the 53 national seats, and in 1985, when the PNC increased its share to 42 of the 53 national seats, amid further allegations of electoral malpractice. As the international team of observers headed by Lord Avebury noted in its report on the 1980 election:

> We came to Guyana aware of the serious doubts expressed about the conduct of the previous elections there, but determined to judge these elections on their own merit and hoping that we should be able to say that the result was fair. We deeply regret that, on the contrary, we were obliged to conclude, on the basis of abundant and clear evidence, that the election was rigged massively and flagrantly.[31]

However, following Burnham's death and his replacement by Desmond Hoyte, the period between 1986 and 1992 saw the gradual breakdown of the authoritarian regime that had been in charge of Guyana for over two decades. This created a degree of political space for opposition parties which were able to organise and protest without overt government interference and this, combined with a new international environment following the end of the Cold War and a freeze on all US aid until electoral democracy was restored, persuaded the Government to negotiate terms for the conduct of free and fair elections in 1992. These included the appointment of a new Elections Commission headed by an independent chairman, provision for the counting of ballots at the place of polling and the admission of international observers.[32] The general election of 1992, which was won by the PNC, was thus generally regarded as the first free and fair election to be held in the country since the PNC had originally acceded to power in 1964.[33] However, the return to power of the PPP did nothing to alleviate the ethnic tensions between the Afro-Guyanese and Indo-Guyanese communities and on

---

[31] Report of the International Team of Observers at the Elections of Guyana, *Something to Remember* (London, Latin America Bureau, 1980).

[32] Hinds, above (n 23) 19.

[33] See *Report of the Commonwealth Observer Group, Guyana General and Regional Elections* (Commonwealth Secretariat, 2001) 5.

election day, when it became apparent that the PNC had won, rioting broke out in Georgetown and continued for four days, only stopping when Desmond Hoyte conceded defeat.

The 1997 election, following Cheddi Jagan's death, which saw his widow Janet Jagan running for President in his place, unleashed an even more prolonged period of ethnic violence, caused by a week-long delay in announcing the results in a number of African communities and the decision of the Chairman of the Elections Commission, notwithstanding this delay, to declare Janet Jagan the winner. In response, the PNC leader vowed to make the country ungovernable as the PNC launched court proceedings to contest the results of the 1997 election and, in the meantime, boycotted Parliament. This was accompanied by a sustained period of post-election rioting and violence, which was only brought to an end when an agreement was reached between the PPP and PNC leaders. The agreement, which was generally known as the 'Herdmanston Accord', provided for the PNC to return to Parliament in return for fresh elections being held within 36 months and the creation of a commission to recommend constitutional reforms.

The report of the Constitutional Commission, which was published in July 1999, made a number of recommendations for further reform of the electoral system. These included the establishment of a permanent electoral task force, the Guyana Elections Commission (GECOM);[34] a requirement that at least one-third of the candidates nominated by parties contesting the election must include women; the abolition of the RDCs; and the introduction of a combination of 'geographical' constituencies and national candidate lists.[35] This meant that all members of the National Assembly would now be elected directly: 25 members being elected from 10 'geographic' constituencies and the remaining 40 being elected from a national 'top-up' list, which also identifies each party's presidential candidate. While this reform went some way to improving the link between constituencies and their elected representatives, which was conspicuously absent from the old system, it did not address the principal criticism of the party list system, namely, that it places too much power in the hands of the party leaders who draw up the list of their party's candidates. More generally, the reforms did little to stem the tide of ethnic violence that followed both the 2001 and

---

[34] Established under the Elections Law (Amendment) Act 2000.
[35] Constitution (Amendment) Act 2000.

2006 elections. This would suggest that whatever its merits in terms of proportionality, the party list system had completely failed to deliver on the promise by the British Government that it would result in the development of a new kind of non-racially aligned politics in Guyana, and that what matters more than the electoral system in place, is having adequate safeguards in place to ensure that the executive is not able to interfere with or manipulate the electoral process to its own ends.

PART III: MANAGEMENT AND ADMINISTRATION OF ELECTIONS

Whichever electoral system is in place, the role of those in control of their management and administration is critical if elections are to be free and fair. This includes fixing and reviewing the number and boundaries of constituencies, the registration of voters and the conduct of elections. Within the Commonwealth Caribbean, these functions are usually assigned to two different bodies, which are both enshrined in the Constitution: the Constituency Boundaries Commissions and Election Management Bodies. In this section I wish to explore the roles played by both of these bodies and to consider the extent to which they are susceptible to political influence and control.

A. CONSTITUENCY BOUNDARIES COMMISSION (CBC)

The FPTP system requires the division of each country into a number of constituencies from which a single representative, gaining the highest number of votes, or being the sole candidate, is elected as a member of the legislature. The task of reviewing and making recommendations to Parliament about the size and number of constituencies in each country is, in most countries in the region, assigned by the Constitution to a separate body, known as the Constituency Boundaries Commission (CBC).[36] The exception is Jamaica, where under section 67 of the

---

[36] In Barbados and Trinidad, the Electoral Commission and Boundaries Commission are combined in one body—the Electoral and Boundaries Commission.

Constitution, this responsibility is assigned to a Standing Committee of the House of Representatives.

In some countries, the jurisdiction of the CBC to determine the size and number of constituencies is to a greater or lesser extent circumscribed by the Constitution. Thus, three Constitutions expressly provide for a fixed number of constituencies: the Constitution of the Bahamas, which provides for a minimum of 38 constituencies;[37] the Constitution of Jamaica, which provides for a maximum number of 60 and a minimum number of 45;[38] and the Constitution of St Vincent, which provides for a fixed number of 13 constituencies.[39] In the multi-island states of Antigua, St Kitts and Trinidad there are special provisions in the Constitution to ensure separate constituencies in the smaller territories of Barbuda (one constituency),[40] Nevis (one-third of the total number of constituencies)[41] and Tobago (at least two constituencies)[42] respectively. Though it is not a constitutional requirement in the other multi-island states, provision is, nevertheless, made for constituencies in the outlying islands. Thus, in St Vincent two constituencies are located in the Grenadines; in Grenada one constituency is located in Carriacou; and there are several constituencies in the outer lying islands of the Bahamas.

Where the Constitution does not provide for a fixed number of constituencies it is, nonetheless, important for CBCs, when recommending the number and size of constituencies, to have regard to the principle of affording equal weight to each vote. While exact equality of constituency size is rarely, if ever, attainable, too great a departure from this principle would be likely to exacerbate the disproportionality between votes cast and seats won that is commonly identified as one of the main drawbacks of the FPTP system. A number of constitutions recognise the importance of this principle by making express provision for maintaining an element of equality between constituencies. The Constitution of Trinidad, for example, provides that the electorate in any constituency shall not be more than 110 per cent, nor

---

[37] s 68(1).
[38] s 67.
[39] s 33(1).
[40] s 62(1).
[41] Sch 2, Constitution of St Kitts and Nevis.
[42] s 70(2).

be less than 90 per cent of the total electorate divided by the number of constituencies.[43] Under the Constitution of Barbados the corresponding figures are 115 per cent and 85 per cent.[44] The Constitutions of the Bahamas,[45] St Vincent[46] and Dominica[47] further provide that these constituencies should contain as nearly equal numbers of inhabitants as is reasonably practical, taking account of factors such as the density of population—in particular the need to ensure adequate representation of sparsely populated rural areas—the means of communication, geographical features and the boundaries of existing administrative areas.[48] As Patrick Emmanuel notes, however, if the limits set by the Constitutions of Trinidad and Barbados represent the optimal norm for variation in constituency size, the only other country to satisfy this norm is St Vincent. Elsewhere in the region there are considerable disparities between constituency sizes, even when account is taken of population density and geographical factors. For example, in St Kitts, all the constituencies fall outside this norm; in Dominica and Grenada the proportion is 86 per cent; Antigua 81 per cent; St Lucia 71 per cent; and Belize and Jamaica 50 per cent.[49]

In recognition of the importance of the task assigned to CBCs there are a number of express provisions within each Constitution designed to combine a measure of political neutrality as well as political balance in the composition of each CBC. The degree of neutrality and balance thus achieved is, however, questionable. For example, in the case of the Bahamas, Dominica, Grenada and St Lucia the chairman is ex officio the Speaker of the House of Assembly. This is presumably intended to 'consecrate' an official link with the House of Assembly and is consistent with the principle that a parliament should have ultimate control over its own composition.[50] However, in these countries, the fact that the Speaker is elected by the government majority in Parliament tends to undermine any claim to political neutrality. As the Eastern Caribbean

---

[43] s 72.
[44] s 31D(1).
[45] s 70(2).
[46] s 33(2).
[47] Sch 2.
[48] See also s 72(5) Constitution of Trinidad and Tobago.
[49] See Emmanuel, above (n 9).
[50] Blackburn, above (n 1) 120.

Court of Appeal noted in *Constituency Boundaries Commission and Another v Baron*[51] (discussed further below):

> The reality of the situation is that when such a Commission is being set up, the respective sides will recommend members whom they are satisfied will look after each side's respective interests. Their concentration will be more on political advantage than constitutional requirements. I agree that the Speaker as Commission Chairman stands in the middle. But again one has to be real. The Speaker was elected by a government majority.

In the case of Antigua and St Kitts, the chairman is even more obviously a political appointee, being appointed, in the case of Antigua, by the Governor General acting in accordance with the advice of the Prime Minister after the latter has consulted the Leader of the Opposition;[52] and, in St Kitts, being appointed by the Governor General, acting in accordance with the advice of the Prime Minister given after the Governor General has consulted the Leader of the Opposition and such other persons as the Governor General, acting in their own deliberate judgement, has seen fit to consult.[53]

In order to achieve political balance, a number of constitutions provide for the appointment of an equal number of members upon the recommendation of the Prime Minister and the Leader of the Opposition respectively.[54] Furthermore, with the exception of the Bahamas, all the other constitutions expressly disqualify members of the legislature and other public officers from being members of the CBC. However, in those cases where the Speaker of the House of Assembly is the chairman and is given a casting vote in the event of a tie between the other members, the government is always able to ensure that its view prevails when the CBC is taking decisions about the review of constituency boundaries.

In Antigua, there is an even greater imbalance as two members are appointed by the Governor General in accordance with the advice of Prime Minister and only one member in accordance with the advice of Leader of the Opposition, thus affording the Prime Minister the final say in the appointment of both the chairman and the majority of the

---

[51] *Constituency Boundaries Commission and Another v Baron* [2001] 1 LRC 25.
[52] s 63(1)(a) Constitution of Antigua and Barbuda.
[53] s 49(1)(a) Constitution of St Kitts and Nevis.
[54] See, eg, s 49 Constitution of St Kitts and Nevis.

members of the CBC.[55] There is a similar imbalance in the appointed element of Bahamas CBC, but here at least the addition of two ex officio members—the Speaker as chairman and a Justice of the Supreme Court as deputy chairman—does mean the government is not guaranteed a majority on the CBC.[56]

CBCs are appointed on an ad hoc basis, but each of the constitutions provides that a review of constituency boundaries must be carried out not less than two years and no more than five years since the last review.[57] Once appointed, members of CBCs usually serve in office until the next dissolution of Parliament and during this period can usually only be removed from office for inability to discharge their functions, following the recommendation of a tribunal appointed by the Governor General.[58] However, in some countries, such as St Kitts, members can be removed by the Governor General acting on the advice of the Prime Minister or Leader of the Opposition, depending on which of these two was responsible for recommending the member for appointment.[59] CBCs can regulate their own procedures, but must reach their decisions by majority vote and are not subject to the direction or control of any other person or authority. Their decisions are, however, open to legal challenge through proceedings for judicial review, but there is a very narrow window within which to bring such proceedings because of an ouster clause contained in each Constitution which requires the proceedings to be brought before the recommendation of the CBC has been implemented by an Order of the Governor General duly approved by Parliament. Once the Order has been approved by Parliament, judicial review is precluded by the following clause:

> [T]he question of the validity of any Order by the Governor General ... and reciting that a draft thereof has been approved by resolution of the House shall not be enquired into in any court of law.[60]

The inclusion of such an ouster clause reflects the presumption that the constitutional basis for the distribution and redistribution of

---

[55] s 63(1) Constitution of Antigua and Barbuda.
[56] s 69 Constitution of the Bahamas.
[57] See, eg, s 64(2) Constitution of Antigua and Barbuda.
[58] See, eg, s 63(6) Constitution of Antigua and Barbuda.
[59] s 33(3)(c) Constitution of St Kitts and Nevis.
[60] See, eg, s 57(7) Constitution of Dominica.

constituencies is ultimately the authority of Parliament rather than the courts.[61] However, the dangers inherent in such a presumption and the importance of allowing the courts to review decisions of CBCs are highlighted by two cases.

The first case, *Constituency Boundaries Commission and Another v Baron*,[62] concerned Dominica's CBC, which had submitted a report to the President recommending that six constituencies should be altered. The report had been submitted to the President pursuant to section 57(1) of the Constitution and, in accordance with section 57(3), the draft Order from the President for giving effect to the recommendations in the report had been laid before the House of Assembly for its approval. However, before the Order had been approved by the House of Assembly, the Respondent had brought proceedings for judicial review in which he succeeded in persuading the court at first instance that the report of the CBC was null and void as it was tainted by bias. On appeal, the Attorney General argued that the courts had no jurisdiction to review the decision of the CBC because Parliament had made no provision for appeal against a decision of the CBC, even though it was empowered to do by section 57(8) of the Constitution. In the view of the Eastern Caribbean Court of Appeal, however, this was not sufficient to oust the Court's supervisory jurisdiction. The Court was obliged to construe the Constitution purposively. Since the Constitution expressly ousted the Court's jurisdiction only in the circumstances outlined in section 57(8), ie, when the draft Order of the President had been approved by the House of Assembly, decisions of the CBC up until that point were justiciable.

Turning to address the question of bias, the Court applied the test laid down by the House of Lords in *R v Gough*,[63] ie, was there a real danger of bias or prejudice? In answering this question in the affirmative, the Court took account of a variety of factors. First, the six constituencies which the CBC had recommended should be altered were all constituencies represented by members of the Opposition party, with the smallest being made even smaller so that a government constituency could be enlarged. Second, a proper enquiry had not been held before the recommendations in the report were made. There was no evidence,

---

[61] Blackburn, above (n 1) 141.
[62] See above (n 51).
[63] *R v Gough* [1993] AC 646.

material, data or information presented to the CBC to enable it in its deliberations to take account of the factors mentioned in Schedule 2 of the Constitution, such as the density of the population and in particular the need to ensure adequate representation of sparsely populated areas, the means of communication, geographical features and the boundaries of administrative areas. Third, the votes taken at the meeting of the CBC were divided equally between the Government appointed members and those appointed by the Opposition, with the vote being won only as a result of the Speaker casting his vote with the Government nominees.

If the first case discloses the potential for bias in decisions of the CBC, the second, *AG St Kitts v Richards and Constituency Boundaries Commission*,[64] reveals just how far a government may go in order to avoid judicial review of a decision of its CBC. In this case the CBC had produced a constituency review report shortly before general elections were due to be held. The Respondent, a member of the Opposition party, had sought and obtained an injunction preventing the CBC from submitting its report to the Governor General pursuant to section 50(1)(a) of the Constitution and, in the event of the report being submitted, the Government from making use of that report. Unbeknown to the Respondent, however, the CBC's report had, in fact, already been submitted to the Governor General and at the hearing of the substantive constitutional motion the Attorney General was granted an adjournment in order to accommodate an emergency sitting of the National Assembly scheduled for that afternoon. This sitting resulted in the Prime Minister laying the CBC's report and the draft proclamation of the Governor General before the Assembly and the Assembly debating and approving the draft proclamation, notwithstanding the existence of the injunction obtained by the Respondent. Though the Respondent subsequently brought proceedings against the Attorney General for contempt for having failed to advise the Court of the purpose of seeking an adjournment of the constitutional motion, and for having failed to inform the National Assembly of the existence of the injunction, the proceedings were dismissed on the ground, inter alia, that the injunction was too wide, vague and imprecise.

---

[64] See *AG St Kitts v Richards and Constituency Boundaries Commission*, Eastern Caribbean Court of Appeal, 2010 HCVAP 2009/009. Available on file with the author.

B. ELECTORAL MANAGEMENT BODIES

Responsibility for the management and administration of the conduct of elections is assigned by each Constitution to a public officer,
a Supervisor of Elections/Parliamentary Commissioner, or to an
Electoral Commission, with the exception of Antigua and St Kitts
where responsibility is shared, somewhat uncomfortably, between the
Supervisor of Elections and the Electoral Commission.[65]

Where responsibility is assigned exclusively to a Supervisor of
Elections/Parliamentary Commissioner, as in the Bahamas, St Vincent
and Grenada, the concern is that the Prime Minister has too much
control over their appointment because of the influence that the Prime
Minister can bring to bear on the Governor General when the latter is
considering who to appoint. As a consequence, there have been calls in
all three countries for the replacement of the Supervisor of Elections
with an independent Electoral Commission. As the Constitution
Review Commission of Antigua noted, in its 2002 report:

> There can be no doubt that the public wish to be assured of maximum
> impartiality and transparency in such politically sensitive activities as control
> of the Supervisor of Elections [and] in the performance of his functions as
> the authority who would be responsible for regulating the registration of vot-
> ers and the conduct of elections in the respective constituencies.[66]

Those who are concerned about the influence of the Prime Minister
over the Supervisor of Elections often point to Antigua as an example
of how easily this can lead to contamination of the electoral process.
Here, responsibility for the management of elections was originally
assigned, exclusively, to a Supervisor of Elections, appointed by the
Governor General on resolutions to that effect by both Houses of
Parliament.[67] However, since the Prime Minister controlled a majority
of the House of Representatives and nominated 10 of the 17 senators
it was inevitable that the Prime Minister would have a considerable say
in which candidate was eventually appointed. As a result, during the
1980s and 1990s, it was widely suspected by the Opposition parties
that the governing Antigua Labour Party (ALP), led by Lester Bird, had

[65] See, eg, s 34(1) Constitution of St Kitts and Nevis.
[66] *Report of the Constitution Review Commission of Antigua* (2002) 89. Available at:
www.ab.gov.ag.
[67] s 67 Constitution of Antigua and Barbuda.

used its influence over the Supervisor of Elections to manipulate the electoral process. Evidence supporting these concerns can be readily found in the several reports of independent observers of the elections, which document some very serious instances of electoral malpractice. These include double-voting, the removal of the names of eligible voters from the electoral register and inflation of the electoral register by 25 per cent with the names of people who had died or migrated.[68] But perhaps the most serious instance of electoral malpractice disclosed in these reports is the undermining of the sanctity of the vote by electoral officers who wrote each voter's registration number on the counterfoil of the ballot paper, thus revealing how they had voted: a frightening prospect for anyone on the government payroll or otherwise obligated to the ALP.[69] Eventually, however, following the recommendations of an independent Commonwealth Observer Group on the conduct of the 1999 elections the Government was finally persuaded to establish an Electoral Commission, which now has joint responsibility with the Supervisor of Elections for the conduct of elections.[70]

Electoral commissions are not, however, themselves entirely immune from political influence because here too the Prime Minister's influence over the Governor General usually secures the appointment of the Prime Minister's chosen candidate for the post of chairman. In some countries, the Prime Minister's influence extends still further to the appointment of the other members of the Electoral Commission, as in Barbados and Belize where three of the five members are appointed in accordance with the advice of the Prime Minister.[71] In St Lucia too, the Prime Minister is able, indirectly, through their influence over the Governor General, to choose the majority of the members of the Electoral Commission.[72] Even where there is a constitutional requirement that the Governor General must consult the Leader of the Opposition when appointing a proportion of the members of the Electoral Commission, this does not necessarily guarantee the participation of the wider opposition in the selection process. For example,

---

[68] See, eg, DW Payne, 'The Failings of Governance in Antigua and Barbuda: The Elections of 1999' (1999) *Policy papers on the Americas*, vol X, study 4.

[69] Ibid, 23.

[70] Representation of the People (Amendment) Act 2001.

[71] s 41A(3) Constitution of Barbados and s 88(2) Constitution of Belize.

[72] s 7(2)(b) Constitution of St Lucia.

in the 2000 general election in St Kitts, the advice of the party which gained the second largest number of votes—the People's Action Movement—was not sought because it did not represent the official opposition in Parliament, having failed to secure any seats despite winning almost 30 per cent of the vote. The exclusion of the second largest party—in what was and is essentially a two-party democracy—from the process of selection of the officials responsible for the management and administration of elections was extremely divisive, and is said to have added greatly to the controversy which surrounded the electoral process in the subsequent elections, in 2004. The Commonwealth Expert Team that observed the 2004 general election, accordingly, included in its list of recommendations wider consultation by the Governor General in the appointment of both the Electoral Commission and the Supervisor of Elections, especially with major national parties that might not be represented in Parliament.[73]

Nor are these concerns about political influence confined to the appointments process, as demonstrated by events in Antigua where the independence of the Electoral Commission has been tested to its limits. First, there was the removal from office of one of the members of the Commission, who was censured for his partisan behaviour in support of the Opposition, ALP, which had originally recommended his appointment as a member of the Commission. This was followed by the resignation of one of the commissioners following 'malicious and unwarranted attacks' by the Prime Minister over the Election Commission's handling of the 2009 elections,[74] which led to the invalidation of the results in a number of constituencies, including the Prime Minister's own constituency. Finally, there was an attempt by the Prime Minister to prevent the chairman of the Commission, Sir Gerald Watt, from resuming his duties, following his suspension pending investigation by a tribunal, even though the tribunal had commended the latter's stewardship of the Commission and recommended that he should not be removed as chairman. At one point, the Prime Minister even went as far as posting 'a squadron of senior members of the Royal Antigua and Barbuda Police Force outside the headquarters

[73] Report available at: aceproject.org.
[74] See statement of Antigua and Barbuda Electoral Commission. Available at: www.abec.gov.ag.

of the Commission to bar his entry'.[75] This was subsequently the subject of judicial review proceedings brought by the chairman in which it was held, inter alia, that the chairman's removal from office by the Governor General on the recommendation of the Prime Minister was unlawful and that he was entitled to and continued to be the chairman of the Electoral Commission.[76] The Prime Minister immediately sought to frustrate the effect of this judgment by signing the Representation of the People Order 2012, which gave retrospective effect to section 22 of the Representation of the People (Amendment) Act 2011, thereby dissolving the Commission of which Sir Gerald Watt was the chairman and, in the process, rendering otiose the order of the court declaring Sir Gerald Watt's removal as chairman unlawful. The actions of the Prime Minister in signing the Representation of the People Order were, however, subsequently declared to be unlawful by the Eastern Caribbean Court of Appeal.[77]

In some countries, at least, efforts have been made to minimise the potential for political influence in the composition and conduct of electoral commissions. Thus, in Jamaica, the Electoral Advisory Committee, which was originally established by the Representation of the People (Interim Electoral Reform) Act 1976, has been replaced by the Electoral Commission (JEC), which was established by the Electoral Commission (Interim) Act 2006. The JEC will remain in force until such time as provision is made in the Constitution for the establishment of an electoral commission and is composed of nine members, four of whom are nominated by the governing and opposition parties (two each) and four other members selected from civil society by the nominated members.[78] There is also a Director of Elections who is a non-voting member. The structure of the JEC thus gives equal weight of voting numbers to party political and civil society members. In Trinidad, the Election and Boundaries Commission (EBC), comprises a chairman and not less than two, nor more than four other members, all of whom are appointed by the President. Though the President must

<hr/>

[75] *The Prime Minister and Another v Sir Gerald Watt*, ANUHCVAP2012/0005. Unreported. Available on file with the author.
[76] See *Sir Gerald Watt v Attorney General Antigua*, Claim No ANUHCV 2011/0025.
[77] *Watt v Prime Minister and Samuel*, ANUHCVAP2012/0042. Unreported. Available on file with the author.
[78] Electoral Commission (Interim) Act 2006. First Schedule.

consult the Prime Minister and Leader of the Opposition, the security of tenure which the President enjoys means that the President is less susceptible to political influence than a Governor General, which may go some way to explaining the cross-party support for the EBC noted by international observers.[79]

Finally, in Guyana, which during the Burnham administration had perhaps the worst record of electoral malpractice in the region,[80] an Elections Commission was first established as part of the negotiated agreement that preceded the 1992 general election. The Elections Commission comprised a chairman (being a judge of a court having unlimited jurisdiction in civil and criminal matters) who was appointed by the President and one member in respect of each political party, including the governing party, which had not less than five seats in the National Assembly. The Commission had a temporary life, in that members had to vacate office within three months of the date of election for which they had been appointed to be commissioners,[81] and was replaced as part of the Herdmaston Accord by a new permanent Elections Commission—the Guyana Elections Commission (GECOM).[82] GECOM comprises seven members, all appointed by the President. The chairman is appointed from a list submitted by the minority leader in the National Assembly. Of the other six members, three are appointed by the President acting in the President's own deliberate judgement and three in accordance with the advice of the Minority Leader.[83] Despite the appearance of political balance there nevertheless remain concerns about the extent of GECOM's political neutrality. As the Commonwealth Expert Team which observed the 2001 general election noted, 'The composition of the Elections Commission and the appointments process, though intended to foster confidence, in practice subjects it to interference and suspicion'.[84] The Commonwealth Expert Team, accordingly, recommended that the appointment and

---

[79] *Report of the Commonwealth Observer Group, Trinidad and Tobago General Election 2000*. Available at: te.gob.mx:89/repo/ArchivoDocumento/17506.pdf.

[80] A Payne, 'Westminster Adapted', above (n 19) 70.

[81] Art 161 Constitution of Guyana 1980.

[82] Established under the Constitution (Amendment) Act 2000, which repealed and re-enacted Art 161.

[83] Art 161 Constitution of Guyana 1980.

[84] See *Report of the Commonwealth Observer Group, Guyana General and Regional Elections*, above (n 34).

management process of GECOM should be completely reviewed to ensure its unfettered independence and that the appointment of the chairman and other members should be vested in Parliament rather than the President, but, to date, this recommendation has not been implemented.

PART IV: FINANCING OF POLITICAL PARTIES AND ACCESS TO THE MEDIA

Competitive elections usually require considerable sums of money: candidates and political parties need funds in order to print election literature, to organise political rallies and to produce election broadcasts. This is no less true of the Commonwealth Caribbean where election costs have increased significantly over the last two decades as campaigning methods have become increasingly 'high-tech'. There has thus been an increasing reliance on media advertising, political rallies have become large-scale productions and US and specialist public relations firms have been recruited, at no small expense, to assist political parties with their election campaigns.[85] For example, in the 1999 general election campaign in Antigua, the ALP is estimated to have spent about US$30 per capita which compares with the US$4 per capita spent by each party in the US presidential election campaign of 1996.[86] This exponential increase in spending on election campaigns by political parties inevitably raises concerns about the potential impact of inequalities of funding as between candidates and parties upon the integrity of the electoral process; or, as Webber has succinctly expressed it, 'the concern that the inequalities of the economic world will dominate the constructed formal equality of the electoral world'.[87] Any system of regulation of financing in its turn, however, raises questions both about who

---

[85] S Ryan, 'Disclosure and Enforcement of Political Party and Campaign Financing in the CARICOM States' in S Griner and D Zovatto (eds), *From Grassroots to the Airwaves: Paying for Political Parties and Campaigns in the Caribbean* (Washington, OAS, 2005) 7.

[86] Centre for Strategic International Studies, *Elections in Antigua and Barbuda 1999*, vol X, study 4.

[87] G Webber, 'The Polycentricity of Political Financing' [2012] *Public Law* 310, 325.

should be entitled to participate in the electoral process and the forms which this participation may take.[88] In this section I will, accordingly, seek to explore the extent to which the financing of political parties and campaign elections as well as access to the media by political parties is regulated across the region.

A. REGULATING THE FINANCING OF POLITICAL PARTIES AND ELECTION CAMPAIGNS

At present only three countries in the region—Antigua,[89] Guyana[90] and Jamaica[91]—have regulations expressly requiring disclosure of political donations, and only three countries—Guyana,[92] Jamaica[93] and Trinidad[94]—impose substantive limits on election campaign spending. Elsewhere in the region—the Bahamas, Belize, Dominica, Grenada, St Kitts, St Lucia and St Vincent—there is simply no regulation of the financing of political parties or of expenditure on election campaigns. There is, instead, what Selwyn Ryan calls, a 'free for all'.[95]

Even in those countries where regulations on the receipt of political donations and election campaign expenditure have been enacted, they are not always effective. In Trinidad, for example, the rules on what can be spent on election campaigns reflect the fact that when they were first enacted independent candidates were the norm and party politics had not yet become entrenched. The rules were never altered to recognise the emergence of political parties and there are, as a consequence, no limits on how much money parties can raise or spend. Nor are there are any obligations on the part of donors to declare what they give to political parties or on the part of the parties to declare what they

[88] Ibid, 312.
[89] s 43 Representation of the People (Amendment) Act 2001.
[90] Arts 120(1)–120(5) Representation of the People (Amendment) Act 2001.
[91] Part VI Representation of the People (Amendment) Act 2011.
[92] Art 118 Representation of the People (Amendment) Act 2001.
[93] Part VI Representation of the People (Amendment) Act 2011.
[94] s 55 Representation of the People Act 1972.
[95] S Ryan, 'Political Party and Campaign Financing in Trinidad and Tobago', OAS Unit for the Promotion of Democracy—International IDEA. Available at: biblio.juridicas.unam.mx/libros/4/1593/56.pdf.

receive.[96] There is, moreover, everywhere general disregard for such regulations as do exist. This is because there is, effectively, no system for scrutinising expenditure reports filed by the candidates' election agents, and the sanctions for breaching the regulations are either non-existent or fail to serve as an effective deterrent. In Antigua, for example, violation of the regulations on acceptance of donations and their disclosure attract a sanction of US$740 per diem,[97] a sum which pales in comparison with the potential amount of money to be raised by violating the regulations. As Selwyn Ryan has observed:

> Disclosure and enforcement regimes are cosmetic and ritualistic, honoured more in the breach than in the observance. The agencies to which candidates and parties are required to report are passive and somnolent and generally lack the capacity or will to monitor such returns as are filed and challenge claims where they seem implausible.[98]

It is, of course, understandable that Commonwealth Caribbean countries, which are among the smallest in the world in terms of their size, population and per capita income, should have correspondingly fewer laws regulating the funding of political parties and election campaigns than larger countries. Such regulation requires administration and that administration requires expenditure, which these small countries can ill afford. In small countries, also, the risk of victimisation of donors is greater if their identities are made public and in Commonwealth Caribbean countries it is thus common for donors to insist on confidentiality.[99] For similar reasons political parties in the region frequently do not themselves maintain records of donations and prevailing habits discourage even intra-party disclosure. Many businesses or individuals make donations directly to the party leader or their nominee or 'bagman' and no attempt is made to formalise the transaction or insist on accountability.[100] Most recently, the Prime Minister of Grenada was obliged to admit, in the face of pressure from the main opposition party, the New National Party, that he had received $US50,000 from an

[96] Ryan, 'Disclosure and Enforcement of Political Party and Campaign Financing', above (n 86).
[97] s 83(6) Representation of the People (Amendment) Act 2001.
[98] Ryan, 'Disclosure and Enforcement of Political Party and Campaign Financing', above (n 86) 36.
[99] Ibid, 7.
[100] Ibid, 29.

unidentified source—a 'friend of Grenada' based in the British Virgin Islands who asked for nothing in return, but did not wish to be publicly identified.[101]

At the same time, however, it is important to understand that these small low-income countries are especially vulnerable to foreign influence and to corruption. When it comes to safe havens for money obtained by international organised crime syndicates or safe storage points for drug traffickers, these microstates are tempting targets.[102] Clifford E Griffin, who has written extensively about the threat to democracy and political stability in the region posed by the 'narcofunding' of political campaigns, cites, for example, the view of an official of the US State Department that 'drug traffickers ... have penetrated the highest levels of society and government institutions' in six Caribbean states, including four members of the Commonwealth. Such allegations are hard to refute because the lack of legislative provisions regulating contributions to political parties and spending on election campaigns means that it is usually impossible to identify the real source of the monies used by political parties to finance their campaigns. As a result, in a number of countries—Antigua, Belize, Jamaica and Trinidad—there is a pervasive suspicion that contributions to political parties are derived from illegal activities such as money laundering, corruption and drug trafficking. There also exists concern about the very narrow base of significant contributors, which in small countries is usually concentrated among the economic elites, who are thus able to use their greater spending power to influence the outcome of elections in order to protect their property and financial interests.

One way of combating such problems is through the public financing of political parties and election campaigns. Not only would this help reduce the type of corrupting influence which results from reliance on private financing, but it would also promote political equality and electoral competition by reducing the barriers to participation confronting smaller or emerging parties and independent candidates.[103] Public

[101] See report, *Caribbean Elections Today* (1 June 2012). Available at: www.caribbeanelections.com.
[102] CE Griffin, 'Democracy and Political Economy in the Caribbean' in IL Griffith (ed), *The Political Economy of Drugs in the Caribbean* (London, Macmillan, 2000) 124.
[103] Webber, above (n 88) 315.

financing could be either direct or indirect. Direct public financing can take the form of grants to members of the legislature, direct public subsidies to parties or political candidates, or reimbursement of election expenditure. Statistics, however, show that the use of such financial subsidies is much less common generally in Commonwealth countries than elsewhere.[104] Within the Commonwealth Caribbean there are only three examples of direct financial subsidies—Barbados, St Lucia and St Kitts—but in each case they represent a relatively inconsequential sum by comparison to the actual election expenditure incurred by the main political parties in these countries.[105] Indirect public financing occurs where instead of providing funds directly to a candidate or a party, access to goods or services to candidates and/or parties is provided at no or reduced cost. In St Kitts, for example, political parties are allowed to bring in vehicles and some other election related materials without paying customs duties. Perhaps the most important example of indirect public financing is, however, the provision of free or subsidised access to the media.

B. REGULATING ACCESS TO THE MEDIA

Despite the recommendation of the Commonwealth Broadcasting Association that it would be appropriate for at least a minimum number of broadcasts for each political party to be publicly funded,[106] only two countries in the region currently afford free access to the media by political parties: one is St Lucia, which offers a small amount of free airtime on the partially government-owned, Radio St Lucia, during election campaigns; the other is Trinidad where, during election campaigns, the state-owned radio and television station allots ten-minute television and radio slots to each political party that fields candidates for at least

---

[104] M Pinto-Duschinsky, *Political Financing in the Commonwealth* (London, Commonwealth Secretariat, 2001) 10.

[105] See further S Griner, 'Political Parties of the Caribbean: Changing the Rules Inside and Out' (Commonwealth Secretariat and Commonwealth Parliamentary Association conference, Port of Spain, 25–27 July 2005). Available at: www.genderandtrade.org/shared_asp_files/uploadedfiles/59512722-B6B0-4BCF-9B03-28B4B72CE92F_PaperbyStevenGriner.pdf.

[106] Commonwealth Election Broadcasting Guidelines. Available at: www.cba.org.uk.

one-third of the seats in Parliament. However, in both countries the allocation of free airtime is dwarfed by the amounts actually spent on airtime by the main political parties during election campaigns.[107]

This failure to provide adequate free or subsidised access to the media is compounded by the general lack of regulation of access to the media across the region. At present, only three countries—Antigua, the Bahamas and Barbados—have enacted laws which seek to regulate access to the media by political parties during election campaigns. Thus, in Antigua, following complaints by opposition parties that the government had been consistently exploiting its access to the state-owned television station to gain an unfair electoral advantage, the Electoral Commission has been authorised to make rules requiring owners of electronic and print media to provide equitable allocation of time and space, in a non-discriminatory manner, to enable political parties and candidates to carry their messages.[108] To date, no such regulations are in place, but statutory recognition of the importance of equal access to the media does seem to have had a positive effect since there were no complaints about media bias in the 2009 elections.[109] In the Bahamas and Barbados the amount of air time on television and radio that each political party can purchase for party election broadcasts is also limited as is the number and duration of electoral advertisements on television and radio for both political parties and their candidates during campaign periods.[110]

Elsewhere in the region, however, the lack of regulation and the market-driven nature of media advertising makes it difficult for smaller opposition parties to have their voices heard, while allowing the better funded political parties to use the broadcasting media to maximum

[107] DW Payne, 'Political Financing: Access of Political Parties to the Media' in S Griner and D Zovatto (eds), *From Grassroots to the Airwaves: Paying for Political Parties and Campaigns in the Caribbean* (Washington, OAS, 2005) 38.

[108] s 36(2) Representation of the People Act 2001. To date no such regulations have been issued.

[109] See *Report of Commonwealth Expert Team, Antigua and Barbuda General Election 2009*. Available at: www.thecommonwealth.org.

[110] In the Bahamas, see the Broadcasting Rules 1992 (the Rules), which are overseen by the Electoral Broadcasting Council. In Barbados, s 4 General Elections (Allocation of Broadcasting Time) Regulations 1990.

advantage as political campaigning has become an 'air war' that is fought via the media.[111]

CONCLUSION

To the extent that Commonwealth Caribbean countries have since independence enjoyed a prolonged period of relative political stability, it may be argued that the FPTP system has served the region well. Despite its manifest drawbacks, the FPTP system has been widely accepted by political leaders across the region and, with the exception of Jamaica in the 1980s, there have been numerous elections, both pre and post-independence, under the FPTP system that have resulted in the peaceful transfer of power from an incumbent government to the former opposition party. As Payne has observed, 'The vitality of electoral politics has long been the most visible and most widely acknowledged characteristic of the post-independence political order of the Commonwealth Caribbean.'[112] The same cannot be said of the party list system in Guyana and while it could be argued that this has nothing to do with the party list system itself and everything to do with the racial politics of that country, it seems unlikely that other counties in the region will be persuaded by Guyana's example to abandon the FPTP system in favour of an alternative based on proportional representation.

However, even if the FPTP system is likely to remain the electoral system of choice for the majority of countries in the region for the foreseeable future, this is not to say that the measures in place for the conduct of free and fair elections have always been as effective as they should be. As we have seen, there has been a number of documented examples of interference with and manipulation of the electoral process by governing parties. This has occurred even where responsibility for the management and administration of elections, and the fixing and reviewing of constituency boundaries, has been devolved to independent

[111] S Ryan, 'Political Party and Campaign Financing in Trinidad and Tobago', above (n 96).

[112] A Payne, 'Westminster Adapted', above (n 19) 67.

bodies, which are constitutionally entrenched and which are not, in theory at least, subject to the direction or control of any person.

There are also concerns about the financing of political parties and expenditure on election campaigns, the more or less unregulated nature of which exposes local politicians to allegations of corruption and of accepting donations from illegal sources. The often lavish sums which are spent by political parties during election campaigns gives them a considerable electoral advantage, and this has been compounded in many countries by the absence of any regulations limiting political parties' access to television and radio stations during election campaigns,[113] as well as the failure to afford free access to these media by those smaller political parties that cannot afford to pay the market price. This has had the effect of not only exacerbating the inherent tendency of the FPTP system to disadvantage minority parties, but also of discouraging large sectors of the population, who may be dissatisfied with the major parties, from voting, thereby permitting the continued alternation in power between the major parties even where their base of electoral support may be diminishing.

It is, of course, unlikely in a region which is composed of so many small countries with a low per capita income that subsidies from public funds for political parties or election campaigning will replace private funding. Subsidies of this nature are not typical of political systems based on the Westminster model, and such is the deep mistrust with which many voters in the region view politicians and parties that they would be unlikely to be willing to allocate scarce public resources to political parties which are seen as insufficiently scrupulous and transparent.[114] However, this means that it is even more imperative to ensure that electoral bodies in the region—the Constituency Boundary Commissions and Electoral Commissions—are truly independent, and to enact measures to regulate the funding of political parties and spending on election campaigns as well achieving greater equality of access to the media.

---

[113] State-owned television and radio stations broadcast in Antigua, the Bahamas, Grenada, Guyana, St Kitts, St Lucia and Trinidad.

[114] S Ryan, 'Disclosure and Enforcement of Political Party and Campaign Financing', above (n 86) 8.

FURTHER READING

PA Emmanuel, *Governance and Democracy in the Commonwealth Caribbean: An Introduction* (Bridgetown, Barbados, Institute of Social and Economic Research, 1993).

D Hinds, *Ethno-Politics and Power-Sharing in Guyana: History and Discourse* (Washington, New Academia Publishing, 2011).

A Payne, 'Westminster Adapted: The Political Order of the Common–wealth Caribbean' in JI Dominguez, RA Pastor and D Worrell (eds), *Democracy in the Caribbean* (Baltimore, John Hopkins University Press, 1993).

RP Premdas, 'Guyana: Ethnic Politics and Erosion of Human Rights and Democratic Governance' in CJ Edie (ed), *Democracy in the Caribbean: Myths and Realities* (Westport, Connecticut, Praeger, 1994).

S Ryan, *Winner Takes All: The Westminster Experience in the Caribbean* (St Augustine, Trinidad, ISER, University of the West Indies Press, 1999).

4

The Executive

———⊱•⊰———

Introduction – The Prime Minister and the Cabinet – The Public Service – Conclusion

PART I: INTRODUCTION

THE CABINET SYSTEM of government, which provides for the government to be drawn from and accountable to the legislature, was introduced into the Commonwealth Caribbean somewhat belatedly by the Colonial Office in the years following the Second World War, as the apparatus of 'Crown Colony rule' was gradually dismantled and the region prepared for independence. Unsurprisingly, having fought so long to attain it, this was the system favoured by the region's political leaders for their newly independent countries and was, accordingly, enshrined in all the Independence Constitutions. Each thus incorporated, either expressly or by implication, the unwritten conventions that underpinned the operation of the Cabinet system of government as it had been evolving in Britain since the mid-nineteenth century.

Under the Cabinet system executive *authority* is vested in the head of state, while executive *power* is vested in the Cabinet, comprising the Prime Minister and such other ministers from among the members of the legislature as the Prime Minister selects. The Cabinet is the principal instrument of policy and it is the Cabinet that is, *collectively*, charged with the general direction and control of government: deciding issues of policy, both domestic and foreign, and how public money should and should not be spent. Since independence, only one country in the region has departed from this template and that is Guyana, which in 1980 abandoned the traditional Cabinet system in favour of an executive presidency, though it has more recently reverted to a semi-presidential system of government.

In this chapter I will begin by outlining the constitutional framework within which Cabinet government functions for all countries in the region, with the exception of Guyana, which I will deal with separately. I will first examine the rules that govern the appointment and removal of members of the Cabinet, including the Prime Minister. I will then explore the powers vested in Prime Ministers and their Cabinets before turning to consider the mechanisms that exist for ensuring that the government is held politically accountable for the exercise of these powers by reference to the principles of collective and individual ministerial responsibility. I will then look at the constitutional framework surrounding the relationship between the government and the public service (or, as it is commonly known in other parts of the Commonwealth—the civil service), which is responsible for the implementation and delivery of government policy. I will consider, in particular, how this relationship has been affected by the region's changing political, social and economic environment.

PART II: THE PRIME MINISTER AND THE CABINET

A. THE PRIME MINISTER

1. Appointment and Removal

It is of the essence of the Cabinet system of government that those who exercise power should be accountable to the legislature. In accordance with this principle, Commonwealth Caribbean constitutions, with the exception of Guyana, provide that whenever the President or Governor General, as the case may be, has occasion to appoint a Prime Minister they must appoint the member of the elected House who appears to them likely to command a majority of the members of that House.[1]

---

[1] The Constitutions of Jamaica and Belize have recently been amended to provide that party leaders cannot be appointed, even if they command a majority of member of the elected House, if they have already served a prescribed number of terms in office.

Once appointed, the Prime Minister remains in office until one of the following events occur. The first is if the Prime Minister ceases to be a member of the elected element of the legislature for any reason other than the dissolution of Parliament: for example, if they are adjudged bankrupt or certified to be of unsound mind.[2] The second is following a resolution of no confidence in the Prime Minister by the elected element of the legislature. In such an event, the Prime Minister is required either to resign from office or to advise the President or Governor General, as the case may be, to dissolve Parliament, within a prescribed period: usually seven days, but in some cases it can be as short as three days.[3] If the Prime Minister does neither, then the President or Governor General, as the case may be, is obliged to revoke their appointment.[4] The third is following the dissolution of Parliament, which a Prime Minister can request at any time during their term of office and which the President or Governor General, as the case may be, if so requested, is bound to grant, even if a majority of the elected element of the legislature does not support the dissolution.[5] The only exceptions to the rule that a Governor General is bound to accede to a Prime Minister's request for the dissolution are Belize, St Lucia and St Vincent. In these countries the Governor General can refuse a request for the dissolution of Parliament if they decide that it would not be in the country's interests and the government of the country could better be carried on without one.[6]

In a number of countries—Antigua, Barbados, Belize, Jamaica, the Bahamas and Trinidad—the Prime Minister automatically vacates office following the dissolution of Parliament, and must then wait to be informed by the President or Governor General, as the case may be, whether they are to be reappointed or whether some other person is to be appointed as Prime Minister.[7] The termination of the Prime Minister's office following the dissolution of Parliament is not, however, always automatic. Thus, the Constitutions of Dominica, Grenada, St Kitts, St Lucia and St Vincent provide for the removal of the Prime

---

[2] See s 40(2) Constitution of Jamaica.
[3] s 71(3) Constitution of Jamaica.
[4] See, eg, s 71(2) Constitution of Jamaica.
[5] See, eg, s 64(5) Constitution of Jamaica.
[6] s 84(4)(a) Constitution of Belize; s 54(4)(a) Constitution of St Lucia; and s 48(5)(a) Constitution of St Vincent and the Grenadines.
[7] s 71(1)(d) Constitution of Jamaica.

Minister following the dissolution of Parliament only if, at any time
between the holding of a general election and the first meeting of the
elected House, the President or Governor General, as the case may be,
considers that as a consequence of changes in the membership of that
House resulting from that election, the Prime Minister will not be able
to command the support of the elected members of that House.[8]

Whether or not the Prime Minister remains in situ or is reappointed
to their office following the dissolution of Parliament depends in each
case on whether the President or Governor General, as the case may
be, adjudges that the Prime Minister can command the support of a
majority of the elected House. Ordinarily, this will be obvious from the
results of the general election, but in the event of a hung parliament the
President or Governor General, as the case may be, is presented with a
dilemma with little in the way of guidance from the constitutional text
on how this dilemma should be resolved. The President or Governor
General, as the case may be, may therefore look for guidance to outside
sources as did the President of Trinidad following the 2001 general
election in Trinidad, which produced an 18:18 tie between the party led
by the Prime Minister, Basdeo Panday, the United National Congress
(UNC), which had its base among the Indian descended population
and the People's National Movement (PNM), led by Patrick Manning,
which had its base among the African descended population.

It was argued by Prime Minister Panday that even though Trinidad
was a republic, the President's power to appoint the Prime Minister
had formerly been vested in the Queen, acting through her Governor
General, and the President ought, therefore, to be guided by the 'incumbency principle' as it is applied in the event of a hung parliament in
Britain.[9] According to this principle, where an election does not result in
an overall majority for a single party, the incumbent government remains
in office unless and until the Prime Minister tenders their resignation to
the sovereign. Thus, an incumbent Prime Minister is entitled to wait until
the new Parliament has met to see if they can command the confidence
of the House of Commons, but is expected to resign if it becomes clear
that they are unlikely to be able to command that confidence and there

[8] s 59(7) Constitution of Dominica.
[9] This account of events draws upon HA Ghany, 'Parliamentary Deadlock
and the Removal of the Prime Minister: Incumbency and Termination Theory in
Trinidad and Tobago' (2006) 12(1) *Journal of Legislative Studies* 76–97.

is a clear alternative. It was also arguable, however, that the incumbency principle had no application in the context of Trinidad because the Constitution expressly provides for the automatic termination of the Prime Minister's office following the dissolution of Parliament:[10] this is quite different from the position in Britain.

Confronted with this constitutional conundrum the President, Arthur Robinson, consulted the distinguished constitutional scholar, Vernon Bogdanor, who concluded that the reappointment of Prime Minister Panday offered the 'least dangerous course'.[11] This was not, however, because Professor Bogdanor adjudged that the incumbency principle had been incorporated into the Constitution of Trinidad and Tobago (on this point his advice appears to have been inconclusive).[12] Rather, it was because Prime Minister Panday had not actually lost the election and for the President to appoint his opponent, who had not positively won the election, would, in the context of the President's highly dysfunctional relationship with Prime Minister Panday, have smacked of personal bias. In tendering his advice, Professor Bogdanor would also have been conscious of the racial tensions that polarised politics and society in Trinidad and which underscored relations between the President, whose main political base when he had been active in politics had been among the African descended population in Tobago, and Prime Minister Panday. In the event, however, the President disregarded Professor Bogdanor's advice and instead appointed Patrick Manning, the Leader of the PNM, as Prime Minister. This proved to be a mistake. Unable to command a sufficient majority of the House of Representatives to secure the election of a Speaker at the House's first sitting after the general election, on the 5 April 2002, Manning had to prorogue Parliament until 28 August 2002 and to request the dissolution of Parliament later that same day after another failed attempt to elect a speaker. Manning's tenure as Prime Minister thus lasted less than six months.

While there was nothing in the Constitution that expressly prohibited the President from appointing Patrick Manning as Prime Minister, by refusing to follow the 'least dangerous course', the President exposed himself to allegations of personal and even racial bias. His refusal also allowed the former Prime Minister and his supporters to justify their

---

[10] s 77(2)(a) Constitution of Trinidad and Tobago.
[11] Ghany, above (n 9) 91.
[12] Ibid, 92.

subsequent actions in refusing to participate in the election of a Speaker for the House of Representatives on the ground that the President had himself acted unconstitutionally by ignoring the incumbency principle. Whether or not this is true is a moot point, but the example of what happened in Trinidad demonstrates the value of the incumbency principle, which allows Parliament rather than the President or Governor General, as the case may be, the final say in who should be Prime Minister, and may thus serve as a precedent for presidents or Governors General, elsewhere in the region who find themselves in a similar predicament in the event of a hung parliament in their country.

2. Powers

I have mentioned above the power of the Prime Minister to request the dissolution of Parliament, and I will explore further below the Prime Minister's powers over their Cabinet, but for the present I wish to focus on the Prime Minister's very extensive powers of appointment over the key figures in the wider institutional framework of government.

At the apex of this structure sits the President or Governor General, as the case may be. As we saw in chapter two, in the case of Governors General, who are formally appointed by the Queen, the convention is that the Queen acts on the recommendation of the Prime Minister when deciding who to appoint and the same convention applies to the Governor General's removal. There is no requirement that in recommending the appointment or removal of the Governor General the Prime Minister must consult any other person or body. As we also saw, this can make it very difficult for a Governor General, even when deciding matters that constitutionally lie within their own judgement or discretion, to act in a way that is contrary to the Prime Minister's wishes. Even in those countries such as Dominica, where the President is elected by the House of Assembly (if the Opposition refuses to endorse the Prime Minister's choice),[13] and Trinidad, where the President is elected by an electoral college (comprising the House of Representatives and the Senate), the Prime Minister's control of the majority of votes in these bodies means that the Prime Minister still has a decisive influence over the selection of the President. While it is true that the President in

---

[13] See s 19(3) Constitution of Dominica.

these countries cannot be removed simply on the recommendation of the Prime Minister, nevertheless a president who chooses to exercise their discretionary powers in a way that displeases the Prime Minister must be prepared to risk incurring the latter's wrath and the accusation that they are behaving like an 'executive' president, as demonstrated by the rancorous relationship between President Patrick Manning and his Prime Minister, Basdeo Panday, discussed above.

The Prime Minister's control of both the elected and nominated elements of the legislature arises from the Prime Minister's power to appoint a majority of the latter and to require the revocation of their appointment, as they see fit. The exception is Belize where, as a result of the Belize Constitution (Sixth Amendment) Act of 2008, the senators nominated by the Leader of the Opposition and non-government organisations now together constitute the majority. Belize apart, however, the power to appoint and revoke the appointment of senators is a powerful political weapon and there are several instances where Prime Ministers have used these powers either to punish dissidents within the Senate or to reward their loyal supporters.

Trinidad furnishes two examples. The first occurred in 2000, when Prime Minister Panday insisted that the President should revoke the appointments of the two senators from Tobago whom the Prime Minister had nominated, but who had subsequently voted contrary to the Government in the Senate. Though reluctant initially, the President ultimately accepted that he was obliged to comply with the Prime Minister's request in accordance with section 43 of the Constitution. The second occurred shortly thereafter, following the 2000 general election, when Prime Minister Panday requested that the President appoint as senators seven of the UNC candidates who had just lost their seats in the election. Though the President initially refused to grant the Prime Minister's request, arguing that if the seven unsuccessful candidates were appointed they would then be eligible to become ministers in the new government, a compromise was eventually reached when the President agreed to appoint the seven senators requested by the Prime Minister upon the understanding that only two would become ministers.[14]

[14] For further discussion of this episode, see the report prepared by Trinidad and Tobago Transparency Unit and Mary King and Associates Ltd for the series National Integrity Systems, Country Study Report 1, 2. Available at: www.archive.transparency.org/policy_research/nis/nis_reports_by_country.

Most recently, in Antigua in 2013, the Prime Minister, purporting
to extend the principle of collective responsibility (discussed in chapter five) to members of the Senate appointed by the Prime Minister,
revoked the appointment of two senators whom he had appointed
because they had sided with the Opposition in defeating a Government
Bill. Two other senators who had been appointed by the Prime Minister
and who had also voted with the Opposition were allowed to remain in
place, but only after they had tendered their resignations and apologised
for the embarrassment caused to the Government.[15]

Though the details vary from country to country the Prime Minister
also has a decisive say in the appointment of a number of the most
important public officials, including, but not limited to: the Chief
Justice and members of the Judicial and Legal Services Commission; the
Chairman and other members of the Public Service Commissions (discussed further below); and members of the Constituency Boundaries
and Electoral Commissions (discussed in chapter three). In recommending their choice of candidate for these appointments the Prime
Minister is, in most cases, required to consult the Leader of the
Opposition,[16] but the nature and extent of the consultation is not generally prescribed; nor, having 'consulted', is the Prime Minister in any
way bound by the views of the Leader of the Opposition. As the report
of the Constitution Review Commission of Antigua notes:

> This system of appointment has its inherent dangers, since to some Prime
> Ministers in the Caribbean, consultation may sometimes mean a short letter
> expressing the Prime Minister's *intention* or even a note from the Cabinet sec-
> retary to the Leader of the Opposition or a telephone message to the same
> effect (emphasis in the original).[17]

Only in the case of Belize, and more recently Guyana (discussed below),
does the Constitution attempt to offer some meaningful content to the
duty to consult by providing that:

> Where any person or authority is directed by this Constitution or any other
> law to consult any other person or authority before taking any decision or

---

[15] See *Caribbean Elections Today* (15 April 2013). Available at: www.caribbeanelections.
com.
[16] See, eg, s 98(1) Constitution of Jamaica.
[17] *Report of the Constitution Review Commission of Antigua* (2002) 46. Available at:
www.ab.gov.ag.

action, that other person or authority must be given a *genuine opportunity* to present his or its view before the decision or action, as the case may be, is taken.[18]

The full effect of this provision was tested in the case of *James Jam Mohammed v AG*.[19] In this case the applicant challenged the validity of the appointment of the Chief Justice just a few days before the general elections were due to take place, and a day before a scheduled meeting between the Leader of the Opposition and the Prime Minister to allow the former to offer his views on the Prime Minister's chosen candidate. In the event, the scheduled meeting never took place and, as the Supreme Court noted, it was clear that the scheduled meeting was, effectively, a sham, the appointment having been made already. The appointment of the Chief Justice was, accordingly, revoked.

However, even if concerns about the issue of lack of consultation are put to one side, the concern remains that the Prime Minister's power to appoint the key public officials in some of the most important institutions and bodies within the wider governmental structure means that their influence extends far beyond their Cabinet. The careers of virtually all the key figures in the governmental structure, both within and without the Cabinet, are dependent on the Prime Minister's patronage. In the context of these small island countries, where the opportunities for advancement may be very limited, and where the end of a political career is likely to spell the end of public recognition and possibly, even, of earning a livelihood, there is unsurprisingly a marked tendency not to be critical of the person who was in the first place responsible for placing the individual in a position of privilege. Prime Ministers are thus able to extract a high level of loyalty and deference from those they have appointed. In addition, by being able to threaten the dissolution of Parliament, the Prime Minister has a very effective way of exerting pressure to secure the support of the members of their party in Parliament. Even if they think that the Prime Minister's continuance in office is not in the best interests of either the party or the country, members of the Prime Minister's party in Parliament may not wish to oppose the Prime Minister at the cost of facing the uncertainties of an election.

---

[18] s 129(2) Constitution of Belize.
[19] Supreme Court of Belize, Action 73 of 1999. Unreported. Available on file with the author.

The cumulative effect of the above is the creation of a perception that the Prime Minister is virtually omnipotent, which can make it all but impossible to challenge the Prime Minister's authority and, as we will see in the next section, this has important implications for the way in which Cabinet government functions within the region.

B. THE CABINET

The Cabinet provides the framework within which the major issues of governmental policy are decided and one of the first tasks of a Prime Minister following an election is, accordingly, to decide on the composition of their Cabinet.

1. Appointment and Removal of Ministers

In those countries with bicameral legislatures ministers may be appointed from either House, while in countries with unicameral legislatures they may be appointed from among the both the elected and nominated element of the legislatures. There are, however, rules about certain ministries and the number of senators that may be appointed as ministers.[20] In Belize, for example, the Minister for Finance must be a member of the House of Representatives[21] and in Dominica the Minister of Finance must be an elected member of the House of Assembly.[22] In Dominica also, the Constitution provides that no more than three ministers may be appointed from among the nominated members of the legislature.[23] In Jamaica, at least two but no more than four ministers must be chosen from the Senate.[24]

The Prime Minister's exclusive power to appoint ministers is, of course, usual under the 'Westminster model', but in the context of the Commonwealth Caribbean there are two particular concerns. First, as we have seen, the Prime Minister's power to appoint nominated senators

---

[20] See, eg, s 69(1) Constitution of Jamaica.
[21] s 41(1) Constitution of Belize.
[22] s 61 Constitution of Dominica.
[23] s 59(4) Constitution of Dominica.
[24] s 69(3) Constitution of Jamaica.

as government ministers is a powerful political tool, which may be used to reward the Prime Minister's supporters even when they have been rejected by the electorate. Second, while a number of Commonwealth Caribbean constitutions provide for a minimum number of ministers, none fix any upper limit. This is problematic because the small size of Commonwealth Caribbean legislatures means that in most countries a majority of the legislators belonging to the ruling party are either already government ministers who are, as a consequence, bound by the principle of collective responsibility to toe the party line, or they are ministers in waiting who are also bound, if they are to have any hope of political promotion, to toe the party line. In Jamaica, for example, under Prime Minister PJ Patterson, 22 out of the 34 elected members of the House of Representatives were government ministers.

Ministers vacate office when any person is appointed as Prime Minister or reappointed as Prime Minister, if they cease to be a member of the legislature, or if their appointment is revoked by the head of state, acting on the Prime Minister's recommendation. In addition, with certain exceptions,[25] ministers automatically vacate office on the resignation of the Prime Minister, and upon the revocation of the Prime Minister's appointment following a vote of no confidence.[26] The political fate of ministers is thus inextricably linked to that of their Prime Minister and this has led to allegations in many countries across the region of prime ministerial 'paramountcy', a term used to express the concern that arises where too much power is concentrated in the office of the Prime Minister, thereby undermining the ideal of Cabinet as a collection of equals (even if the Prime Minister is *primus inter pares*), which is so crucial to the functioning of the Cabinet. As one local Prime Minister, Ralph Gonsalves, of St Vincent, has observed, the dominance of the Prime Minister in relation to their Cabinet has meant in many countries that, 'Parliamentary Government is reduced not merely to Cabinet Government but to Prime Ministerial Government'.[27] The devastating consequences of this style of government is perfectly illustrated by the actions of the Prime Minister of St Kitts, in 1986, in guaranteeing a loan of US$25,330,000 (representing one-third of the country's

---

[25] Antigua and Barbuda, the Bahamas, Barbados and Trinidad and Tobago.
[26] s 71(d) Constitution of Jamaica.
[27] See National Integrity Systems, *Transparency International Country Study Report: Caribbean Composite Study 2004*, 29. Available at: www.transparency.org.

annual budget) to purchase three hydrofoils (which left St Kitts never to return) without ever bothering to discuss the legal implications of the guarantee with his Cabinet colleagues and without subjecting the terms of the guarantee to scrutiny by his ministers.[28]

2. Functions of Ministers

Ministers are assigned portfolios, including the administration of a government department, by the Prime Minister. The number and responsibilities of ministries varies considerably from country to country within the region. Typically, the number of ministries ranges from 11 to 13 in the case of the smaller islands and to 26 in the case of Trinidad, which has easily the largest number of ministries in the region, considerably exceeding Barbados, which, with 18 ministries, has the second highest number in the region. Generally, one person heads each ministry and is expected to exercise overall direction and control over that department, though the day-to-day supervision of the department is entrusted to a Permanent Secretary (a senior public servant). In the case of some of the larger government departments the minister may be assisted by more junior ministers: a Parliamentary Secretary and a Minister of State who may be assigned to deal with a defined range of departmental work, such as receiving visitors and meeting a wider section of the public than the minister may have time for in explaining the details of government policy.[29]

The degree to which ministers rely on their Permanent Secretaries and other senior officials in the running of their departments varies from country to country and between ministries, but if Cabinet ministers are to discharge their primary constitutional responsibility—focusing on developing policies and directing the work of their department—it is expected that they will delegate many of their decision-making powers

---

[28] Report of the Commission of Inquiry, *The Tale of the Three Hydrofoils and Other Acts of Financial Management in St Kitts and Nevis 1980–1999* (established 14 July 1999 and submitted to the Governor General on 3 February 2000) 42–45. Available at: www.cuopm.com.

[29] See *Manual of Cabinet and Ministry Procedure*, Bahamas, para 16. Available at: www.bahamas.gov.bs.

to their junior ministers and other officials within their departments.[30] This has not, however, always proved to be the case. Instead, in a number of countries, ministers have been reluctant to delegate their decision-making powers, particularly with regard to any matter that offers an opportunity for the exercise of patronage and the consolidation of their electoral base. This has sometimes resulted in ministers involving themselves in administrative decisions concerning relatively minor matters that could properly have been delegated to officials within their department. As a consequence, ministers have, on occasion, been accused of spending too much of their time in performing low grade tasks, such as responding to routine requests for assistance from their constituents, to the detriment of their policy-formulation and other duties.[31]

This over centralisation of decision-making can also occur, not just within government departments, but within Cabinet itself. While the principle of collective responsibility requires that all major matters of policy, and matters on which there may be doubt regarding the attitude of other members of Cabinet, should be put before Cabinet,[32] the dominance that some Prime Ministers in the region have exercised over their Cabinets has resulted in their ministers taking this principle to unnecessary extremes, with ministers being overly cautious when deciding matters of policy and reluctant to make decisions on their own for fear of censure.[33] A study carried out in Trinidad in 1985, for example, disclosed that the number of notes submitted to Cabinet for consideration amounted to several thousand per annum through the 1960s and 1970s, reaching a peak of 5176 in 1981; the subject matter of these notes included, for example, the rental of portable chemical toilets and a request from Texaco Trinidad to quarantine a dog. As the authors of the study noted, a new form of collective responsibility had evolved in

---

[30] This is sometimes known as the *Carltona* principle in reference to the case of *Carltona v Works Commissioners* [1943] 2 All ER 560.

[31] B Samaroo, 'Public Service Reform in the Era of Structural Adjustment' in S Ryan and AM Bissessar (eds), *Governance in the Caribbean* (St Augustine, Trinidad, Sir Arthur Lewis Institute of Social and Economic Studies, University of the West Indies Press, 2002) 494, 501.

[32] See *Manual of Cabinet and Ministry Procedure*, Bahamas, above (n 29) Part I.

[33] See P Sutton, 'Public Sector Reform in the Commonwealth Caribbean: A Review of Recent Experiences' (2008) Caribbean Paper No 6, 6. Available for download at www.cigionline.org.

Trinidad whereby all decisions, regardless of their policy import, were being channelled through the Cabinet as ministers would seek to justify all their actions or their inaction by reference to the Cabinet (which was widely assumed to mean, in effect, the Prime Minister).[34] In Jamaica, while never quite reaching this scale, the number of notes submitted to Cabinet between 1981 and 1983 was 1571, well above the 139 submitted to the British Cabinet during the same period.[35]

C. MINISTERIAL ACCOUNTABILITY

1. Collective Responsibility

It is a fundamental principle of all Commonwealth Caribbean constitutions that Parliament retains the power to dismiss the government and a government which loses a vote of no confidence in Parliament must resign.[36] In practice, this has been a somewhat remote possibility for a number of reasons. The first is the frequency with which post-independence elections have produced large majorities for the winning party. The second is the dominance of Commonwealth Caribbean legislatures by government ministers, who are bound by the principle of unanimity, discussed below, to support their Prime Minister. The third is the ability of the government to control the parliamentary schedule and to refuse to afford time to debate a motion of no confidence lodged by the Opposition for as long as possible. This occurred in 2013 in St Kitts,[37] leading to the Opposition boycotting the presentation of the national budget in protest at the Government's continuing refusal to table motion of no confidence that had been filed on 11 December 2012.

A fourth reason is the ability of the Prime Minister, in the event that it is not possible to further delay the debate of a motion of no confidence, to request a prorogation or dissolution of Parliament rather than

---

[34] Public Service Review Task Force, 'Over-Centralization: The Question of Submissions to Cabinet' in Ryan and Bissessar (eds), *Governance in the Caribbean*, above (n 31) 306.
[35] Ibid.
[36] See, eg, s 69(2) Constitution of Jamaica.
[37] *Nation News* (25 March 2013).

face the risk of defeat on a vote of no confidence. This has occurred on a number of occasions since independence. Thus, for example, in Grenada in 1989, the Prime Minister, Herbert Blaize, acted to pre-empt the possibility of a defeat on a vote of no confidence by instructing the Governor General, Sir Paul Scoon, to prorogue Parliament, thereby enabling a minority party to remain indefinitely in control of the government until the Prime Minister chose to advise the Governor General to dissolve Parliament and to fix a date for a new election.[38] The actions of Herbert Blaize were strongly criticised, not only by opposition politicians in Grenada, but also by political leaders in Dominica, St Lucia and St Vincent, who argued that since the Parliament in Grenada was reaching the expiry of its term it would have been preferable instead for the Parliament of Grenada to have been dissolved so that an election could take place. Nevertheless, the precedent was set and, more recently in 2012 in very similar circumstances, the Prime Minister of Grenada, Tilman Thomas, faced with the threat of defeat on a vote of no confidence, instructed the Governor General to prorogue Parliament some 10 months before a general election was due to be held. More often, however, the Prime Minister will simply request a premature dissolution of Parliament as was the case in Trinidad, in 2010, when Prime Minister Patrick Manning requested a premature dissolution in order to avoid facing defeat on a vote of no confidence.

As a result of the above, there has only been one occasion on which a government has actually been defeated on a vote of no confidence. This was in Barbados, in 1994, when a number of members of the governing Democratic Labour Party (DLP) broke ranks; the incumbent Prime Minister, Erskine Sandiford, was obliged to request a premature dissolution of Parliament and the DLP was defeated in the subsequent election. Nevertheless, even if governments rarely lose votes of confidence the mere threat of a vote of no confidence remains a powerful sanction in so far as it can force a Prime Minister to request a premature dissolution of Parliament, rather than risk defeat on a vote of no confidence. Such was the case in Trinidad, in 2010, when Prime Minister Patrick Manning was obliged to request a premature dissolution and went on to lose the subsequent general election. Indeed, even when a Prime Minister survives a no confidence vote, as in the case of Bruce Golding,

[38] Ibid.

in Jamaica in 2010, winning the motion by 30 votes to 28, the damage done to the Prime Minister's standing can be fatal, with Golding resigning from office the following year.

Beyond the requirement that a government that loses a no confidence vote must resign or be dismissed, the content of the doctrine of collective responsibility is not further elaborated upon in the text of Commonwealth Caribbean constitutions. However, it is clear, both from political discourse within the region and from the attempts to elaborate the meaning of the doctrine in the Codes of Conduct for Ministers which have been published by the Jamaican and Bahamian Governments,[39] that it is understood to embrace a 'confidentiality rule' and a 'unanimity principle'.[40]

The first of these can be summarised very briefly as requiring ministers to respect the confidentiality of Cabinet proceedings. This means that all subjects coming before Cabinet and all discussions within Cabinet are treated as 'secret'. Two justifications are offered for this rule. The first is that outside knowledge that Cabinet is considering any subject might hamper free discussion, or might give rise to undesirable speculation, or might result in embarrassment to members of Cabinet through attempts by interested parties to influence them.[41] The second, is that members must be able to express themselves freely in Cabinet without fear that individual opinions put forward may become public knowledge whether at an early date or in the future. Accordingly, the obligation of 'secrecy' continues to be binding after the resignation or dismissal of that member from Cabinet or the dissolution of a government.[42]

The unanimity principle requires a more detailed explanation. In essence, the principle requires ministers to support and defend policies and decisions of their government; hence the requirement that all major policy decisions must be disclosed to Cabinet. For so long as a minister remains in government they may not speak in public or private against a decision of Cabinet or against an individual decision of

---

[39] Code of Ethics for Ministers and Parliamentary Secretaries introduced by the Prime Minister, Hubert Ingraham, in the Bahamas in 2002; Code of Conduct for Ministers introduced in Jamaica in 2002, Ministry Paper No 19 of 2002. Unpublished. Available on file with the author.

[40] G Marshall, *Ministerial Responsibility* (Oxford, Oxford University Press, 1989) 2–4.

[41] *Manual of Cabinet and Ministry Procedure*, Bahamas, above (n 29).

[42] Ibid.

another minister, and ministers must not speak or vote on any measure debated in either House of Parliament otherwise than on the lines agreed in Cabinet.[43] If any minister is unable to support a decision taken by Cabinet then they must resign or face dismissal.[44] The force of this principle is illustrated by the numerous reports from across the region of ministers being dismissed for failure to publicly support government policy. For example, in 2004, Sarah Flood-Beaubrun, St Lucia's Home Affairs Minister, was dismissed when she publicly criticised a government Bill to legalise abortion in special circumstances.[45] Again, in St Lucia, in 2007, the Foreign Minister Rufus Bousquet was dismissed for criticising the Prime Minister's decision to maintain diplomatic relations with China. In Belize, in May 2007, the Prime Minister dismissed his Minister for National Development, Mark Espat and his Minister for Defence, Cordel Hyde for refusing to support a government motion.

However, resignation or dismissal for breach of this principle is not always automatic, as demonstrated by the controversy in Jamaica surrounding Portia Simpson-Miller's failure to resign after she abstained on an Opposition resolution in Parliament criticising the Government's underfunding of the fire service. Simpson-Miller, an extremely popular MP for the People's National Party (PNP), was, at the time of her abstention in 2004, Minister of Local Government and Sport and thus responsible for the fire service. Though the Government comfortably defeated the Opposition's resolution, this did nothing to prevent the opprobrium heaped upon Simpson-Miller by some of her Cabinet colleagues and other members of the PNP in the House of Representatives who portrayed her abstention, not only as a breach of an important constitutional principle, but also as a betrayal of her duty of loyalty to her party. Those who defended her actions, by contrast, argued that the unanimity principle was symptomatic of the archaic nature of the whole Westminster model, and that Simpson-Miller had not breached any constitutional principle in placing the national interest above the interests of the PNP.[46]

[43] Ibid.
[44] Ibid.
[45] BBC Caribbean (24 March 2004).
[46] See CAD Charles, 'Newspaper Representations of Portia Simpson-Miller's Abstention in Parliament and Westminster Politics in Jamaica' (2009–10) 8 *IDEAZ* 25–49.

The debate surrounding Simpson-Miller's abstention perfectly highlights the ambivalent nature of the unanimity principle itself. On the one hand, the principle is very much in the interests of the political party in power because it allows the Government to present a unified front against the Opposition, and unlike most other constitutional principles it does not seek to confine or limit the exercise of executive power, but rather to bolster its efficacy.[47] On the other hand, it could be argued that the principle, nonetheless, serves an important constitutional function in so far as it insists upon the loyalty of ministers to policies which have been approved by the electorate. This dual function is implicitly recognised by the declaration in the Bahamas Ministerial Code:

> [The] doctrine of collective responsibility is the basis on which the system of ministerial government rests. Without it the ministerial system cannot be effective and cannot survive, as a method of Government *developed to work in accordance with the wishes of the people* (emphasis added).

In the event, Simpson-Miller survived and, indeed, went on to become not only leader of the PNP, but also Prime Minister of Jamaica for a brief period between March 2006 and September 2007, and again in 2011. This would suggest that, whatever the criticisms of Simpson-Miller, the unanimity principle is far from sacrosanct. So long as she continued to enjoy the support of the Prime Minister and the wider support of the rank and file of her party Simpson-Miller was able to resist calls for her resignation. Thus, much clearly depends upon the support a delinquent minister enjoys within the party at large, and this applies with equal force to the principle of individual ministerial responsibility, which I will now consider.

2. Individual Ministerial Responsibility

The constitutional requirement that ministers must be members of the legislature reflects the underlying principle that some minister is responsible to Parliament and through Parliament to the public for every act of the executive. Commonwealth Caribbean constitutions thus expressly

---

[47] See E Daly, 'Residual Conventions of the Irish Constitution: The Incongruous Example of Collective Responsibility' [2011] *Public Law* 703, 705.

provide that ministers are *responsible* for the administration of their departments.[48]

What this entails in practice is, however, not entirely clear as the responsibility of ministers for the administration of their departments encompasses two distinct obligations. The first is the obligation to give an account to Parliament of the conduct of their departments. This includes the duty to give Parliament and the public the fullest information as possible about the policies, decisions and actions of the government, and not to deceive or mislead Parliament and the public.[49] The second obligation requires ministers to accept responsibility for the actions of their departments—in the sense of having to take the blame themselves when something has gone wrong. The problem with this latter obligation is that it is generally accepted that ministers cannot be expected to be responsible for everything that goes on within their departments. This means that where something has gone wrong it is not always easy to decide whether this was as a result of the actions of an official within the department or the actions of the minister, and the problem has only been compounded by the introduction of Executive Agencies, which I discuss below. As a consequence, ministers are not usually therefore required to resign as a result of the failings of their departments.

Instead, they are much more likely to resign as a result of a personal sexual or financial scandal, which may have little to do with failings in the administration of their departments. This would suggest that the principle of individual ministerial responsibility goes beyond the administration by ministers of their departments and that there is an implied standard of conduct for ministers which arises simply by virtue of their public office. Thus, for example, the Bahamas Immigration Minister, Shane Gibson, was obliged to resign amid the fallout over his involvement with Anna Nicole Smith, the former *Playboy* 'Playmate of the Year' and billionaire's widow, including allegations that he had fast-tracked her application for residency in the Bahamas. In Jamaica, the Minister of State in the Ministry of Transport, Joseph Hibbert, was obliged to resign amid allegations made in fraud proceedings brought by the Serious Fraud Office in Britain that he had accepted bribes worth

---

[48] See, eg, s 71(1) Constitution of Antigua and Barbuda.
[49] See *Manual of Cabinet and Ministry Procedure*, Bahamas, above (n 29).

£100,000 in return for government contracts, one of them worth £14 million, with a British bridge-building company.[50] While in Trinidad, the former national security minister, Jack Warner, resigned in the most dramatic circumstances, following allegations of financial wrongdoing during his presidency of the Caribbean Football Union, which were contained in a report prepared on behalf of the Confederation of North, Central American and Caribbean Association Football by Sir David Simmons, the former Chief Justice of Barbados.

As originally conceived, the principle of individual ministerial responsibility meant that a minister who had failed in the administration of their department or whose conduct of their personal affairs fell below the implied standard could be required to resign following a vote of censure in Parliament. The possibility of Parliament holding a minister to account in this way is now, however, vanishingly small because for so long as the Government controls a majority of the votes in Parliament the Opposition cannot force the resignation of a minister unless the minister has also lost the confidence of their own party. As a result, Parliament no longer serves as the primary forum for enforcing ministerial accountability, but has been supplemented, and even to some extent supplanted, in the Commonwealth Caribbean as elsewhere, by ministers' accountability to a wide network of extra-parliamentary actors, including investigatory bodies and the media.[51]

This can be seen in the establishment in a number of countries—Jamaica, Trinidad, the Bahamas, Dominica and St Lucia—of statutory bodies such as Integrity Commissions and Corruption Prevention Commissions (discussed further in chapter five), which are charged with monitoring the income, assets and liabilities of ministers as well as those of their spouses and immediate family. In addition, a number of ministers have been held to account by specially created Commissions of Inquiry. Thus, for example, in Jamaica, in 2002, Karl Blythe's resignation as Minister of Water and Housing was the direct result of a damning report by a Commission of Inquiry investigating the management of the National Housing Development Corporation and its Operation PRIDE

---

[50] See D Leigh and R Evans, 'British firm Mabey and Johnson convicted of bribing foreign politicians' *The Guardian* (London, 25 September 2009). Available at www.theguardian.com/business/2009/sep/25/mabey-johnson-foreign-bribery.

[51] RAW Rhodes, J Wanna and P Weller (eds), *Comparing Westminster* (Oxford, Oxford University Press, 2009) 146.

project, the latter being a low-income housing project to upgrade squatter settlements established during the PJ Patterson administration in the 1990s. Blythe had been found to have not only ignored a Cabinet decision to suspend work on a number of PRIDE projects, but also to have improperly meddled in the day-to-day operations of the project. More recently, in 2010, Ronald Robinson, a junior minister in Jamaica's Ministry of Foreign Affairs and Trade, was obliged to resign after a Commission of Inquiry concluded that he had acted improperly in contacting a US law firm to advise the Jamaican Government on how it should respond to a request by the United States' authorities for the extradition of a Jamaican national, Christopher Coke, to face trial for charges of drugs and gun trafficking. Coke was widely rumoured to have helped the Jamaica Labour Party (JLP) to secure victory in the constituency of the Prime Minister, Bruce Golding, and it was suspected that the principal purpose of engaging the US law firm was to find a way of delaying or even avoiding Coke's extradition.

In addition to these extra-parliamentary bodies, the media is increasingly assuming an important, if not the paramount role in holding ministers to account. Each country in the region has a number of television and radio stations as well as several newspapers, and ministers are liable to be interrogated on a regular basis by the media.[52] According to a Freedom House Survey conducted in 2003, in terms of being 'free' from government interference, Commonwealth Caribbean countries are among the top quartile of the 193 countries rated in the survey.[53] While there have been some notable exceptions, such as in Antigua under the Bird dynasty and in Guyana during the Burnham era,[54] there is, as a general rule, no censorship, formal or informal: journalists suffer no prosecution or harassment and allegations and stories of corruption of public officials are regularly carried in the media.

The increasing involvement of the media and the waning of Parliament's power to hold ministers to account does not, however, necessarily mean that the principle of individual ministerial responsibility is

---

[52] See *Caribbean Composite Study 2004*, above (n 27) 73.

[53] Available at: www.freedomhouse.org.

[54] For a chilling account of the suppression of the media in the Bunham era in Guyana, see RP Premdas, 'Guyana: Ethnic Politics and Erosion of Human Rights and Democratic Governance' in CJ Edie (ed), *Democracy in the Caribbean: Myths and Realities* (Westport, Connecticut, Praeger, 1994) 46.

entirely without meaning. As we have seen, there is still an expectation that ministers must account to Parliament for the actions of their department. One of the principal criticisms of Ronald Robinson, discussed above, was that by instructing the US law firm to act on behalf of the JLP rather than the Government, Robinson was attempting to avoid his obligation as a minister to account to Parliament for the handling of the matter. Moreover, the various examples where resignations have occurred would suggest that the principle of individual ministerial responsibility still has considerable political force even if the conditions under which it functions have changed, making it now more likely that the condemnation of the media or a Commission of Inquiry, rather than the censure of Parliament, forces a resignation.

D. GUYANA: FROM EXECUTIVE PRESIDENCY TO SEMI-PRESIDENTIALISM

Under its 1980 Constitution, the Cooperative Republic of Guyana abandoned the Westminster model of Cabinet government in favour of an executive presidency. According to Forbes Burnham, the decision to pursue a socialist path to development required the introduction of new concepts and institutions, bringing the executive branch of government into line with that of other developing socialist states.[55] However, the 1980 Constitution was forever dogged by the controversy surrounding the discredited referendum which had preceded its adoption, and by the suspicion that the real purpose of the switch to an executive presidency was to enable the Peoples National Congress (PNC) to entrench itself in office by increasing the power at its disposal over the other organs of state.[56] Accordingly, the 1980 Constitution was significantly revised as a result of the recommendations of the Constitutional Reform Commission, which had been established following the disputed election results of 1997 (discussed earlier in chapter three), and Guyana

---

[55] R James and H Lutchman, *Law and the Political Environment in Guyana* (Georgetown, Guyana, Institute of Development Studies, University of Guyana, 1984) 88.
[56] Ibid.

has, since 2001, functioned under what may loosely be described as a semi-presidential system of government.[57]

Under the revised Constitution the supreme organs of democratic power are the Parliament, the President and the Cabinet. The office of the President, nevertheless, remains the most powerful office under the Constitution. The President is not only the head of state and Commander-in-Chief of the Armed Forces, but also the supreme executive authority. Unlike the position under the 1980 Constitution, however, both the President and their Cabinet are now accountable to the National Assembly and must resign if the government is defeated on a vote of no confidence by a majority of all members of the National Assembly, though the President can, like Prime Ministers elsewhere in the region, avoid a vote of no confidence simply by proroguing or dissolving Parliament.

Despite the President's accountability to the National Assembly on a vote of no confidence, their relationship with the National Assembly is in a number of other respects quite different from that of a Prime Minister. Thus, in addition to the President's power to dissolve Parliament a president can, at any time they consider Guyana to be at war, require the National Assembly to extend the life of Parliament by 12 months at a time for a further maximum period of five years.[58] The President may attend and address the National Assembly at any time as well as sending messages to the National Assembly which must be read at the first convenient sitting of the Assembly after the message is received. Conversely, the President has no corresponding duty to provide an account to the National Assembly for the business of their government: this is instead left to the Prime Minister. The President also has the power to withhold their assent to legislation approved by the National Assembly. While the presidential veto has been modified somewhat by amendments to the Constitution in 2001 the existence of the veto still underlines the imbalance of power between the President and the National Assembly, since the latter can only overturn a presidential veto by a vote of not less than two-thirds of all the elected members of the National Assembly. Even then the President can avoid giving their assent to legislation so approved by the National

---

[57] M Duverger, 'A New Political System Model: Semi-Presidential Government' (1980) 8 *European Journal of Political Research* 52.
[58] Art 70(4) Constitution of Guyana.

Assembly by exercising their right to dissolve the National Assembly. The imbalance resulting from the presidential veto is illustrated by the failure of a Bill to amend the Constitution to prohibit discrimination on grounds which included 'sexual orientation'. The Bill, which was approved by Parliament in 2000, was vetoed by the President after 'representations by various groups including religious leaders'.[59]

The President's control over the Cabinet is absolute. The Cabinet comprises, in addition to the President, the Prime Minister, the Vice Presidents, who are appointed for the express purpose of assisting the President in the discharge of the President's functions, and such other ministers as the President might appoint,[60] each of whom may be dismissed by the President at any time.[61] The Prime Minister is appointed from among the elected members of the National Assembly and is the President's principal assistant in the discharge of the President's executive functions, as well as being the leader of government business in the National Assembly. Vice Presidents and other ministers are appointed from elected members of the National Assembly or from those who are qualified to be elected as members of the National Assembly. The Cabinet collectively is responsible for aiding and advising the President in the general direction and control of the government, but the President is not bound to follow their advice. The President presides over Cabinet meetings and allocates ministerial responsibilities for the conduct of government business and the administration of government departments. The President is, in theory, charged with responsibility for any government business not so assigned, but only in the sense that they must appoint a minister or Parliamentary Secretary 'to be answerable therefor to the National Assembly'.[62]

The President's powers of appointment of the key figures in the wider governmental structure are at least as extensive as those of Prime Ministers elsewhere in the region. However, they no longer include appointing the Leader of the Opposition, following a constitutional amendment in 2001, which provides that the Leader of the Opposition is elected at a meeting of the non-governmental members

[59] Guyana Government Information Agency (23 July 2003).
[60] Art 106 Constitution of Guyana.
[61] Art 108 Constitution of Guyana.
[62] Art 107 Constitution of Guyana.

of the National Assembly.[63] When appointing key figures, such as the members of the Public Service Commission, the President is also now required to engage in 'meaningful consultation' with the Leader of the Opposition,[64] or such other person or body as the Constitution may specify. The interpretation of this term is now set out in an addition to Article 232, which requires that the person consulted is given a reasonable opportunity to express their views on the matter, and the person consulting must prepare a record of the consultation and circulate the decision to each of the persons consulted. Furthermore, the ouster clause in the 1980 Constitution which precluded the courts from enquiring whether the President had received or acted in accordance with such advice or recommendation, or whether such consultation had taken place, has since been repealed.[65]

Nevertheless, the immunity clause included in the 1980 Constitution has been retained. This provides, inter alia, that the President shall not be answerable to any court for the performance of the functions of their office or for any act done in the performance of those functions.[66] The original justification for the inclusion of such a clause in the 1980 Constitution was that it was standard practice around the world to include such clauses and that it was 'a mere sort of carry-over of the British principle that the Crown can do no wrong'.[67] Quite apart from the irony of invoking British constitutional practice to justify the inclusion of an immunity clause, having so emphatically rejected the Westminster model of government, the analogy with the British Crown is quite inapposite. Under the British Constitution, the Crown acts, for the most part, by and through her ministers; under the Guyanese Constitution, by contrast, executive power is vested in the President whose ministers merely serve as the President's aides and advisers. As we have seen, however, in chapter two, the effect of this immunity clause has been mitigated to a certain extent by the decision of the Court of Appeal of Guyana in *Baird (Michael) v Public Service Commission*, in which it was held that the clause would not prevent a court from offering a remedy against the State for

---

[63] Art 184 Constitution of Guyana.
[64] See, eg, Art 198(2)(b) Constitution of Guyana.
[65] Art 231, 1980 Constitution of Guyana.
[66] Art 182 Constitution of Guyana.
[67] 'Forbes Burnham Speaks of Human Rights' (Publication Division, Ministry of Information, August 1980) 14, cited by James and Lutchman, above (n 55) 105.

the President's wrongdoing even if the President would themselves be immune from court proceedings: 'it is the President who is immune from curial processes, not his acts'.[68]

This is an important decision because it offers the possibility of some form of legal remedy being provided for abuse of executive power in the absence of any constitutional requirement for the President personally to account to Parliament for their actions and where the possibility of removing the President through a vote of no confidence or through the impeachment process, which requires the support of not less than two-thirds of the members of the National Assembly, is remote.[69]

PART III: THE PUBLIC SERVICE

Under the Westminster model the public service has traditionally been treated as an extension of the government.[70] Senior public servants are expected to inform and advise ministers, and to manage on their behalf the programmes for which their respective ministers are responsible.[71] In terms of constitutional theory, public servants are exclusively responsible to their departmental minister who is, in turn, responsible to Parliament for the actions or omissions of their department.

This traditional view of the role of public servants assumes a public service that is based on the principles of the Northcote–Trevelyan report of 1854, the essential characteristics of which are: a permanent bureaucracy staffed by neutral and anonymous officials; recruitment and promotion based on merit; self-sufficiency; and a strict separation of powers between the minister who decides policy and the public servant who administers it.[72] In the Commonwealth Caribbean, however, the relationship between the government and the public service has never quite lived up to this idealised version for a variety of reasons that

---

[68] See further, *Karanathilaka v Commissioner of Elections* [1999] 4 LRC.

[69] Art 180(2) Constitution of Guyana.

[70] *Report of the Royal Commission on Australian Government Administration* (Coombs Report) 1976 (Canberra, Australian Government Printing Service) para 2.1.4.

[71] See *Manual of Cabinet and Ministry Procedure*, Bahamas, above (n 29).

[72] Northcote-Trevelyan, *Report on the Organisation of the Permanent Civil Service.* Reprinted in: *Committee on the Civil Service (Fulton Report) 1968* (Cmnd 3638, 1968) Appendix 3.

I explore below. In doing so it will be necessary to take account not only of the formal constitutional framework which regulates the relationship between the government and the public service, but also how the changing political, social and economic environment has affected this relationship.

A. PUBLIC SERVICE COMMISSIONS (PSCS)

The Constitutions of all the countries within the region make provision for the establishment of PSCs, the underlying rationale for which was summarised thus by Lord Diplock in *Thomas v AG:*

> The whole purpose of Chapter VIII of the Constitution, which bears the rubric, The Public Service, is to insulate members of the Civil Service, the Teaching Service and the Police Service in Trinidad and Tobago from political influence exercised directly upon them by the Government of the day. The means adopted for doing this was to vest in autonomous commissions, to the exclusion of any other person or authority, power to make appointments to the relevant service, promotions and transfer within the service and power to remove and exercise disciplinary control over members of the service.[73]

Members of the PSC, including the chairman, are appointed by the President or Governor General, as the case may be, usually after consultation with the Prime Minister and, in some cases, the Leader of the Opposition.[74] A number of Constitutions also make provision for the Prime Minister to consult appropriate representative bodies before advising the President or Governor General, as the case may be, about whom to appoint.[75] In order to secure their independence from the executive and the legislature, each Constitution imposes strict conditions on eligibility for membership of a PSC, length of appointment and security of tenure. Thus, former public officers and members of the legislature are usually disqualified,[76] and there is also usually a quarantine period during which a person who has held office or acted as a member of a PSC cannot

---

[73] *Thomas v AG Trinidad* [1982] AC 113.
[74] See, eg, s 99(1) Constitution of Antigua and Barbuda and s 120(1) Constitution of Trinidad and Tobago.
[75] See, eg, s 84(1)(b) Constitution of Dominica; s 83(1) Constitution of Grenada; and s 124(2) Constitution of Jamaica.
[76] See, eg, s 77(2) Constitution of St Kitts and Nevis.

be eligible for appointment to another public office. This is in order to avoid any risk of a member of a PSC being influenced in favour of the executive by considerations of advancing their own career after stepping down from the PSC.[77] Appointments to the PSC are for a fixed term, the minimum being two years, as in the case of Antigua, and the maximum being five years, as in the case of Jamaica, with the office being vacated on expiry of the fixed term or if the member is disqualified for some other reason, for example, election to the legislature or nomination to the Senate.

Members of the PSC may only be removed from office by the President or Governor General, as the case may be, for inability to discharge the functions of their office whether arising from infirmity of mind or body or any other cause or for misbehaviour, and then only if their removal has been recommended by a tribunal, comprising a chairman and two other members appointed by the Chief Justice.[78] The salaries and allowances of members of the PSC are usually standing charges on the Consolidated Funds. There is also usually a provision that their conditions of service shall not be altered to their disadvantage. In this way members of the PSC enjoy the same level of immunity as is afforded to Supreme Court judges. Moreover, the provisions surrounding the appointment and composition of the PSC are heavily entrenched, usually at the deepest level.[79]

Notwithstanding these safeguards, the risk of political interference with the functions of the PSC remains a profound concern. George Eaton, for example, writing about the operation of the PSC in Grenada has argued that:

> It is naïve to suppose that persons appointed through a process of political patronage to a legally independent, but functionally very important body, will thereafter become immune to political sensitivities … It simply means that political persuasion is exercised surreptitiously or, as in the case of Grenada, under the Gairy regime, by the outright usurpation and subversion of the functions and responsibilities of the [PSC].[80]

---

[77] See, eg, s 126(2) Constitution of Trinidad and Tobago and *Thomas v AG Trinidad* [1982] AC 113 [5].

[78] See, eg, ss 77(5) and 77(6) Constitution of St Kitts and Nevis.

[79] See s 42(2) Constitution of Dominica.

[80] G Eaton et al, 'The Public Service Commission in Grenada' in Ryan and Bissessar (eds), *Governance in the Caribbean*, above (n 31) 210.

Even where governments may not directly usurp the functions of the PSC they may seek to subvert the jurisdiction of the PSC by employing non-established workers, thereby avoiding the necessity for party members whom they wish to appoint having to present the minimum required qualifications and ensuring that they are not subject to the same disciplinary arrangements as 'established' public servants. In Antigua, for example, in 2002, almost two-thirds of those on the government payroll were 'non-established' workers.[81]

For those public servants who remain subject to the jurisdiction of the PSC, however, the possibility exists at each stage of their career for interference by a politically directed PSC, the decisions of which are not judicially reviewable as a result of the ouster clause in respect of PSCs to be found in most Constitutions in the region.[82] Unsurprisingly, this has had a baleful effect upon the relationship between government and the public service across the region, which has been further exacerbated by a number of other factors which we will examine in the next section.

B. INDEPENDENCE, RACIAL DIVISIONS, IDEOLOGICAL DIFFERENCES AND THE PROBLEMS OF SMALL ISLAND STATES

In the immediate post-independence period relations between newly appointed ministers and their public servants tended to be characterised by 'friction, mutual suspicion and conflict'.[83] Senior public servants, who regarded themselves as better educated and of a superior social status, and accustomed under the colonial system to performing powerful roles as policy makers, resented the intrusion of elected political

---

[81] *Report of the Constitution Review Commission of Antigua*, above (n 17) 47. The figures for established and non-established posts can be difficult to obtain with any accuracy, but for an estimate of the extent of non-established workers in other countries in the region see Sutton, above (n 33) 13.

[82] s 99(11) Constitution of Antigua and Barbuda; s 105(13) Constitution of Belize; s 84(12) Constitution of Dominica; s 83(12) Constitution of Grenada; s 136(c) Constitution of Jamaica; s 77(11) Constitution of St Kitts and Nevis; s 85(12) Constitution of St Lucia; and s 77(12) Constitution of St Vincent and the Grenadines.

[83] GE Mills, 'Conflict between Ministers and Civil Servants' in Ryan and Bissessar (eds), *Governance in the Caribbean*, above (n 31) 265.

heads and found difficulty in adjusting to their new subordinate status.[84] For their part, newly appointed ministers were anxious to assert their authority and to make it clear that they were now the new masters.[85]

During this period public servants were frequently accused by ministers of 'foot dragging' or, even worse, 'overt sabotage'.[86] In Grenada, where a senior public servant hid important files from his minister, the latter responded by boarding up the official's office. Such was the atmosphere of mutual distrust in St Kitts that the Attorney General was heard to declare that any public servant found sabotaging or working against the Government would be dismissed: 'Constitution, or no damn Constitution'.[87] In Antigua, 16 senior public servants were 'retired in the public interest' on the ground that their conduct was regarded as inconsistent with the continuance of their relationship as 'employees of the Government'. It was subsequently discovered that the public servants in question were known not to have supported the governing party during the elections.[88] In Trinidad, the Prime Minister, Eric Williams, used every available public platform to criticise the public service, even alleging at one point that 'a small ambitious group of technocrats were scheming to take over the country outside of the Constitution'.[89] This led to the interdictment and suspension of both his Permanent Secretary and Economic Adviser for actions that were subsequently established to have been authorised by the Prime Minister.

To an extent this tension between ministers and public servants was to be expected as each became accustomed to their new roles in the postcolonial landscape. However, in some countries such as Guyana and Trinidad, the tension never entirely dissipated and was exacerbated by racial divisions between those of African and those of Indian descent, which mirrored the racial divisions between the supporters of the two main political parties in each country.

Thus, in Guyana, under Forbes Burnham, it was generally understood that the route to advancement within the public service was membership in the PNC. The idea of the neutrality and independence

---

[84] Ibid.
[85] Ibid.
[86] Ibid.
[87] Ibid.
[88] Ibid.
[89] Quoted by S Ryan, 'Administrative Improvement in the Commonwealth Caribbean' in Ryan and Bissessar (eds), *Governance in the Caribbean*, above (n 31) 450.

of the public service was rejected by PNC ministers as 'a device created by the imperialists to further their own interests and was never operated in the interests of the working class or the working people'.[90] Instead, the active participation, commitment and loyalty of public servants to the PNC, its policies and programmes were regarded as virtues to be encouraged. Police officers and soldiers were even obliged to declare their loyalty to the PNC. When the Indian-dominated People's Progressive Party (PPP) finally came to power, in 1992, it was thus faced with a public service predominantly staffed by those of African descent in which 'there was no pretence of bureaucratic neutrality'. During the period from 1973 to 1979, for example, it was noted that five out of a total of 55 chairmen of the various boards and commissions were Indians and, out of a total membership of 487 members, 365 were Africans while 96 were East Indians.[91] By way of response, the PPP moved aggressively to remove officials across the public service, nearly all of whom were of African descent, replacing them with their own supporters, leading to charges by public service unions of 'political victimization' and 'ethnic cleansing'—accusations that continue to be made to this day.[92]

In Trinidad, there may not have been the same requirement of allegiance to the PNM, but the mere fact that the PNM had dominated the machinery of government since independence meant that its relationship with the public service was perceived by the Government's opponents as far too close.[93] This meant that when, in 1986, the PNM was replaced by the National Alliance for Reconstruction (NAR)—a union of Indian and anti-PNM, Afro-Trinidadian political leaders—NAR ministers, particularly those of Indian descent, suspected their senior public servants of racial bias. They also believed that their efforts at reform were being blocked by public servants still loyal to the PNM[94] and,

---

[90]   Quoted by James and Lutchman, above (n 55) 81.

[91]   S Debiprashad, 'East Indians in the Caribbean' in IJ Bahadur Singh (ed), *Indians in the Caribbean* (Bangalore, Sterling Publishers, 1987).

[92]   Sutton, above (n 33) 5.

[93]   Ibid.

[94]   Allegations of discrimination by Indians, particularly at the senior level, were confirmed by *Ethnicity and Employment Practices in Trinidad and Tobago* (1994), a report carried out by the Centre of Ethnic Studies in Trinidad, commissioned by the PNM government in 1991 and quoted in A Bissessar, 'The Introduction of New Public Management in Small States' in Ryan and Bissessar (eds), *Governance in the Caribbean*, above (n 31) 509.

accordingly, set about the removal of Permanent Secretaries appointed during the PNM administration.[95] As the Constitution Commission noted in its 1974 review of the Constitution of Trinidad and Tobago:

> These officials are so directly concerned with the formulation of policy and supervision of its implementation that they must be acceptable to the political chiefs with whom they must have a close working relationship. This does permit some measure of political influence in purely public service appointments but is necessary on purely practical grounds.[96]

However, the NAR did not stop at senior public servants, but instead insisted upon the wholesale reorganisation of ministries, and the removal or transfer of public servants regardless of experience and competence.

Even without the complicating factor of racial divisions, fundamental ideological differences between an outgoing and incoming government have, on occasion, put an immense strain on relations between ministers and their senior public servants, testing the presumed *neutrality* of the public service to its limits. This can be seen especially in the case of Michael Manley's PNP administration, which came into office in 1972 with the avowed aim of introducing democratic socialism into Jamaica. In order to bring about this change Manley insisted that it was necessary to introduce special advisers into government with a strong political commitment to the PNP's policy goals. According to Manley, these special advisers would serve as 'pipelines' and thus enable ministers to have access to 'the huge reservoir of ideas and thinking' represented by 'the opinions and views of the people at large'.[97] Unsurprisingly, the introduction of special advisers was unpopular with senior public servants.[98] Ministers were no longer obliged to rely exclusively on their advice, but were free to seek and receive advice from a range of sources and inevitably ministers would seek out sources whose advice would be ideologically more attractive than the advice that they could expect to receive from their Permanent Secretaries. As a result, concerns were

[95] S Ryan, 'Political Transitions in Trinidad and Tobago 1986–1992' in Ryan and Bissessar (eds), *Governance in the Caribbean*, above (n 31) 283.

[96] Constitution Commission of Trinidad and Tobago, *Report of the Constitution Commission* (Port of Spain, 1974). Available at: www.ttparliament.org.

[97] M Manley, 'Politicians and Civil Servants' in Ryan and Bissessar (eds), *Governance in the Caribbean*, above (n 31) 509.

[98] Mills, above (n 83) 267.

expressed not only about the special advisers' lack of neutrality, but also the possible confusion and conflict in the lines of authority and responsibility between ministers, their special advisers and their senior public servants.[99]

The use of special advisers is today much more commonplace in government ministries across the region and attracts much less controversy. This is, in part because of their familiarity, but it is also, in large part, because the ideological consensus between governments in the region—which all broadly pursue a neoliberal economic agenda—confines special advisers to a mainly technocratic role which is quite different from the more overtly political role that they had played in the past.[100] Nevertheless, fundamental concerns about the role of special advisers remain. Unlike public servants who operate within a defined constitutional framework, there are no controls over special advisers; there are no mechanisms for checking their character on appointment; no formal process for enquiring into their identity or financial connections; and no limits on the gifts and hospitality that they can receive from outside sources.[101]

Quite apart from racial divisions and ideological differences between governments, one of the greatest difficulties confronting the public service in the region is the small size of many of these countries. While Commonwealth Caribbean constitutions may envisage a distinction between policy *formulation*, being the preserve of ministers, and policy *implementation*, being the responsibility of their public servants, this distinction can be very difficult to maintain in a small developing country where senior public servants are often required to play a central role in the economic and social development of their countries.[102] Moreover, in such small highly personalised societies, where the political sympathies and loyalties of individuals tend to be widely known, it can be difficult to preserve the anonymity that is supposed to shield public servants from exposure to public criticism. But without this guarantee of anonymity it can be difficult for public servants to offer the best possible

---

[99]   Ibid.

[100]   Sutton, above (n 33) 5.

[101]   J Tindigarukayo and SJ Chadwick, *Civil Service Reform in Jamaica*, 38. Available at: www.mirror.undp.org/magnet/Docs/psreform/civil_service_reform_in_jamaica.htm.

[102]   See, eg, *Manual of Cabinet and Ministry Procedure*, Bahamas, above (n 29) paras 11 and 16.

advice on policy to ministers.[103] They may become associated with particular policies and in the event of a change of government are likely to find themselves in a 'precarious and uncomfortable situation'.[104]

This blurring of the distinction between the respective roles of ministers and their public servants is not, however, the only way in which the chain of responsibility between ministers, their departments and Parliament has been weakened as we will see as we turn to consider the impact upon both the public service and the principle of ministerial responsibility following the introduction of the principles of New Public Management (NPM).

C. NEW PUBLIC MANAGEMENT (NPM)

In the 1980s, several of the larger countries in the region underwent structural adjustment programmes as one of the prerequisites for loans and aid from international development agencies. In economic terms, this meant a reorientation away from the public sector towards private-sector-led development, and a more market-driven economy.[105] This coincided with a growing recognition that reform of the public service within the region was also essential in order to deal with the problems of political patronage and of waste in the public sector. A report published by the Caribbean Community and Common Market (CARICOM) in 1995, and endorsed by the Heads of Government of CARICOM, proposed tackling these problems by reforming the public sector in accordance with the principles of NPM.[106] NPM comprises a number of different elements, but the two that have been most enthusiastically embraced by governments in the region are the introduction of semi-autonomous Executive Agencies, and the contracting out of public service provision to the private sector. Both raise concerns about the nature of the relationship between government and the public service.

---

[103] Sutton, above (n 33) 3.

[104] S Ryan, 'Politics and Public Servant: An Overview' in Ryan and Bissessar (eds), *Governance in the Caribbean*, above (n 31) 261.

[105] S Ryan, 'Administrative Reform: An Overview' in Ryan and Bissessar (eds), *Governance in the Caribbean*, above (n 31) 435.

[106] See *Report of CARICOM Ministerial Roundtable on Public Management in the Caribbean* (CARICAD, 1992).

1. Executive Agencies

The most extensive network of Executive Agencies (Agencies) is, undoubtedly, to be found in Jamaica where, to date, 10 Agencies have been established as part of its 'Public Sector Modernisation Programme'. The aim of these Agencies is to reduce the central control of government over the provision of designated public services by delegating responsibility for delivery of these services to a senior public servant within the department concerned, who is appointed the Chief Executive Officer (CEO) of the Agency. A framework document sets out the basic elements of the contract between the CEO and the minister.

CEOs enjoy a considerable degree of autonomy in terms of operational matters, being free to run the affairs of their Agency in a more flexible way than a government department might be.[107] However, the Agency remains located within the government department concerned, and CEOs must still report to the relevant minister who remains ultimately responsible for matters of policy. This is intended to maintain the chain of responsibility between ministers and Parliament. In practice, however, the distinction between policy and operations can be difficult to draw as they inevitably impact on each other and this has implications for democratic control and accountability: how to determine who is responsible for what, who is to be held accountable and by what means when an Agency malfunctions.[108] This may be illustrated by the example of the Child Development Agency (CDA), in Jamaica, where the CEO was obliged to resign following mounting criticism of her performance as a result of findings of abuse at children's homes from 2005 to 2006, and a damning report into a fire that had occurred at a Juvenile Correction Centre. While accepting responsibility for what had and had not been achieved by the CDA, the CEO sought to argue in her defence that limited resources and a constant shifting of expectations by government authorities had hampered the work of the CDA.[109]

---

[107] See *Executive Agencies in Jamaica: The Story Thus far and the Central Management Mechanism.* Available at: www.cabinet.gov.jm.

[108] G Drewry, 'The Executive: Towards Accountable Government and Effective Governance?' in D Oliver and J Jowell (eds), *The Changing Constitution*, 5th edn (Oxford, Oxford University Press, 2004) 280.

[109] See 'CDA head confirms resignation', *Jamaica Observer* (25 February 2010).

However, when the Minister of Health, who was ultimately responsible for the CDA, delivered his report to Parliament there was not a single mention of the CDA or of the difficulties reported by its CEO.[110] In other words, responsibility in terms of accepting blame for what had gone wrong had been accepted by the CEO, but there was no corresponding accountability to the Jamaican Parliament for the failings of the department that was responsible for supervising the CDA.

2. Privatisation of Public Services

In accordance with the principles of NPM, statutory bodies have been established in a number of countries to take over functions that had previously been carried out by central government. In the case of non core governmental activities this is relatively unproblematic and does not give rise to any major constitutional concerns, other than the role to be played by the PSC in supervising the transfer, reassignment or retirement of the public servants concerned. However, where it is proposed to privatise core governmental activities the position is constitutionally much more complex as we can see by comparing and contrasting the decisions of the Judicial Committee of the Privy Council (JCPC) and the Court of Appeal of Guyana on this issue.

In *Perch v Attorney General of Trinidad and Tobago*,[111] the appellants, who had been postal workers employed by the Government of Trinidad, objected to being forced to choose between voluntary retirement or transfer to the Trinidad and Tobago Postal Corporation (TTPC),[112] a body established by the Trinidad and Tobago Postal Corporation Act (TPCA). The appellants' challenge to the constitutionality of the Government's actions was principally concerned with the exclusive responsibility of the PSC for the transfer of public officers, but the wider constitutional context in which the challenge arose brought to the surface an even more fundamental question about the constitutionality of privatising a formerly public service.

In answering this latter question, the JCPC drew a distinction between two kinds of privatisation. The first involves the divestment

110 Ibid.
111 *Perch v Attorney General of Trinidad and Tobago* [2003] UKPC 17.
112 Pursuant to s 36(2) Trinidad and Tobago Postal Corporation Act.

by governments of functions previously carried out by them directly or indirectly, but forming no part of the core functions of government and lending themselves to commercial non-governmental operation in the interests of efficiency and economy: such as operating telephones, trains, lotteries, meteorological offices, scientific laboratories, libraries or hospitals. The second involves the devolution of the core functions of government, such as defence, the maintenance of law and order and the administration of justice. In the latter case, the JCPC considered that there would be a strong case for arguing that the transfer of such functions to a statutory corporation contradicted the assumptions upon which the Constitution was based. Though the JCPC did not consider it necessary to elaborate on these assumptions, the judges may have had in mind the rationale underpinning the existence of PSCs, as elaborated by Lord Diplock in *Thomas*, and the implied constitutional principle of the separation of powers, which the JCPC had declared in *Hinds v AG Jamaica* to be a fundamental principle of Commonwealth Caribbean constitutions.[113] The transfer by the executive to the private sector of core governmental functions such as defence, the maintenance of law and order and the administration of justice would not only offend this principle, but would also defeat the whole purpose of vesting control over the appointment, transfer, removal and discipline of such public officers in the PSC.

In *Chue and Another v Attorney General Guyana*,[114] however, the Court of Appeal of Guyana reached a quite different conclusion on the same issue. In this case, the Government of Guyana had transferred to a Revenue Authority, established by the Revenue Authority Act, the functions and powers of the Inland Revenue and Customs Departments. The appellants were a Comptroller of Customs and Excise and a Director of Customs and Excise who sought declarations, inter alia, that while it was open to Parliament to transfer functions, which were not intrinsically governmental 'from the purview of the public service to a public corporation', it was not open to Parliament to so transfer core or essential functions of executive government such as revenue assessment and collection to a corporate body without constitutional amendment.

---

[113] *Hinds v The Queen* [1977] AC 175.
[114] *Chue and Another v Attorney General Guyana* (2006) 72 WIR 213.

The Court of Appeal, however, rejected this submission and held that even if the functions performed by the Inland Revenue and Customs Departments were core government functions, their transfer to a statutory body was permitted by Article 99(2) of the Constitution which, in the Court's view, allowed Parliament to confer functions on persons or authorities other than the President. Since Article 99(2) draws no distinction between core and non-core governmental functions there could be no warrant, in the Court's view, for seeking to restrict Parliament in the exercise of its powers under Article 99(2) by drawing such a distinction. It is curious, however, that there is no mention in *Chue* of the JCPC's decision in *Perch*. While Guyana had abolished the right of appeal to the JCPC when it became a republic in 1970, the decision in *Perch*, even if only of persuasive authority, is so directly relevant to the issue in *Chue* that it should at least have given the Court of Appeal pause for thought. The constitutional framework in both cases is similar[115] and there is no reason for supposing that the principle of the separation of powers is not implied in the Constitution of Guyana. The decision in *Chue* would, in effect, permit the creation of a privatised police force or even a privatised army, thereby defeating the underlying rationale for the vesting of control over such personnel in the PSC, which is at least as much a feature of the Guyanese Constitution as it is of the Trinidadian Constitution.

CONCLUSION

In the period immediately prior to independence political leaders in the Commonwealth Caribbean were gradually introduced to the practices and conventions of Cabinet government. This is the system that they adopted upon independence and to which they have adhered, with the exception of Guyana, ever since. The problems with this system of government—its concentration of power in a small group of ministers, and in the office of the Prime Minister—are well known, but have been exacerbated in the Commonwealth Caribbean by a variety of

---

[115] s 74(3) Constitution of Trinidad and Tobago is in identical terms to Art 99(2).

factors. These include the extensive powers of appointment vested by Commonwealth Caribbean constitutions in the Prime Minister, which affords Prime Ministers a greater than usual capacity to exercise political patronage in rewarding their most loyal supporters and silencing their critics. They also include the failure of local legislatures to act as a sufficient check on the exercise of executive power. As we will see in the next chapter this is due, in part, to the fact that their small size and limited resources means that there is not the system of specialised select committees which exists in other countries operating under the Westminster model, and which have the ability and the capacity to scrutinise government policy as well as the administration of government departments. The small size of local legislatures also means that they tend to be dominated by government ministers who are bound to support government policy and the remaining backbenchers, who may be dependent upon the Prime Minister for their candidacy, and opposition MPs, are not usually a sufficient counterweight to hold the government, in any meaningful sense, to account.

This is not to say that there are no checks on executive power, but rather that the conventions which underpin the operation of Cabinet government, such as collective responsibility and the individual responsibility of ministers, which originally depended upon ministers being held to account by Parliament, do not function quite as intended. Governments can still be held to account, collectively, by a vote of no confidence and ministers are still under a duty to give an account to Parliament of the administration of their department. However, in the circumstances described above, it is highly unlikely that a government could be defeated on a vote of no confidence or that ministers could be forced to resign following a vote of censure in Parliament. Instead, ministers are more likely to be held to account by the media and by extra-parliamentary bodies for breach of the principles of collective or individual ministerial responsibility.

It is, however, in relations between the government and the public service that there has been perhaps the greatest breakdown in the conventions that underpin the operation of the Westminster model—in particular, the presumption of a public service composed of neutral and anonymous public servants. Although much has changed since the early days of independence, the degree of influence which the Prime Minister is able to exert over PSCs means that these bodies have not always been able adequately to insulate the public service from interference by the government of the day and has, in some cases, resulted in a public service which is dominated by one racial group or is perceived to be politically partisan. The role of the PSCs has also been undermined in some cases by the establishment of non-established workers and the privatisation of public services with the threat that, in the case of Guyana at least, these could include core public services.

Notwithstanding its manifest drawbacks, the majority of countries remain fundamentally committed to the principle of Cabinet government and the Cabinet system has now become firmly established in every country across the region, with the exception of Guyana. Though there have been recommendations by some constitutional reform commissions for a shift to a more executive presidential system, this has generally been regarded as a reform too far. As we will see in chapter eight, rather than replacing the existing system of Cabinet government such reforms as have been introduced have instead sought to work within the framework of Cabinet government with a view to improving its accountability.

FURTHER READING

CJ Edie (ed), *Democracy in the Caribbean: Myths and Realities* (Westport, Connecticut, Praeger, 1994).

HA Ghany, 'Parliamentary Deadlock and the Removal of the Prime Minister: Incumbency and Termination Theory in Trinidad and Tobago' (2006) 12(1) *Journal of Legislative Studies* 76–97.

R James and H Lutchman, *Law and the Political Environment in Guyana*, (Georgetown, Guyana, Institute of Development Studies, University of Guyana, 1984).

RAW Rhodes, J Wanna and P Weller (eds), *Comparing Westminster* (Oxford, Oxford University Press, 2009).

S Ryan and AM Bissessar (eds), *Governance in the Caribbean* (St Augustine, Trinidad and Tobago, Sir Arthur Lewis Institute of Social and Economic Studies, University of the West Indies Press, 2002).

P Sutton, *Modernizing the State: Public Sector Reform in the Commonwealth Caribbean* (Kingston, Jamaica, Ian Randle Publishers, 2005).

5

Parliament

———————

Introduction – **Membership and Structural Organisation of Commonwealth Caribbean Parliaments** – **Parliament's Law-Making Powers** – **Scrutiny of the Executive** – **Conclusion**

PART I: INTRODUCTION

PARLIAMENT IS A key component of the 'Westminster model' of governance and, as such, is expected to perform a multiplicity of functions. These include, in addition to forming the government of the day: serving as a forum for debating issues of public importance; representing the will of the people; and the approval of government expenditure. For the purposes of this chapter, however, we will concentrate on what are generally regarded as Parliament's two most important functions: law-making and scrutiny of the executive. Before considering the role of Commonwealth Caribbean parliaments in discharging these functions it is, however, necessary first to provide an overview of their membership and structural organisation, since both have a direct bearing on each parliament's ability to perform these key functions.

PART II: MEMBERSHIP AND STRUCTURAL ORGANISATION OF COMMONWEALTH CARIBBEAN PARLIAMENTS

With the exception of Dominica, Guyana, St Kitts and St Vincent, which each have unicameral parliaments, all the remaining countries in the region opted, upon independence, for bicameral parliaments. In these

countries Parliament comprises both an Upper House—the Senate—
composed of nominated members, and a Lower House—known either
as the House of Assembly or the House of Representatives—composed
of elected members. Though unicameral, the Parliaments of Dominica,
St Kitts and St Vincent include both an elected and a nominated element. Guyana, which abandoned the Westminster model when it
adopted a 'socialist' Constitution in 1980, is now wholly composed of
directly elected members.

A. MEMBERS OF PARLIAMENT (MPS)

1. Elected Members

As we have seen in chapter three, with the exception of Guyana, elections to Commonwealth Caribbean parliaments take place under the
'first past the post' (FPTP) system. Qualifications for election vary
slightly from country to country. In some cases—Grenada, Jamaica and
St Vincent—any Commonwealth citizen is entitled to stand for election so long as they satisfy the residency and age requirements. In the
case of St Kitts, either the candidate or one of their parents must have
been born there.[1] Elsewhere, candidates actually have to be citizens
of the country concerned. Everywhere—apart from the Bahamas and
Barbados—there is also an English language requirement. The matters that disqualify candidates from standing for election are numerous
and include undischarged bankruptcy, insanity, imprisonment, prior
convictions for offences of dishonesty, election offences or holding
a religious ministry.[2] However, one disqualification in particular—the
'voluntary acknowledgment of allegiance, obedience or adherence to a
foreign state or power'—has proved to be especially problematic in a
region which contains some of the most migratory people in the world,
and where it is not at all unusual for a citizen of a country to be born
and have their residence there yet also be a citizen of another country.
As a result, there have been a number of instances across the region
of successful candidates in general elections having their nominations

---

[1] s 27 Constitution of St Kitts and Nevis.
[2] See, eg, s 39 Constitution of Antigua and Barbuda.

challenged subsequently on the ground that they were disqualified by reason of their dual citizenship.

Some of the most well known examples where this has occurred involve the Jamaican general elections of 2007. In the first of four cases to be brought by disappointed People's National Party (PNP) candidates, *Dabdoub v Vaz*,[3] the defeated PNP candidate, Abraham Dabdoub, filed an election petition, in which he argued that the winning Jamaica Labour Party (JLP) candidate, Daryl Vaz, was disqualified because he had 'by virtue of his own act acknowledged allegiance, obedience or adherence to a foreign power'.[4] Vaz had been born in Jamaica, his mother was a US citizen who had registered his birth at the US Embassy in Jamaica, and as a child he had been added to his mother's passport. Subsequently, Vaz had acquired a US passport in his own right, which he had used to travel abroad on numerous occasions and which he had also renewed. Dabdoub having conceded that a person who had obtained foreign citizenship by an act of law without any application on their part would not be so disqualified,[5] the central question for the Jamaica Supreme Court was whether or not the acquisition, renewal and use by Vaz of his US passport as an adult amounted to an acknowledgment by his own act of his allegiance to the United States. In finding that Vaz's actions did indeed amount to such an acknowledgment of allegiance, the Court declared that:

> It is not the owing of allegiance to the USA by virtue of being a citizen of that country that is a ground for disqualification from sitting in the House of Representatives but rather the voluntary taking of steps to acknowledge that citizenship that causes the disqualification.[6]

Accordingly, the Court ordered that there would have to be a by-election, which Vaz went on to win, having renounced his US citizenship.

The decision in *Dabdoub* set a precedent for three further petitions filed by disappointed PNP candidates, which resulted in the JLP candidate

---

[3] *Dabdoub v Vaz*, Supreme Court Jamaica, 2007 HCV 03921. Unreported. Available on file with the author.

[4] Contrary to s 40(2)(a) Constitution of Jamaica.

[5] As held by the Court of Appeal of Trinidad and Tobago in *Chaitan v AG* (2001) 63 WIR 244 and an unreported case of the Eastern Caribbean Supreme Court, *Spencer v Smith*, 23 June 2003.

[6] At [33].

in each case being held to have been disqualified from standing for election; though in each case the disqualified candidate, having renounced their US citizenship, managed to win the subsequent by-election. In retaliation, the JLP launched its own legal challenges to PNP candidates whom they alleged were equally disqualified on the grounds of holding US passports. The first of these, *Hayles v Hamilton*,[7] was settled after the PNP candidate, Hayles, renounced his US citizenship and won the subsequent 2011 election before the election petition against him could be heard. The second challenge was also concluded without trial, but not before the PNP candidate, Sharon Hay Webster, had resigned from the PNP to sit as an independent MP and had, unsuccessfully, stood as a candidate for the JLP in the General Election of 2011.[8]

The decision in *Dabdoub* also sent shockwaves reverberating across the region as winning candidates in elections in both St Kitts[9] and Grenada found their victories being challenged on the ground of their dual citizenship. It is, however, in Dominica where the impact of *Dabdoub* has had probably the most profound effect since it led directly to a challenge to the nominations of Prime Minister, Roosevelt Skerritt, and his Education Minister, Petter Saint Jean, following the 2009 general election, on the ground that they had both held French citizenship on nomination day.[10] The candidates themselves having acknowledged that they had acquired French citizenship through their mothers, the central issue in the case concerned whether or not the candidates had also held French passports. However, the answer to this question was never ultimately determined by the courts. Instead, the High Court of Dominica dismissed the election petitions against both the Prime Minister and the Education Minister on the rather unsatisfactory basis that the petitioners had not been able to discharge the evidential burden required to establish that either the Prime Minister or his Education Minister had held French passports; the latter having refused to answer questions

[7] *Hayles v Hamilton* [2010] JMCA Civ 27. Unreported. Available on file with the author.

[8] 'Hay-Webster dual citizen case abandoned', *Jamaica News Online* (12 June 2012).

[9] See *Liburd v Hamilton* ECCA 2011. Unreported. Available on file with the author.

[10] *Green v Petter Saint Jean* ECSC from Dominica High Court Civil Claim No 6 of 2010 and *Joseph v Skerritt*, Civil Claim No 7 of 2010. Unreported. Available on file with the author.

on this point by invoking the privilege against self-incrimination, and a *subpoena duces tecum* to produce their passports having been overturned.

Though a right to stand for election is not protected in any of the Commonwealth Caribbean constitutions, the right is recognised either expressly[11] or impliedly in a number of international human rights treaties which, in turn, inspired the fundamental rights guaranteed by these constitutions.[12] The European Court of Human Rights, for example, has held that Article 3 of Protocol 1, which requires the High Contracting Parties to hold free elections at reasonable intervals, includes the individual right to stand for election.[13] In this regard it is notable that the new Jamaican Charter of Fundamental Rights and Freedoms, approved by the Jamaican Parliament in March 2011, expressly includes the right to vote.[14] On the other hand, it has also been widely accepted that the right to stand for election is not absolute and may be subject to limitations provided that any such limitations are, for example, in pursuit of a legitimate aim and are proportionate. In *Dabdoub*, the Court identified the principal aims of the dual citizenship prohibition as twofold: first, to avoid legislators having perceived or actual conflicts of interest arising as a result of divided loyalties; and, second, to prevent improper political influence by foreign governments. There is no doubt, therefore, that the prohibition is in pursuit of a legitimate aim, but whether or not it is proportionate remains a vexed question.[15]

Those who argue for the removal of the prohibition point out that first, the possession of dual citizenship does not, without more, render an MP incapable of possessing the requisite degree of loyalty; second, there may be less restrictive measures than a blanket prohibition of dual citizens, for example, restricting the prohibition to the posts of Prime Minister and selected Cabinet ministers, or letting the electorate decide by replacing the disqualification with a prior duty of disclosure of a candidate's dual citizenship; and third, a significantly high percentage of Caribbean nationals are potentially affected by it. In the case of

---

[11] Article 25(b) International Covenant on Civil and Political Rights.

[12] See comments of Lord Wilberforce in *Minister for Home Affairs v Fisher* (Bermuda) [1979] UKPC 21.

[13] *Mathieu-Mohin v Belgium* (1988) 10 EHRR 1.

[14] s 13(3)(m) Jamaica Charter of Fundamental Rights and Freedoms.

[15] For a discussion of the proportionality issue see A Johns, 'Dual Citizenship and the Right to Candidacy: An Analysis of Jamaica's Foreign Allegiance Parliamentary Disqualification' (MPhil thesis, University of Oxford, 2013).

Jamaica, for example, it has been estimated that approximately 10 per cent of the worldwide Jamaican population (estimated at 4.7 million) are disqualified by the prohibition.[16] This means that not only are Jamaican voters being denied access to the widest possible pool of candidates but, since many of those who have lived abroad and have acquired dual citizenship are among the most highly educated members of Jamaican society, the voters are also being denied access to potentially the most able pool of candidates. To avoid this problem the Government of Belize sought to amend the Constitution to remove the prohibition against dual citizenship altogether, but a provision to this effect in the Constitution (Seventh Amendment) Bill 2009, was rejected by the Senate and had to be removed.

The maintenance of a prohibition against dual citizenship is also potentially very destabilising politically. In Dominica, for example, the Opposition boycotted Parliament for a period of two years after the elections in which the Prime Minister and his Education Minister won their seats. Moreover, the High Court's ruling, failed to resolve questions raised about the status of the Prime Minister and his Education Minister to everyone's satisfaction and the ruling was, subsequently, appealed to the Eastern Caribbean Supreme Court, which finally ruled in favour of the Prime Minister and his Education Minister in March 2013, some four years after the election.[17] To avoid such a situation arising in St Kitts, legislation was enacted in 2009 requiring candidates seeking election to the National Assembly to declare on oath or affirm that they are duly qualified in accordance with section 28 of the Constitution, which disqualifies candidates with dual citizenship.[18]

2. Nominated Members

It is one of the paradoxical features of constitutional development within the Commonwealth Caribbean that, notwithstanding the prolonged

[16] See A Bennett et al, *Dual Citizenship and Political Representation in Jamaica: Insights From Comparative Research* (Caribbean Policy Research Institute 2008). Available at: www.capricaribbean.org.

[17] *Ronald Green v Petter Saint Jean* and *Maynard Joseph v Roosevelt Skerrit* DOMHCVAP 2012/001. Available at: www.eccourts.org.

[18] National Assembly Elections (Amendment) (No 2) Act 2009.

struggle to remove the nominated element from colonial legislatures and replace it with an elected element, all the post-independence parliaments in the region (with the exception of Guyana), whether unicameral or bicameral, contain a nominated element (senators) alongside the elected element. Among unicameral parliaments the ratio of elected to nominated members varies quite considerably from 15:6 in St Vincent, 21:9 in Dominica and 11:3 in St Kitts.

The inclusion of a nominated element was intended not only to ensure more robust deliberation of legislation, but also to provide an additional set of checks and balances over executive decision-making, while at the same time enhancing the diversity of representation in the legislature. Furthermore, since a special majority of the Upper House is required for certain constitutional amendments to the Constitution, it was envisaged that the Upper House would have an important role in preventing the government of the day using its majority in the elected House to force through such amendments. Whether or not the nominated element in Commonwealth Caribbean parliaments is able to serve any or all of these important constitutional functions is, however, largely determined by the extent to which they are independent of the executive and this, in turn, depends on the provisions surrounding their appointment and removal.

The majority of senators are appointed by the head of state on the recommendation of the Prime Minister, or the Leader of the Opposition, as the case may be.[19] Their appointment is for a fixed term of five years, corresponding to the life of a parliament. However, they may be removed at any time on the recommendation of whoever, whether the Prime Minister or the Leader of the Opposition, recommended their appointment. In the Bahamas, the Prime Minister nominates nine of the 16 senators; in Barbados, the Prime Minister nominates 12 of the 21 senators; in Jamaica the Prime Minister nominates 13 of the 21 senators; and in Trinidad the Prime Minister nominates 16 of the 31 senators.[20] In the Bahamas, the Prime Minister is additionally required to consult

[19] As is the case for elected MPs, there are a number of eligibility requirements relating to age and residence in the country concerned, as well as a wide range of disqualifications. The latter include insanity, undischarged bankruptcy and prior criminal convictions. In Antigua, the list of those disqualified includes ministers of religion. See, eg, s 29 Constitution of Antigua and Barbuda.

[20] s 39(2) Constitution of the Bahamas; s 36(2) Constitution of Barbados; s 35(2) Constitution of Jamaica; and s 40(2)(a) Constitution of Trinidad and Tobago.

the Leader of the Opposition in the appointment of three senators, over and above the four senators already appointed in accordance with the latter's advice.[21] The purpose of the consultation is to ensure that the political balance of the Senate reflects that of the House of Assembly.[22] However, while the Prime Minister may be required to consult, the Prime Minister is not bound to follow the advice of the Leader of the Opposition when appointing these three senators and the court will only review the appointment of such senators by the Prime Minister if it can be shown to be *Wednesbury* unreasonable.[23]

In some countries in the region, constitutional provisions attempt to ensure that the nominated element is not confined solely to those with political affiliations to the two main parties. In these countries, the Governor General is empowered to appoint senators who represent a wide range of interests in the community: such as religious, economic, social or other such interests as they think ought to be represented.[24] Such constitutional measures help to enhance the legislature's claim to representativeness in these countries and there have been calls by the constitutional review commissions of a number of countries to increase the number of senators without political affiliations.[25]

Elsewhere in the region, however, senators are usually affiliated either to the party in power or to the opposition party. As a member of the Constitutional Review Commission of St Vincent wryly observed with regard to the appointment of senators in that country:

> Ninety-nine times out of a hundred, four or five of the six [senators] are people who have just contested the elections and lost—on both sides ... Renwick Rose contested and he was expected to win. He lost. You must find a job for the boy; appoint him a senator. Very often you not only appoint him a senator, he becomes a minister as well.[26]

---

[21] ss 39(3) and 39(4) Constitution of the Bahamas.

[22] s 40 Constitution of the Bahamas.

[23] *Christie v Ingraham* (2008) 74 WIR 1.

[24] See, eg, s 36(4) Constitution of Barbados; s 61(2)(c) Constitution of Belize; s 24(2)(c) Constitution of St Lucia; and s 40(2)(c) Constitution of Trinidad and Tobago.

[25] See, eg, *The Bahamas Constitutional Review Commission Preliminary Report and Provisional Recommendations 2006*. Available at: www.islandwoo-ivil.tripod.com.

[26] Renwick Rose, 'Constitution Review: The Experience of St Vincent and the Grenadines'. Available at: www.crforumtt.org.

This has led to the nominated element of Commonwealth Caribbean parliaments being characterised, respectively, as 'puppets of the government' or opposing 'for opposition's sake'.[27] Whether or not this is a fair description the reality is that so long as the Prime Minister is guaranteed a majority of the nominated element in both unicameral and bicameral legislatures, and so long as the Prime Minister can revoke the appointment of the senators that the Prime Minister has nominated who do not toe the party line, the level of influence which the nominated element can bring to bear on the legislative process and executive decision-making is negligible. As we will see below, however, opposition and independent senators may, in some countries, still have a role to play in blocking those amendments to the Constitution which require a special majority over and above the ordinary majority guaranteed by the Prime Minister's nominees.

B. LEADER OF THE OPPOSITION

The Westminster model is unusual, if not unique, among political systems in so far as it makes provision for a permanent role for a political 'Opposition'.[28] Originally, this was to ensure that the monarch was given the option of an alternative administration in the event that the incumbent fell out of favour or lost the confidence of the monarch.[29] However, even today, the Opposition remains a crucial element within the system: an 'executive-in-waiting', its members working through the system and learning its norms and conventions so that when the call comes, it is ready to govern.[30] At the same time, the Opposition is expected to provide policy alternatives to those of the present government and to ensure that there is a continual debate on the Government's performance. The office of Leader of the Opposition is thus enshrined

---

[27] *Report of the Constitution Reform Commission of Antigua* (2002) 80. Available at: www.ab.gov.ag.
[28] See RAW Rhodes, J Wanna and P Weller (eds), *Comparing Westminster* (Oxford, Oxford University Press, 2009) 206.
[29] Ibid.
[30] Ibid, 207.

in all the Commonwealth Caribbean constitutions. In Guyana, the Leader of the Opposition is referred to as the Minority Leader.[31]

When appointing the Leader of the Opposition the Governor General or President, as the case may be, must select the member of the elected House who appears to them most likely to command the support of a majority of the members of the House who do not support the Government. If no member of the House appears to the President or Governor General to command such support, they must appoint the member of the House who appears to them to command the support of the largest single group of members of the House who do not support the Government.[32] In the very small parliaments of the Commonwealth Caribbean, however, this has not always been an easy task, particularly since there has been a tendency for the winning party to gain a disproportionately high number of seats to votes cast in post-independence elections. The Constitutions of Antigua and St Vincent anticipate just this sort of problem by providing that where there are two or more members of the House of Representatives who do not support the Government, but none of them commands the support of the other, or the other members of the House of Representatives, the Governor General may appoint any one of them.[33] In exercising their discretion in such a case the Governor General must have regard to the seniority of each based on their length of service as a member of the House of Representatives, by the number of votes cast in favour of each at the last election, or by both.

A different kind of problem, however, arises for a Governor General or President, as the case may be, where there is no one at all to appoint as Leader of the Opposition because one party has won all the seats in the election. This has occurred no fewer than six times since independence: in Trinidad in 1971; in Jamaica in 1983; in Grenada in 1999 and 2013; and in St Vincent in 1989 and 1994. It can be just as problematic if a party has managed to win a seat in the election but the Constitution precludes the possibility of a 'one person' Opposition:[34] for example, by providing that a member of the House of Representatives cannot

[31] Arts 110 and 184 Constitution of Guyana.
[32] See, eg, s 79 Constitution of Antigua and Barbuda.
[33] s 79(2) Constitution of Antigua and Barbuda and s 59(2) Constitution of St Vincent and the Grenadines.
[34] See s 58(2) Constitution of St Kitts and Nevis.

be eligible for appointment unless that member commands the support of at least one other member of the House of Representatives. Thus, in St Kitts, in 2000, a vacancy arose even though the Concerned Citizens' Movement (CCM) had won two of the seats in Nevis because the Prime Minister appointed one of the two CCM members to his Cabinet, thereby disqualifying the other member of the CCM from being appointed Leader of the Opposition because he was unable to secure the support of the only other member of the National Assembly who was opposed to the Government (being a member of the Nevis Reformation Party).

The absence of a Leader of the Opposition for either of the above reasons is clearly undesirable from a democratic perspective because it means there is no official Opposition in Parliament to hold the government to account or to provide alternatives to government policy. Moreover, it presents the President or Governor General, as the case may be, with a very practical problem when exercising those functions that the Constitution stipulates they can only exercise after consulting the Leader of the Opposition, such as the appointment of senators as well as a number of senior public officials. In such a situation Commonwealth Caribbean constitutions broadly offer three alternative solutions—with the exception of the Constitution of St Vincent, which does not make any provision for such a situation. The first is to permit the head of state to act in their own deliberate judgement. This occurred in Grenada, following the 1999 election, when the Governor appointed three senators whom he believed would ordinarily have been opposed to the Government;[35] and again, following the 2013 elections, when the Governor appointed three former ministers of the opposition National Democratic Congress to fill the Opposition seats in the Senate.[36] The second is to remove the requirement for any constitutional function to be performed on advice or after consultation with the Leader of the Opposition.[37] The third is to substitute the advice of the Prime Minister for that of the Leader of the Opposition, as occurred in Jamaica in 1983

---

[35] HA Ghany, 'The Office of the Leader of the Opposition: An Examination of the Whitehall Version in the Commonwealth Caribbean' (2001) 7(2) *Journal of Legislative Studies* 105–22, 113.

[36] *Caribbean Elections Today* (26 March 2013). Available at: www.caribbeanelections. com.

[37] Art 185(4) Constitution of Guyana; s 83(6) Constitution of Trinidad and Tobago; and s 47(6) Constitution of Belize. In the case of Belize, see further s 61(3).

when the JLP, led by Edward Seaga, won all the seats in the House of Representatives.[38]

In practice, however, the subservient nature of the relationship between Governors General and the Prime Minister, as discussed in chapter two, means that even where a Governor General may be empowered to act in their own deliberate judgement the likelihood is that they will be influenced, to a greater or lesser degree, by the advice of the Prime Minister. This is of particular concern with regard to the appointment of Opposition senators who may have an important role to play when it comes to amending the Constitution. In the absence of a cohort of senators selected by the Leader of the Opposition to counter-balance the Government's majority in the Senate there is a danger that the Government will be able to make amendments to the Constitution completely unopposed. Only the Constitution of Belize seeks to guard against this danger. Here the Governor General is required, in the event of a vacancy in the office of the Leader of the Opposition, to select a person, in their own deliberate judgement, to advise them on the appointment of Opposition senators; or select two persons, in their own deliberate judgement, to advise them on the appointment of one senator each.[39]

C. THE SPEAKER

Speakers were introduced into Commonwealth Caribbean legislatures as part of a wider package of constitutional reforms that were introduced in the region by the Colonial Office, following the end of the Second World War, with the aim of increasing the measure of responsibility for government borne by colonial legislatures.[40] The Speaker thus replaced the Governor as the Chairman of the Legislative Council,[41] and it was

---

[38] s 81 Constitution of Jamaica.

[39] s 61(3) Constitution of Belize.

[40] See dispatch from Arthur Creech Jones, Secretary of State to the Colonies to Sir John Shaw, Governor of Trinidad, CO 1031/1393, Trinidad No 10 7 January 1949, para 9.

[41] Jamaica (Constitution) Order-in-Council 1944, SRO 1944 No 1215, 378; and Trinidad and Tobago (Constitution) Order-in-Council 1950, SI 1950 No 510.

intended that, like the Speaker in the British Parliament, they would be responsible for the orderly conduct of debate in the legislature.

Initially, the question of whether the Speaker should be elected by members of the Legislative Council—as happened in the British Parliament—or appointed by the Governor, was a matter of some controversy.[42] The problem of following the British practice and permitting members of the Legislative Council to elect the Speaker was that in the absence of an established party system in the region each member of the Legislative Council fought as an independent candidate. This meant that there was no guarantee that an elected Speaker would not be required to fight an election; or that, in such an eventuality, the constituents could be relied upon to ensure that the Speaker was returned. In the longer term, however, with the emergence of political parties in the period leading up to independence, it proved impossible to withstand local demands for an elected Speaker. This was particularly true in a country like Trinidad where the Deputy Speaker, who had been elected, proved to be extremely popular and a more than competent substitute for the Speaker appointed by the Governor when the latter was taken ill.[43] Thus, by the time of independence, elected Speakers had become the norm and each of the Independence Constitutions made provision for a Speaker to be elected when Parliament first meets after any general election and before it proceeds to the despatch of any other business.[44] In the case of the Bahamas, Barbados and Jamaica, the Speaker must be elected from among members of the Lower House;[45] everywhere else in the region, the Speaker may be elected from among persons who are not members of the Lower House, but are qualified to be elected as such. Members of Cabinet and Parliamentary Secretaries are disqualified from being elected either as Speakers or Deputy Speakers.[46]

Though the decision to allow someone who is not a member of the Lower House to be elected as Speaker was a departure from the practice of the British Parliament it is clear that, in all other respects, the Speaker was intended to function in the same way as their counterpart

---

[42] See HA Ghany, 'Parliamentary Crisis and the Removal of the Speaker: The Case of Trinidad and Tobago' (1997) 3(2) *Journal of Legislative Studies* 112–38, 122.

[43] Ibid, 126.

[44] See, eg, s 43(1) Constitution of Jamaica.

[45] s 50(1) Constitution of the Bahamas; s 117(1) Constitution of Barbados; and s 43(1) Constitution of Jamaica.

[46] See, eg, s 32(2) Constitution of St Kitts and Nevis.

in the British Parliament. In the case of the latter, however, there are a number of conventions which serve to emphasise the Speaker's political neutrality—such as the practice of a retiring Speaker being replaced by someone from the other side of the House of Commons[47]—which are not replicated in the Commonwealth Caribbean. In the absence of such conventions, regulating the Speaker's election and their conduct while in office, it has proved to be extremely difficult in the Commonwealth Caribbean to establish a Speakership which is seen to be impartial and which can thus earn the respect and trust of all political parties. Instead, the tendency has been for the office of Speaker to be regarded as the privilege of the party in power, thus making it almost impossible to disassociate the Speaker from party politics.

In Antigua, for example, there has been for nearly a decade a protracted dispute between the Antigua Labour Party (ALP) and the Speaker of the House of Representatives, Giselle Isaac-Arrindell, whom the ALP believes has consistently favoured the governing party in her management of business in the House of Representatives. In the course of this dispute Gaston Browne, an ALP member of the House of Representatives, unsuccessfully sought to challenge the legality of the Speaker's appointment on the ground that she was disqualified because she was the holder of a public office, namely Executive Secretary to the Board of Education.[48] Though it is impossible to establish whether this was by coincidence or not, the day after his legal challenge to the Speaker's appointment was dismissed by the High Court[49] Browne was suspended indefinitely from Parliament by the Speaker for protesting too vocally about the legitimacy of Baldwin Spencer's Government.[50]

The office of Deputy Speaker, though less prestigious, has been no less afflicted by party politics and has, in a number of cases, been used by the Opposition as a vehicle for causing maximum embarrassment for the Government. For example, in St Lucia, when the Deputy Speaker, who was also the lone backbencher from the governing United Workers Party, resigned and crossed the floor of the House, the Opposition

[47] See P Laundy, *The Office of the Speaker in the Parliaments of the Commonwealth* (London, Quiller, 1984).

[48] Contrary to s 39(1)(g) Constitution of Antigua and Barbuda.

[49] *Browne v Giselle Isaac-Arrindell*, High Court Antigua, 16 June 2010. Unreported. Available on file with the author.

[50] 'Gaston Suspended' *Antigua Observer* (16 June 2010). Available at: www.antiguaobserver.com/gaston-suspended.

St Lucia Labour Party (SLP) refused to nominate a Deputy Speaker in an attempt to force a government minister to resign and fill the vacant office. When no Government minister resigned, the SLP walked out of the House of Assembly in a somewhat disingenuous protest at the Speaker's decision not to adjourn proceedings in the House until a Deputy Speaker had been found.[51] In the event, with elections pending, the Deputy Speaker's post remained vacant until after the election, a not uncommon occurrence in the region. In St Kitts also, the Government found itself in an awkward position when, having appointed the former Deputy Speaker to a Cabinet post, the Opposition parties refused to nominate one of their own members for the post of Deputy Speaker, arguing that it could prevent them from fully participating at all times in parliamentary debates. As a result, the Minister for Tourism was obliged to resign his post in order to fill the vacant Deputy Speaker's office.[52]

By far the greatest crisis to affect the office of Speaker in the region has been, however, the removal of the Speaker of the Parliament in Trinidad in very controversial circumstances in 1995.[53] In this case, the Speaker, who had been implicated in fraud proceedings brought against a third party, initially resisted all parliamentary attempts to remove her by way of a motion of no confidence. Accordingly, the Government sought to introduce a Bill to amend the Constitution by providing for a specific procedure for suspension of the Speaker prior to the latter's removal from office by Order of the House. The Speaker's response to the introduction of this Bill was to adjourn the House to a date when private member's business was to have precedence. When the Leader of Government Business protested that this was irregular the Speaker suspended him for six months.

Eventually, a date was fixed for consideration of the Bill to amend the Constitution. On 3 August, but before the Bill could be considered, the Government allegedly received information that the Speaker, supported by certain members of the Opposition, planned to reduce the Government's majority in the House of Representatives by improperly

---

[51] 'FM says Deputy Speaker's post "may remain vacant"', *Antigua Observer* (23 September 2011). Available at: www.antiguaobserver.com/fm-says-deputy-speaker%E2%80%99s-post-%E2%80%98may-remain-vacant.

[52] W Archibald 'Tangled Webs', *St Kitts-Nevis Observer* (5 March 2010). Available at: www.thestkittsnevisobserver.com/2010/03/05/washie.html.

[53] The account that follows is drawn from Ghany, 'Parliamentary Crisis and the Removal of the Speaker', above (n 42).

suspending a number of its members from the House, thereby ensuring that the Bill would not be passed. In response to this information, late in the evening of 3 August, a state of emergency was declared around the area where the Speaker's official residence was located and a detention order was issued, confining the Speaker to her official residence. On the following day, the Bill, which had already been approved by the Senate, was passed in the Speaker's absence by a margin of five votes. In his address to the nation on the evening of 4 August, the Prime Minister defended the Government's actions in the following terms:

> Having steadfastly refused to respond to approaches behind closed doors, the Speaker's response to the motion of no confidence was even more startling. The Speaker, aided and abetted by those who do not wish us well, reacted by seizing control of the parliament through arbitrarily dismissing relevant Standing Orders. Make no mistake ... the full effect of a loss of control by the House through the use of the Standing Orders and a substitution by the intervention of the Speaker is tantamount to nothing short of a palace coup where the elected members of the House are now at the mercy of the discretion of a Speaker at large.[54]

The Government's account of these events was disputed by the Opposition but, whether or not the Government's account is true, the incident vividly demonstrates what can happen where no provision is made in the Constitution for the removal of the Speaker and where the office of Speaker becomes embroiled in party politics.

D. PRIVILEGES OF PARLIAMENT

The privileges of parliaments under the Westminster model traditionally consist of the rights and immunities which parliaments possess in order to enable their members to carry out their parliamentary functions effectively. Without these privileges and immunities, it is said, the ability of parliaments to confront the executive and to serve as a forum for expressing the anxieties of citizens would be profoundly diminished.[55] Thus, parliaments traditionally claim 'exclusive cognizance of [their]

---

[54] Quoted by Ghany, 'Parliamentary Crisis and the Removal of the Speaker', above (n 42) 133.

[55] *First Report of the Joint Committee on Parliamentary Privilege, 1999.* Available at: www.parliament.the-stationery-office.co.uk.

proceedings' and a number of other privileges, by far the most important of which is freedom of speech.[56] However, unlike the position in Britain, for example, where the privileges of its Parliament derive from the law and custom of Parliament, which as a matter of common law is recognised by the courts, the privileges of Commonwealth Caribbean parliaments derive, in the main, from the text of the Constitution and from laws enacted by Parliament. Each of the region's Constitutions thus provide: first, that no civil or criminal proceedings may be instituted against any member for words spoken before, or written in a report to, the House or to a committee of the House;[57] and, second, that Parliament may by law determine the privileges, immunities and powers of its respective Houses and its members.

1. Freedom of Speech

Absent freedom of speech, it is argued, MPs would be unable to perform their duties because of fear of the consequences that might arise from what is said in Parliament.[58] Hence, the constitutional immunity from civil or criminal suits afforded to members of Commonwealth Caribbean parliaments for words spoken before, or written in a report to, the House or to a committee of the House.

The nature and extent of this constitutional immunity has, however, tended to be interpreted very narrowly by the courts as we can see from the following three decisions. The first is the decision of the High Court of Trinidad in *Boodram v Attorney General*,[59] in which it was held that the immunity afforded by section 55 of the Constitution did not extend to a decision by the Government to table in Parliament the report of a Commission of Inquiry (the Report) into the extent of drug abuse in Trinidad. As a result, the applicant successfully argued that the publication of the Report, which identified a number of alleged drug dealers

---

[56] Ibid.

[57] See, eg, ss 48(2) and 48(3) Constitution of Jamaica. This protection is commonly supplemented by legislation, which extends immunity from legal process to officers of Parliament and individuals who appear as witnesses before parliamentary committees.

[58] See *Prebble v Televison New Zealand Ltd* [1995] 1 AC 321.

[59] *Boodram v Attorney General*, TT 1989 HC 62. Unreported. Available on file with the author.

including the applicant, while criminal proceedings against the applicant
were still pending, violated his constitutional rights to due process and
equality before the law, to be presumed innocent and to a fair hearing. As the Court observed, the immunity afforded by section 55 is
expressed to be 'subject to the provisions of [the] Constitution':

> A democracy which claims not only to have respect for the fundamental
> rights of its citizens but which makes express provision in its Constitution
> to entrench and preserve those rights should never appear to entertain the
> suggestion that members of parliament are free to do what they like provided
> it is done within its walls ... Members are entrusted with an awesome burden
> of responsibility and it goes without saying that that 'freedom of speech'
> which they enjoy is not a license to defame and to malign the citizens of the
> country within its walls, much less, to infringe their fundamental rights.

The second case is the decision of the Judicial Committee of the
Privy Council (JCPC) in *Toussaint v Attorney General St Vincent and the
Grenadines*.[60] Here it was held by the JCPC that the appellant, whose
property had been compulsorily purchased by the Government, should
be allowed to adduce in evidence in proceedings for constitutional
relief a statement made by the Prime Minister during the budget debate
in the House of Assembly which, it was alleged, revealed the true reason for the compulsory purchase of the appellant's land. The JCPC
acknowledged the constitutional importance of ensuring that MPs were
able to speak freely and without fear of the consequences. However,
the Board also pointed out that it had made it clear in its earlier decision, in *Prebble v Televison New Zealand Ltd*, that if at trial a party wished
to allege the occurrence of events or the saying of certain words in
Parliament without any accompanying allegation of impropriety or any
other questioning, there could be no objection to that course. In the
instant case, the only allegation of impropriety related to action taken by
the Government outside the House of Assembly, there being no allegation that the Prime Minister had misled the House or acted improperly
within the House. Moreover, the evidential importance of the Prime
Minister's statement, when coupled with the appellant's specific right of
access to the courts in respect of constitutional violations, justified its
admission in evidence. In the JCPC's view, to ring-fence what ministers
say to Parliament by prohibiting its admission in evidence would be

---

[60] *Toussaint v Attorney General St Vincent and the Grenadines* (2007) UKPC 48.

'bizarre': 'A source of protection of the legislature against the executive and the courts would be converted into a source of protection of the executive from the courts and the rule of law'.[61]

The third case, *Richards v Attorney General St Christopher and Nevis*,[62] involved the alleged breach of an injunction by the Attorney General in connection with advice that he had given to the Prime Minister with regard to the publication of a report by the Constituency Boundaries Commission (CBC), as disclosed by the Prime Minister in a statement which he made to Parliament. The Attorney General had sought to argue that he was protected by the immunity from process, which was granted by section 45 of the Constitution for words spoken in Parliament. However, the Eastern Caribbean Supreme Court held that since it was not statements made by the Attorney General in Parliament that were in issue, but rather statements made by the Prime Minister in Parliament concerning advice that he had received from the Attorney General outside Parliament, the Prime Minister's statement could be adduced in evidence.

In the first and second of the above cases it is clear that, when asked to strike a balance between freedom of speech in Parliament and the constitutional rights of those affected by the exercise of this freedom, the courts preferred to strike the balance in favour of the latter. It might be argued that, as a matter of constitutional principle, this is the correct approach and that the freedom of speech of MPs must give way where it impinges on an individual's rights. It might also be argued that this properly reflects the difference between a country, such as Britain, where Parliament has traditionally been regarded as sovereign or supreme, and the countries of the Commonwealth Caribbean where it is the Constitution that is supreme.

On the other hand, it could also be argued that in the first case, at least, the Court went much further in its reasoning than the facts of the case strictly required. For, if the immunity afforded by the Constitution of Trinidad and Tobago does not provide protection for MPs from civil or criminal proceedings for what is said 'within its walls', if it is defamatory or maligns the citizens of the country, then it would seem that the central purpose of the immunity, which is to allow MPs to perform their

[61] At [17]. Quoting from the *First Report of the Joint Committee*, above (n 55) para 51.
[62] *Richards v Attorney General St Christopher and Nevis*, HCVAP 2009/09. Unreported. Available on file with the author.

duties without fear of the consequences, is significantly compromised. Furthermore, in the third case, where no constitutional rights were directly involved, the Court, nevertheless, still adopted a very restrictive interpretation of the immunity clause contained in the Constitution of St Kitts. In so doing, it could be argued, the Court's approach may have a 'chilling effect' on the freedom of speech which MPs are meant to enjoy in order that they may effectively discharge their duties. Instead of being allowed to speak without fear of the consequences members of Commonwealth Caribbean parliaments must always have regard to the wider, perhaps unanticipated, use to which their statements in Parliament may be subsequently put.

2. Control of Parliamentary Affairs

A parliament's 'exclusive cognizance of its own proceedings' has been defined thus by Sir William Blackstone in his *Commentaries on the Laws of England*:

> The whole of the law and custom of Parliament has its origins from this one maxim, that whatever matter arises concerning either House of Parliament ought to be examined, discussed and adjudged in that House and not elsewhere.[63]

While the original justification for this privilege—protecting MPs from interference by the monarch—may no longer apply, the privilege continues to be justified by reference to the constitutional theory, implicit in the Westminster model, which assumes that MPs should be able to exercise their functions free from interference by non-members and from any limitations on that freedom by the courts.[64] I consider below how the principle of 'exclusive cognizance' has been applied in the context of the law-making powers of Commonwealth Caribbean parliaments, but here I wish to focus on how it impacts on their power to regulate their internal affairs by punishing those who violate parliamentary privileges or for contempt.

Discussion of this aspect of parliamentary privilege in the context of the Commonwealth Caribbean is complicated by the fact that

---

[63] W Blackstone, *Commentaries on the Laws of England*, 17th edn, vol 1 (1830) 163.
[64] D Feldman, *Public Law* (Oxford, Oxford University Press, 2004) 117.

it had already been firmly established by the time of independence that colonial legislatures did not *inherently* enjoy privileges of the sort established for the House of Commons by the law and custom of Parliament.[65] Instead, colonial legislatures *inherently* enjoyed only such privileges as were deemed reasonably necessary for any legislative body to secure the conduct of its proceedings.[66] This left colonial legislatures at something of a disadvantage compared with the British Parliament when regulating their internal affairs. In order to make good this disadvantage Commonwealth Caribbean parliaments are expressly empowered by their Constitutions 'to make laws determining the privileges, immunities and powers of their respective Houses and their members'.[67] Such 'laws' are to be found in the various Privileges Acts, which have been enacted across the region and in the Standing Orders of each Parliament, though as we shall see, the legal status of the latter has been called into question in at least one case.

The Privileges Acts to be found across the region commonly empower the Speaker to grant or refuse permission for statements made in Parliament to be adduced in evidence in court proceedings.[68] The Standing Orders also commonly empower the Speaker to maintain the order of the House by suspending members[69] upon the recommendation of a Privileges Committee, established by the Standing Orders. These Privileges Committees usually comprise the Speaker as chairman and such other members as may be prescribed by Standing Orders, who are nominated by the House at the commencement of each session of Parliament.[70] Each Privileges Committee is empowered to deal with matters affecting the powers and privileges of their respective House which are referred to the Committee, and to make recommendations and report back to the House. The precise nature and scope of the power of Commonwealth Caribbean parliaments to punish their members for breach of parliamentary privilege or for contempt, as well as the role of the courts in reviewing the exercise of this power, remains, however, a highly contentious topic.

---

[65] *Kielley v Carson* (1842) 4 Moo PCC 63, 88.
[66] Ibid.
[67] See, eg, s 53(1) Constitution of the Bahamas.
[68] See, eg, s 16 Privileges Act, St Vincent and the Grenadines.
[69] Trinidad, House of Representatives, Standing Order No 92.
[70] Trinidad, House of Representatives, Standing Order No 75.

Thus, in *Sabaroche v Speaker of House of Assembly Dominica*,[71] the applicant, an MP who had been suspended for remarks that he had made about another member, sought to challenge his suspension from Parliament on the grounds, inter alia, that the House of Assembly had no power to punish him for contempt. On behalf of the House of Assembly it was argued that the House enjoyed exactly the same privileges as the British House of Commons, including the power to punish for contempt, by virtue of Standing Order No 87, which provides, inter alia that: 'In any matter not herein provided resort shall be had to usage and practice in the House of Commons of Parliament for Great Britain'.

In the Court's view, however, Standing Orders are rules made by the House of Assembly, which has no authority to make any laws providing for an alleged breach of parliamentary privilege—such a power residing exclusively in the Parliament of Dominica by virtue of section 43 of the Constitution. Parliament, not having any passed any such legislation and the House, not having acquired any privileges under common law by virtue of ancient usage and prescription, the only privileges which the House of Assembly possessed were those which were essentially necessary for the exercise of its functions. This did not include the power to punish the appellant for a past misconduct. Nor was the Court persuaded by the Attorney General's suggestion that it did not have jurisdiction to enquire into the conduct of proceedings in Parliament. In the Court's view, the supremacy of the Constitution from which the House of Assembly derived its authority meant that the Court as 'the sentinel of the Constitution' had a positive duty to act 'when any authority acts in non-conformity with any rules or laws which it derives under the very constitution'. The Court could, therefore, rule on the legality of the applicant's suspension from the House of Assembly.

By contrast, in *Musa v Attorney General Belize*,[72] the Supreme Court of Belize refused to entertain a challenge by the Leader of the Opposition to his suspension from Parliament, on the grounds, inter alia, that the House of Representatives had no power to punish him for contempt. Having determined that the House of Representatives enjoyed the same powers as the British House of Commons to punish one of its members

---

[71] *Sabaroche v Speaker of House of Assembly Dominica*, DM 1999 CA 4. Unreported. Available on file with the author.
[72] *Musa v Attorney General Belize*, BZ 1998 SC 6. Unreported. Available on file with the author.

for contempt, by virtue of the Imperial Laws (Extension) Act, which specifically incorporates English common law into the law of Belize, the Supreme Court declared that the judiciary had no power to interfere in the internal proceedings of the legislature.

It is possible to distinguish between the decisions in *Sabaroche* and *Musa* on the ground that, in the case of the former, the Court was merely asserting its jurisdiction to enquire into the existence and extent of any privilege or power claimed by Parliament; whereas, in the case of the latter, having established the existence of the power, the Court properly declined to enquire into the mode of its exercise. This is a well-established distinction, which respects the principle of Parliament's exclusive cognizance of its own proceedings. However, for so long as Commonwealth Caribbean parliaments' inherent power to punish breaches of privilege or contempt is defined by reference to 'whatever is deemed reasonably necessary to secure the conduct of its proceedings' the precise scope of the power is always likely to be in issue and so too will be the courts' power to intervene in a particular case. As the High Court of Dominica noted, in *James v Speaker of House of Assembly*,[73] in which the Court was asked to find the House of Assembly in contempt for failing to obey a court injunction prohibiting the Privileges Committee from presenting a report to the House of Assembly concerning the conduct of the applicant:

> [T]he fact that the House cannot punish the claimant for contempt by way of committal, does not bar an investigation into conduct where a breach of privilege is asserted. The question is whether the alleged misconduct of the claimant, not being a vocal or physical interruption of the House, is a matter that the House could rightly inquire into as constituting a breach of its common law privileges and whether such an inquiry is a matter of internal proceedings with which the Court ought not to interfere.

Moreover, the Court's refusal to interfere with the internal proceedings of Parliament once the existence of the power to punish is established can be highly problematic if questions arise as to the integrity or fairness of the whole process. Recommendations of the Privileges Committee are voted on by the legislature, which means that a government can use its majority in the legislature to support or reject the recommendations

---

[73] *James v Speaker of House of Assembly*, DM 2004 HC 6. Unreported. Available on file with the author.

of the Privileges Committee, irrespective of the integrity or overall fairness of the process which produced the recommendations. As the Court noted in *Sabaroche*, the vote by the House of Assembly on the motion for the appellant's suspension had been passed along strictly party lines.

More recently, in Trinidad, the suspension of the former Prime Minister, Patrick Manning, by the Privileges Committee in connection with allegations that he had made regarding the source of funding for the construction of the current Prime Minister's private home was bitterly opposed by Manning and his supporters in the People's National Movement. It was argued not only that Manning had not been given proper notice of the hearing by the Privileges Committee, but also that the latter should have questioned the Prime Minister about the source of the funding.[74] Whether or not there was any substance to these allegations, the principle of exclusive cognizance meant that there was no possibility of these arguments being tested in the courts and thus no opportunity to dispel the suspicion that the former Prime Minister had been treated unfairly or that the whole process had been tainted by political bias.

E. REGULATING THE FINANCIAL INTERESTS OF MPS

The privileged access to central government and to the levers of power which is enjoyed by members of Commonwealth Caribbean parliaments poses the problem of how to ensure that they do not abuse their public office for private gain and that they perform their parliamentary duties free of undue influence from financial and business interests outside Parliament. In order to guard against such potential conflicts of interest, each Commonwealth Caribbean constitution disqualifies anyone who has an interest in any government contract from standing for election unless they have previously disclosed the nature of the contract and of their interest therein.[75] Each Constitution also provides that an MP will automatically vacate office if the MP becomes interested in a government contract, unless before becoming interested in such a contract or

---

[74] 'TT Parliament Suspends PM', *Jamaica Observer* (18 May 2011).
[75] See, eg, s 40 (2)(c) Constitution of Jamaica.

as soon as practicable thereafter, the MP discloses to Parliament the nature of the contract and their interest therein and Parliament agrees to exempt the MP from vacating their seat.[76]

In addition, in a departure from the principle of parliamentary self-regulation which we considered in the last section, extra-parliamentary Integrity Commissions have been established in a number of countries across the region in response to the numerous corruption scandals involving members of the executive, including in some cases the Prime Minister, which have been revealed by various Commissions of Inquiry. These have included the drugs for arms scandal concerning the shipment of Israeli-made weapons through Antigua to the Medellin Drug Cartel in Colombia, which was revealed by the Louis Blom-Cooper enquiry in Antigua, and which involved Vere Bird Junior, the son of the Prime Minister who was at the time Antigua's National Security minister.[77] They also include the Ramsahoye Commission of Inquiry, in St Lucia, which investigated a number of actions by the SLP Government between 1997 and 2006, and found that the Prime Minister, Kenny D Anthony, had contravened the requirements of the Finance Act which required foreign borrowing to be conducted only with the consent of the House of Assembly.[78] Finally, in Trinidad, a report of a Commission of Inquiry into the construction of the Piarco Airport, which was never published, disclosed that there had been a criminal conspiracy to manipulate the award of consulting, construction and maintenance contracts with respect to the construction of the Piarco Airport in order to create inflated construction contract prices. The conspirators included public servants—government officials who helped to rig the bidding process so that various contracts and subcontracts were awarded to a complex maze of corporate vehicles.[79]

In some countries these Integrity Commissions have been established by the Constitution,[80] in others they owe their creation to

---

[76] See, eg, s 41(1)(f) Constitution of Jamaica.

[77] See further, L Blom-Cooper, *Guns for Antigua* (London, Duckworth, 1990).

[78] See C Barrow-Giles, *Regional Trends in Constitutional Developments in the Commonwealth Caribbean* (2010) 15. Available at: www.agora-parl.org/search-resources-results?combine=trends%20in%20constitutional%20development%20in%20the%20commonwealth%20caribbean.

[79] See *Report of the World Bank*. Available at: www.star.worldbank.org.

[80] See, eg, Constitution of St Lucia.

statute.[81] In either case the Integrity Commission is responsible for receiving and supervising the filing of declarations in writing by MPs, containing details of their assets, liabilities and income. In a number of countries the Integrity Commission is also responsible for implementing a Code of Conduct which governs the standards of ethical conduct of MPs and other public officers, including members of the Diplomatic Service, advisers to the government and any person appointed by a Service Commission or the Statutory Authorities' Service Commission, as well as the monitoring and investigating of conduct, practices and procedures which are dishonest or corrupt.[82]

In each case, the Integrity Commission is charged with making such independent enquiries and investigations relating to a statutory declaration as it thinks necessary; investigating cases of non-compliance; and dealing with complaints of breaches of the Code of Conduct and offences of corruption. For the purpose of discharging its responsibilities, the Integrity Commission is usually empowered to summon witnesses, require the production of documents and do all such things as it considers necessary or expedient for the carrying out of its functions. Failure to file the requisite annual declaration or filing a false declaration is an offence, for which an offender is liable on conviction to be punished by a fine or a term of imprisonment. Breaches of the Code of Conduct and offences of corruption are also liable on conviction to a fine or a term of imprisonment.

Though the precise composition of the Integrity Commission varies from country to country, there is a requirement in most cases that it includes at least one experienced lawyer and one experienced accountant.[83] As with the Public Service Commissions examined in chapter four, however, the Prime Minister has a considerable say in the appointment of members of the Integrity Commission, and even where the Prime Minister may be required to consult the Leader of the Opposition, there is considerable scepticism about the degree of consultation that actually takes place. As Basdeo Panday has caustically observed, when describing the arrangements for appointments to the Integrity Commission when he was the Leader of the Opposition in Trinidad: 'I am consulted by a letter written by the President's secretary

---

[81] See, eg, Integrity in Public Life Act 2004, Antigua and Barbuda.
[82] See s 138(2)(d) Constitution of Trinidad and Tobago.
[83] See, eg, s 4 Integrity in Public Life Act 2004, Antigua and Barbuda.

to me saying that they are going to appoint so and so and if I have any comments or objections. That is the level of consultation'.[84]

Indeed, even where the Leader of the Opposition has an autonomous choice in the appointment of one or more members of the Integrity Commission, tensions can arise between the Government and the Leader of the Opposition with regard to the latter's nominee. For example, in Dominica, the Deputy Leader of the governing Dominica Labour Party, went so far as to commence proceedings for judicial review to challenge the Leader of the Opposition's nominee—Dave Bruney—for appointment to the Integrity Commission,[85] on the basis of public statements the latter had made which were critical of the Prime Minister and the Government.[86] It is arguable, however, that such tensions are inevitable in the context of small island states where it is virtually impossible to select suitable members of the Integrity Commission 'whom everybody in public life would be satisfied could look into their personal affairs'.[87]

Members of the Integrity Commission are normally appointed for a term of three years. As we shall see below, however, they do not always serve a full term of office, either because they resign prematurely, or are removed from office by the President or Governor General, as the case may be. In the latter case, a member of the Integrity Commission can only be removed for inability to exercise the functions of their office, physical or mental infirmity or misbehaviour and only then if a tribunal, appointed by the President or Governor General, as the case may be, has recommended their removal.[88]

The record of Integrity Commissions within the region has been, to say the least, very mixed. In Antigua, for example, only 200 out of the

---

[84] Ironically, Panday was himself the subject of criminal proceedings brought against him as a result of an investigation by the Integrity Commission in Trinidad (discussed below).

[85] The Opposition's former media coordinator who gave evidence in the dual citizenship case against the Prime Minister, Ronald Skeritt: *Joseph v Skeritt*, Civil Claim No 7 of 2010. Unreported. Available on file with the author.

[86] Contrary to s 4(3) Integrity in Public Office Act.

[87] Report of the Commission of Inquiry, *The Tale of Three Hydrofoils and Other Acts of Financial Management in St Kitts and Nevis 1980–1999*, 98. Available at: www.cuopm.com.

[88] See, eg, s118(5) Constitution of St Lucia.

300 public officials required to file declarations in 2010 had done so.[89] In St Lucia, a Commission of Inquiry into standards of conduct in public life, which reported in 1999, revealed that throughout the conduct of the Inquiry no mention was ever made at any stage by any participant in the Inquiry (which included a Permanent Secretary and a former Prime Minister) of the existence of the Integrity Commission. Indeed, the chairman of the Commission, Sir Louis Blom Cooper, admitted that he himself had been entirely unaware of the existence of the constitutional requirement for the establishment of an Integrity Commission.[90] In Belize, in 2007, a leaked memorandum from the US Embassy revealed that the most recent annual report from the Integrity Commission showed a mere 27 per cent filing rate.[91] There have also been numerous complaints about the ineffectiveness of Integrity Commissions in punishing non-compliance and breaches of the Code of Conduct. In Belize, for example, the same leaked memorandum referred to above, noted that in the 13 years since the establishment of the Integrity Commission, only one complaint had been investigated relating to the conduct of the Minister of Foreign Affairs, the Minister of Trade and the Solicitor General, but had not resulted in any prosecutions. In Jamaica, also, where an Integrity Commission was first established in 1973, it was some 30 years before the first case against an MP for failure to file a declaration was brought to court.[92]

Part of the explanation for the relative ineffectiveness of Integrity Commissions was outlined in a report of the Dominica Integrity Commission, in 2011, in which it complained that it was being hampered in the performance of its functions by inadequate resources and the absence of an able pool of candidates with the required skills and qualifications from which to draw.[93] The Integrity Commission also complained that while it had laid two reports before Parliament, there

[89] 'Integrity Commissioners threaten Court Action', *Antigua Observer* (Antigua, 13 October 2011). Available at: www.antiguaobserver.com/integrity-commissioners-threaten-court-action.

[90] See L Blom Cooper, Commission of Inquiry Report, *Standards in Public Life in St Lucia* (1998) 78. Available at: www.slucia.com.

[91] Wikileaks Reference ID 07BELMOPAN700, released 30 August 2011.

[92] T Munroe, *Transparency International Country Study Report: Caribbean Composite Study* (Berlin, Transparency International Secretariat, 2004) 36.

[93] See Integrity Commission Dominica, *Third Annual Report, Year ended 31 August 2011*, 14. Available at: www.integritycommission.gov.dm.

had been scant reference to these reports either in questions, motions, statements or speeches before the House of Assembly.

It would be wrong, however, to assume that Integrity Commissions are entirely ineffective. In Trinidad, for example, as a result of an investigation by the Integrity Commission, criminal proceedings were brought against the former Prime Minister, Basdeo Panday, for failure to reveal bank accounts in London held in his name and that of his wife. These resulted in the former Prime Minister being sentenced before a magistrates' court to a term of imprisonment of two years, although the conviction was subsequently quashed by the Court of Appeal on the ground that the Chief Magistrate who presided over the trial of the former Prime Minister may have been biased and a retrial was ordered, which is still pending.

Ironically, however, it is also in Trinidad where the Integrity Commission has faced probably the greatest challenges in the performance of its functions. Here, the Integrity Commission has been mired in controversy for nearly a decade, having gone through no less than five different chairmen between 2003 and 2011. In 2009, the chairman and all the other members of the Commission were obliged to step down after the High Court had ruled that they had acted in bad faith by filing a report with the Director of Public Prosecutions (concerning the alleged siphoning of materials from a government hospital site to a development project in which the wife of the Leader of the Opposition had an interest) without having allowed the Leader of the Opposition or his wife a chance to be heard during the investigation.[94] This was followed by a period of nine months when the Integrity Commission was unable to function at all because of the President's failure to appoint any new members between May 2009 and March 2010, for which the President was severely criticised by the High Court in *Maharaj v AG*.[95] As the Court observed:

> The complaint mechanism [provided by the Integrity Commission] is a vital provision when considering the protection of the law clause. The various acts and conduct of persons in public life which the Act seeks to deal with can have both a direct and indirect impact on individuals and groups. Corruption

---

[94] *Rowley v The Integrity Commission*, CV 2007-00185. Unreported. Available on file with the author.

[95] *Maharaj v AG*, CV 2009-03591. Unreported. Available on file with the author.

takes away resources, which may properly be channeled, to individuals and groups ... The complaints mechanism is a way in which these violations can be discouraged, exposed, remedied and punished. ... The allocation of resources in a plural society, such as Trinidad and Tobago is, can be very contentious. There is a strong public interest factor in the functioning of the Integrity commission.

Though new members were eventually appointed, the Integrity Commission collapsed again soon afterwards when its new chairman stepped down in the face of accusations of plagiarism and issues related to canon law. This was followed a week later by the resignation of all the remaining members. The newly appointed Commission however, fared no better. Its chairman was obliged to resign after he had been chastised on a number of occasions for speaking about the confidential business of the Commission, but still proceeded to reveal to a newspaper reporter that the chairman of one of the Government's agencies was under investigation.[96] Then a dispute between the most recently appointed chairman and the deputy chairman, regarding the investigation of a complaint against the former Attorney General, led to the suspension of the deputy chairman and the appointment of a tribunal to investigate complaints against her.[97] In the event, the deputy chairman's term of office expired before the tribunal had completed its investigation, leaving the Integrity Commission inquorate and therefore unable to function. Four new members have since been appointed. However, at the time of writing there have been calls for the resignation of the current chairman who is embroiled in a controversy regarding a meeting that took place with the Leader of the Opposition at the former's home to discuss a cache of emails in the latter's possession, which allegedly contained evidence of a conspiracy—between the Prime Minister, the Attorney General and two Government ministers—to discredit the judiciary.

[96] Editorial 'Get Integrity Commission Going Again', *Guardian Media* (Trinidad, 18 October 2011). Available at: guardian.co.tt/editorial/2011/10/17/get-integrity-commission-going.

[97] C Head 'Gafoor sues Max, Integrity Commission', *Trinidad Express* (3 March 2012). Available at: www.trinidadexpress.com/news/Gafoor-sues-Max-Integrity-Commission-141322383.html.

PART III: PARLIAMENT'S LAW-MAKING POWERS

Each Commonwealth Caribbean constitution empowers its Parliament, 'subject to the provisions of the Constitution', to make laws 'for the peace order and good government of the country'. Before I consider what, if any, constraints, these two clauses impose on the region's parliaments' law-making powers, however, I will briefly outline the procedure laid down for the passage of legislation through Parliament, and the respective roles of the Senate and the Governor General or President, as the case may be, in the passage of legislation.

A. THE LAW-MAKING PROCESS

Broadly speaking, the procedure for the enactment of legislation by Commonwealth Caribbean parliaments is modelled on the procedure adopted by the British Parliament. Public Bills, which seek to alter the general law, are usually introduced into Parliament by a minister; though any MP may, with the exception of Money Bills, introduce a Bill.[98] Private Bills, which aim to alter the law relating to a particular locality or to confer rights on or relieve from liability a particular person or body of persons, may also be introduced, but are usually subject to separate Standing Orders relating to private business. In the case of bicameral legislatures Bills may be introduced in either House, with the exception of Money Bills, which must always be introduced first in the elected House, and neither House can proceed upon a Bill which has the aim of raising taxes without the consent of the Cabinet.

After a Bill has been introduced, it must pass through several stages known as 'readings', during the course of which the Bill is debated and scrutinised in detail, either by a select committee or, more usually, by a committee of the whole House. In either case, the Government's majority ensures that no amendment can be made at the committee stage without the Government's agreement. For those countries with bicameral legislatures, Bills which originate in the elected House are then sent to the Senate, where they go through the same procedure. Though the

---

[98] See, eg, s 55 Constitution of Jamaica.

Senate has no power of veto over Bills approved by the elected house, it does have a power of delay for Bills other than Money Bills.[99] The length of the power of delay varies from country to country. In Antigua, for example, the Senate can delay a Bill for a maximum of two sessions.[100] This power of delay is, however, very unlikely to be exercised in practice because, as we have seen above, the Prime Minister not only recommends the appointment of the majority of senators, but can also recommend the removal of any senator they have appointed: senators who vote against a government Bill are likely to be very quickly replaced.

Once a Bill has passed through all its stages it then only requires the assent of the Governor General or President, as the case may be, to become law. In some countries, as we saw in chapter two, the Constitution appears to contemplate that the Governor General or President, as the case may be, can in certain circumstances refuse assent to legislation approved by Parliament, thus mirroring the reserve powers of the monarch under the British Constitution.[101] What these circumstances are, however, is not spelled out in the text of any of the region's constitutions and the power to refuse assent to legislation has never, as yet, been put to the test. By contrast, the Guyanese Constitution expressly empowers the President to withhold their assent to legislation approved by the National Assembly and, as we have seen, in the case of the attempt to amend the Constitution to prohibit discrimination on the grounds of 'sexual orientation', a president will not be afraid to exercise their power of veto if they consider it politically expedient to do so.[102]

B. CONSTRAINTS ON PARLIAMENT'S LAW-MAKING POWERS

Though the law-making *procedures* of Commonwealth Caribbean parliaments are, with the exception of Guyana, clearly modelled on those

---

[99] See, eg, s 55(1) Constitution of Antigua.

[100] Ibid.

[101] s 63(4) Constitution of the Bahamas; s 58(3) Constitution of Barbados; s 45(2) Constitution of Grenada; s 60(3) Constitution of Jamaica; s 42(2) Constitution of St Kitts and Nevis; and s 61(2) Constitution of Trinidad and Tobago.

[102] Arts 170(2)–170(4) Constitution of Guyana.

of the British Parliament, the law-making *powers* of Commonwealth Caribbean parliaments, unlike those of the British Parliament, are expressly made 'subject to the Constitution'. In this section I will, accordingly, examine the nature and extent of the limitations imposed on their Parliament's law-making powers by the region's constitutions.

1. Procedural Limitations

Commonwealth Caribbean constitutions usually contain a raft of procedural limitations, which range from the interval that must elapse between a Bill's final reading in the House of Representatives and its introduction in the Senate, to the requirement of the Cabinet's approval before a Money Bill can proceed. The question whether the rules of procedure of each Parliament also act as a limitation on that Parliament's law-making powers was considered by the JCPC in *Bahamas District of the Methodist Church in the Caribbean and the Americas v Symonette and Others.*[103] In this case, the JCPC was concerned with the limitation imposed by Article 59(1) of the Constitution of the Bahamas, which provides that any member may introduce any Bill in any House subject to the provisions of the Constitution and that 'the same shall be debated and disposed of according to the rules of procedure of that House'. The appellants had sought to challenge the enactment of a private Bill on the ground that the Bill had not been debated according to the rules of procedure of the Bahamas House of Assembly. In responding to this challenge to the constitutionality of the legislation so enacted, the JCPC had regard to the principle of the exclusive cognizance of Parliament, discussed above, as it had been applied by the House of Lords in the context of a similar breach of the Standing Orders of the British House of Commons in the case of *Edinburgh & Dalkeith Railway v Wauchope*:

> All that a court of justice can do is to look to the parliament roll: if from that it should appear that a Bill has passed both Houses and received the Royal Assent, no court of justice can inquire into the mode in which it was introduced into parliament, or into what was done previous to its introduction,

---

[103] *Bahamas District of the Methodist Church in the Caribbean and the Americas v Symonette and Others* [2000] UKPC 31.

or what passed in parliament during its progress in its various stages through both Houses.[104]

As the JCPC acknowledged, however, the decision in *Edinburgh & Dalkeith Railway* was based on two principles which were specific to the British Parliament: the legislative supremacy of Parliament and Article 9 of the Bill of Rights. The question here was whether in the context of a country, such as the Bahamas, where it is the Constitution rather than Parliament which is supreme, the principle of exclusive cognizance is displaced by a provision such as Article 59(1). In the JCPC's view it was not. This is because by Article 55(1), subject to contrary provision in the Constitution, each House 'may regulate its own procedure'. While a number of Articles in the Constitution do make contrary provision, restricting the freedom of each House—for example, Article 59(3) which precludes the House of Assembly from proceeding on any Bill for the raising of tax except on the recommendation of the Cabinet, and Article 60 which restricts the power of the Senate regarding Money Bills—the same is not true of Article 59(1). In the JCPC's view, Article 59(1) is essentially permissive, enabling any member of the House to introduce a Bill and providing for the debate of a Bill thus introduced. Though Article 59(1) does refer to the rules of procedure of the House this was not in the JCPC's view intended to deprive either House of the power given by Article 55(1) to regulate its own affairs:

> Clearer language would be required before it would be right to construe this provision as having the far-reaching effect of opening up to court scrutiny the procedures followed in parliament on all Bills … initiated by members.[105]

In a significant departure to this approach to Parliament's exclusive cognizance the High Court of St Kitts has recently struck down a Bill— The Senators (Increase of Numbers) Act 2013—on the ground, inter alia, of the participation in voting on the Bill of the Attorney General, whose appointment as Attorney General was held to be invalid because he was not at the time of his appointment a member of the National Assembly, contrary to section 52(4) of the Constitution.[106] It must be

---

[104] *Edinburgh & Dalkeith Railway v Wauchope* (1842) 8 Cl and F 710, 725.
[105] At [51].
[106] No report of the proceedings is currently publicly available, but see summary in *Caribbean Elections Today* (1 March 2013). Available at: www.caribbeanelections.com.

emphasised, however, that this is a first instance decision and is, at the time of writing, the subject of an appeal.

Another set of procedural constraints on the region's parliaments' law-making powers concerns amendments to the Constitution itself which, depending upon the country and the constitutional provision concerned, may require not only a special majority in Parliament, but also a majority or even a special majority of citizens in a referendum. Thus, for example, in the case of Jamaica, certain provisions of the Constitution, such as the chapter dealing with fundamental rights and the immunity of MPs from civil and criminal proceedings, can only be amended by a two-thirds majority in both Houses of Parliament. Other provisions, such as the composition of the House of Representatives and the Senate, are more deeply entrenched and must be approved not only by a majority in both Houses, but also by a majority of the citizens qualified to vote in a referendum. The rationale for requiring a special majority for altering certain provisions of the Jamaican Constitution was explained thus by Lord Diplock in *Hinds v The Queen*:

> The purpose served by this machinery, for 'entrenchment' is to ensure that those provisions which were regarded as important safeguards by the political parties in Jamaica, minority and majority alike, who took part in the negotiations which led up to the constitution should not be altered without mature consideration by the Parliament and the consent of a larger proportion of its members than the bare majority required for ordinary laws.[107]

The requirement of a special majority of both Houses of Parliament ensures that the Government cannot use its majority in the lower House, which can often be overwhelming, to force through constitutional amendments. As discussed above, in such circumstances the role of Opposition and/or Independent senators becomes crucial. In the case of the unicameral parliaments of Dominica, St Kitts and St Vincent, the votes of nominated senators do not count towards the two-thirds majority needed for the enactment of constitutional amendments, and the role of the Opposition in the parliamentary process is, as a consequence, greatly diminished.[108] However, in these countries a referendum is also required for certain constitutional amendments. For example, in St Kitts a Bill to alter the fundamental rights chapter

---

[107] *Hinds v The Queen* [1977] AC 195.
[108] See, eg, s 38(2) Constitution of St Kitts and Nevis.

of the Constitution, or the provisions surrounding the office of the Governor General, as well as numerous others must be approved in a referendum.[109] In such cases the Opposition, even if they cannot block the Bill in Parliament, may still have an influence on the outcome of the referendum. As we saw, in chapter two, in the case of St Vincent, the decision of the Opposition to withdraw their support for constitutional reform and to campaign against the Constitution Reform Bill was a significant factor in its rejection by a majority of the citizens of St Vincent in the referendum.[110]

Where constitutional amendments are concerned, however, the requirement of a special majority of the legislature or in a referendum may not be the only limitations on a parliament's law-making powers. As we shall see in the next section, there may also be substantive limitations.

2. Substantive Limitations

In addition to a supreme law clause which provides that their parliaments' law-making powers are 'subject to the Constitution' and any laws inconsistent with the Constitution are, to the extent of the inconsistency, null and void, Commonwealth Caribbean constitutions also provide that their parliaments may 'make laws for the peace, order and good government' of the country concerned. This, in turn, raises the question of whether the court might strike down legislation which is adjudged not to be 'for the peace, order and good government' of their country?

The phrase can be traced back to the imperial statutes which sought to vest in local representative legislatures the largest possible measure of authority. The plenary nature of the power thus granted was recognised by the JCPC, even in an era when emphasis was given to the character of colonial legislatures as subordinate law-making bodies, in a series of

---

[109] See s 38(3)(b) Constitution of St Kitts and Nevis.

[110] ML Bishop, 'Slaying the "Westmonster" in the Caribbean? Constitutional Reform in St Vincent and the Grenadines' (2011) 13 *British Journal of Politics and International Relations* 420–37.

historic decisions at the close of the nineteenth century.[111] Thus, for example, in *Riel v The Queen*, Lord Halsbury rejected the contention that a statute was invalid if a court concluded that it was not calculated as a matter of fact and policy to secure 'peace, order and good government'.[112] More recently—albeit in the context of the exercise of the royal prerogative—the JCPC has affirmed that, 'the words "peace, order and good government" have never been construed as words limiting the power of a legislature'.[113] As the High Court of Australia explained, in *Nationwide News Pty Ltd v Willis*,[114] a court cannot hold a law invalid merely on the ground that the law is not 'for the peace, order and good government of the country', as the court sees it. It is not for the court to concern itself with the wisdom or expedience of the legislative power. Otherwise, there could be no logical limit to the grounds on which legislation might be brought down. In this way, the courts pay the deference due to the legislative sovereignty of Parliament.[115]

Recently, however, the extent of the plenary power conferred on the legislature by the phrase, 'peace, order and good government' has been questioned by the Supreme Court of Belize, in two cases, in the context of amendments to the fundamental rights provisions of the Constitution of Belize. In the first case, *Bowen v Attorney General*,[116] a group of landowners sought to challenge the constitutionality of the Belize Constitution (Sixth Amendment) Bill 2008 (the Sixth Amendment). The Sixth Amendment was intended to enable the Government to exploit the recent discovery of oil in the country and Clause 2 of the Sixth Amendment, accordingly, sought to disapply the protection afforded by section 17(1) of the Constitution to the owners of

> petroleum minerals and accompanying substances, in whatever physical state located on or under the territory of Belize … the entire property and control over which are exclusively vested, and shall be deemed always to have been so vested, in the Government of Belize.

---

[111] *R v Burah* (1878) 3 App Cas 889; *Hodge v The Queen* (1883) 9 App Cas 117; and *Powell v Apollo Candle Company* (1885) 10 App Cas 282.

[112] *Riel v The Queen* (1885) 10 App Cas 675.

[113] *Bancoult (No 2)*, [50].

[114] *Nationwide News Pty Ltd v Willis* (1992) 108 ALR 681.

[115] HP Lee, 'The Australian High Court and Implied Fundamental Guarantees' [1993] *Public Law* 606, 624.

[116] *Bowen v Attorney General*, BZ 2009 SC 2. Unreported. Available on file with the author.

The purported effect of the legislation was thus to deny to the owners of any such interests in land the right to apply to the courts for compensation in the event of being arbitrarily deprived of their interests in the land by the State.

Lawyers for the Attorney General argued that since the Sixth Amendment had been approved by the special three-quarters majority required by section 69 of the Constitution, this was sufficient to dispose of the claimants' challenge to its constitutionality. Chief Justice Conteh, however, disagreed. In his view the law-making powers of the Belizean Parliament were not unlimited because the Belizean Parliament cannot legitimately make laws that are contrary to the 'basic structure' of the Constitution itself.[117] In the Chief Justice's view, this included not only the fundamental rights guaranteed by Chapter II of the Constitution—in particular the right to redress from the courts for the arbitrary deprivation of property by the State—but also the principles, ideas, beliefs and desires of the people of Belize as enshrined in the Preamble of the Constitution. These include, among other things, respect for the rule of law and the right of the individual to the ownership of private property. The Chief Justice also had regard to the principle of the separation of powers, which had previously been recognised by the JCPC in *Hinds v The Queen* to be a basic feature of the structure of the Westminster type constitutions adopted by Commonwealth Caribbean countries upon independence. This principle would be violated if the citizens of Belize were to be denied access to the courts for compensation for the arbitrary derivation of their property by the State.

But, was the approval of the legislation by a special majority of the National Assembly to count for nothing? In the Chief Justice's view, section 69 was a mere 'manner and form' requirement, no more than a 'procedural handbook',[118] and was certainly not determinative of the constitutionality of legislation enacted by Parliament. In addition to the formal procedures laid down by section 69, any prospective amendment of the Constitution had to conform to the Constitution's *normative* requirements as captured by section 68, which provides that all laws

---

[117] Invoking the 'basic structure' doctrine which had been famously expounded by the Supreme Court of India in *Golak Nath v State of Punjab*, AIR 1967 SC 1643 and in *Kesavananda v State of Kerala*, AIR 1973 SC 1461.

[118] *Bowen v Attorney General* [101].

enacted by Parliament must be 'subject to the Constitution'.[119] Any other view would entail subordinating the supremacy of the Constitution in favour of parliamentary supremacy for once the required majority for an amendment is obtained then absolutely no constitutional provision would be beyond alteration or revocation.[120]

Following the judgment, the Government amended clause 2 of the Sixth Amendment to provide that nothing in the amended section 17 would affect the rights of the owner of any private land beneath which any petroleum deposits are located to receive royalties from the Government.[121] That did not mean, however, that the Government accepted that Parliament's law-making powers were limited in the ways suggested by Chief Justice Conteh.

In the second case, *British Caribbean Bank Ltd v AG Belize*,[122] the applicant had originally challenged the constitutionality of the Belize Telecommunications (Amendment) Act 2009 (TCA 2009), the purpose of which had been to enable the Government compulsorily to acquire the properties, rights and interests held by the applicants in Belize Telemedia Ltd. The latter is a major provider of telecommunications services in Belize and one of its major shareholders is BB Holdings Ltd, the chairman of which is Michael Ashcroft, who is also the deputy chairman of the British Conservative party, and who was a major funder of the Opposition party, the People's United Party, led by Michael Musa. Though the claim to the constitutionality of the legislation had been dismissed at first instance, it had been upheld by the Court of Appeal on the grounds, inter alia, that the TCA 2009 was contrary to the right to property under section 17(1) of the Constitution because it did not prescribe the principles on which reasonable compensation was to be paid for the acquisition of the applicant's property within a reasonable time.

In response to the Court of Appeal's judgment the Government secured the enactment of the Belize Telecommunications (Amendment) Act 2011 (TCA 2011), which sought to address some of the problems with the TCA 2009 that had been identified by the Court of Appeal.

---

[119] Ibid, [105]–[107].
[120] Ibid, [120].
[121] For an account of the *Bowen* litigation, see *Prime Minister Belize v Vellos* [2010] UKPC 7.
[122] Claim No 597 of 2011. Unreported. Available at: www.belizelaw.org.

At the same time, and in order to put the re-nationalisation of various public utilities, including the telecommunications industry, beyond doubt, the Government also secured the enactment of the Belize Constitution (Eighth) Amendment Act 2011 (the Eighth Amendment). The Eighth Amendment not only sought to disapply the 'supreme law' clause of the Constitution to 'a law to alter any of the provisions of this Constitution which is passed by the National Assembly in conformity with s 69 of the Constitution', but also expressly declared that 'the provisions of [s 69] are all-inclusive and exhaustive and there is no other limitation, whether substantive or procedural, on the power of the National Assembly to alter this Constitution'. As the Prime Minister frankly admitted, this was in direct response to the judgment of the Supreme Court in *Bowen*.[123] Additionally, the Eighth Amendment added a new Part XIII to the Constitution, the effect of which was, first, to define the meaning of 'public utilities'; second, to vest majority ownership and control of all public utility providers in the Government; and, third, by section 145(1) and 145(2), to declare that the Government's acquisition of such public utilities was duly carried out for a public purpose.

A challenge to the constitutionality of the Eight Amendment was, however, upheld by the Supreme Court, which concurred with the judgment of Chief Justice Conteh in *Bowen* in concluding that the National Assembly is not legally authorised to make any amendment to the Constitution that would remove or destroy any of the basic structures of the Constitution of Belize.[124] Since the cumulative effect of the Eighth Amendment was to prevent the Court from determining whether the deprivation of property by the Government was for a public purpose, the Eighth Amendment offended the principle of the separation of powers and the basic structure of the Constitution. To this extent the amendments to the Constitution were unlawful, null and void.

Though the basic structure doctrine has now been prayed in aid by the Belize Supreme Court on two occasions, it has not yet been endorsed by any higher court in the region; an appeal to the Caribbean Court of Justice (CCJ) against the Court of Appeal's refusal to award consequential relief to the applicants following its original judgment in *British Caribbean Bank Ltd v Belize*, having been stayed pending the

[123] See A Fiadjoe, 'Legal Opinion on the Ninth Amendment Bill of Belize' (2011) 20. Available at: www.thehaywardcharitablebelizetrust.com.
[124] At [45].

challenge to the TCA 2011.[125] It is also worth noting that the doctrine is very difficult to reconcile with the following dicta of Lord Diplock in *Hinds v The Queen*:

> Where … a constitution on the Westminster model represents the final step in the attainment of full independence by the peoples of a former colony or protectorate, the Constitution provides machinery whereby any its provisions, whether relating to fundamental rights and freedoms, or to the stratum of government and the allocation to its various organs of legislative, executive or judicial powers, may be altered by those peoples through their elected representatives in the Parliament acting by specific majorities, which is generally all that is required.[126]

It is true that, in *Hinds*, Lord Diplock was not addressing the issue of an amendment to the Jamaican Constitution that sought to derogate from a fundamental right, but rather the compatibility with the Constitution of ordinary legislation, setting up the so-called 'Gun Courts' in that country, and his remarks are to that extent, strictly *obiter*. Nevertheless, it is clear that Lord Diplock did not contemplate there being any implied limit on the legislature's power to alter the Constitution. It therefore remains to be seen whether other courts in the region, when faced with a challenge to a constitutional amendment based on the basic structure doctrine, will prefer the approach of Lord Diplock in *Hinds* or will opt to follow the lead of the Supreme Court of Belize.

PART IV: SCRUTINY OF THE EXECUTIVE

As we saw in chapter four, the fact that ministers have to be members of the legislature reflects the fact that they are deemed to be accountable to Parliament for the stewardship of their ministries. In turn, Parliament is assumed to be responsible for continuously scrutinising the competence of ministers in running their departments and for their handling of the public finances.

---

[125] *British Caribbean Bank Ltd v AG Belize* [2012] CCJ 1 (AJ) (R).
[126] At 214.

A. SCRUTINY OF POLICY AND ADMINISTRATION

Formally, at least, the traditional institutional conventions associated with Parliament's scrutiny function still exist across the region, including ministerial questions and debates. Ministers, including the Prime Minister, are still expected to attend and be prepared to answer questions from their opponents in Parliament,[127] and while the government of the day may control the business of the Lower House, time is still set aside for debates proposed by the Opposition.

In practice, however, a number of factors have seriously curtailed the ability of Commonwealth Caribbean parliaments to scrutinise their governments effectively. First, the tendency of the FPTP electoral system to result in disproportionate majorities for the winning party means that the size of the opposition is often quite small, and lacking the resources to mount an effective challenge to the government of the day. Second, the absence of a cap on the number of MPs who can be appointed government ministers, and are thereby bound by the convention of collective responsibility, means that the number of backbenchers who might be capable of holding the government to account is also quite small. Third, a tradition of authoritarian leadership, and the power of political patronage vested in the Prime Minister, means that the few remaining backbenchers are unlikely to challenge the government. Fourth, a culture of 'clientilism' in those countries where the State is the primary source of economic power means that constituents may be more interested in their MP's ability to access state resources than their MP's willingness to challenge government policy. Even in those countries with bicameral parliaments, the Prime Minister's powers of appointment and removal of a majority of the senators means that the Senate cannot seriously be relied upon to mount an effective opposition to the government, save, possibly, in relation to constitutional amendments.

Commonwealth Caribbean parliaments also generally lack the multitude and range of departmentally related parliamentary committees that are such a distinctive feature of the parliaments of countries such as Britain, Canada and Australia, where much of the scrutinising function is actually undertaken. Linked to the departments of central government, the role of these committees is to keep the work of the departments

---

[127] See, eg, Trinidad, House of Representatives, Standing Order No 13.

of central government under continuous review. Membership of these committees is cross party and they are generally seen as providing a very effective and less partisan forum for scrutiny of the executive than occurs during debates and ministers' questions. They are also seen as having a valuable, albeit invisible, deterrent effect on ministers who have to consider how their actions might appear if they are subsequently subject to scrutiny by a select committee. The small size of Commonwealth Caribbean parliaments, however, has meant that it has not proved practicable, with limited exceptions, to develop a meaningful system of oversight by departmentally related committees.

Such committees as do exist in the region's parliaments can be divided into three broad categories. First, there are those of a general nature, appointed at the commencement of each session, which are concerned mainly with the regulation and control of proceedings in Parliament. These include: the Standing Orders Committee (which advises on such matters connected with the Standing orders as are referred to it); the House Committee (which advises on matters connected with the comfort and convenience of members of the House); the Regulations Committee (which is responsible for reviewing all such secondary legislation as is required to be laid before the House); and the Privileges Committee (discussed above).[128] All these committees, with the exception of the House Committee, have the power to summon persons to appear before them and to make request for documentary evidence to be provided to them.[129] The second category is the Special and Joint Select Committees, which are composed of an agreed number of members of the lower and upper Houses, and which are appointed on an ad hoc basis to assist their Parliament with its legislative and policy-making functions. Finally, there are the so-called 'watchdog' committees, by far the most important of which is the Public Accounts Committee, which we will examine in more detail in the next section.

Two countries which have, however, attempted to establish something resembling a network of departmentally related committees are Guyana and Belize. Thus, in Guyana, four sectoral committees were established following reform of the 1980 Constitution: the Committee on Natural Resources, the Economic Services Committee, the Foreign

---

[128] For a definition of the work of each of these committees, see Trinidad, House of Representatives, Standing Orders.

[129] See, eg, Trinidad, House of Representatives, Standing Order No 80.

Relations Committee and the Social Services Committee. Each of these sectoral committees has responsibility for the scrutiny of the relevant area of government policy and administration. In the exercise of this responsibility they have the power to examine all policies and administration for each sector to determine whether the execution of government policy is in consonance with the principle of good governance and in the best interest of the nation. A revision to the Standing Orders in 2006 provides for ministers and public servants to be summoned to appear before these sectoral committees, since which time several ministers, including the Prime Minister, have been called to appear before the four sectoral committees to answer issues relating to policy and performance of their sectors. Meetings of the four sectoral committees are open to the public and the media.[130]

In Belize, in 2009, Parliament established 12 Standing Committees of the House of Representatives. These include committees on Finance and Economic Development, Public Utilities, Transport and Communication, Health, Education, Foreign Affairs, the Environment, National Security and Immigration, and Agriculture and Fisheries. In 2000, the list of Standing Committees was further expanded to include an Ombudsman Reports Committee. Each of these Standing Committees is charged with considering and examining all matters relating to their portfolios as referred to the Standing Committee by the House of Representatives and to report back to the House within 60 days. The Standing Committees have the power to oversee the expenditure, administration and policy of government departments and their associated public bodies and may send for persons, papers and records and specialist advisers, where necessary. Ministers are specifically required to attend before committee hearings when requested, unless unavoidably prevented from doing so on good and reasonable grounds, in which case they are required to send their Permanent Secretaries or other senior public officers in their place. In order to encourage bipartisan participation by committee members, each committee must include in its membership at least two parliamentarians who do not support the government. In 2000, the Standing Orders were amended to allow committees in all cases except legislation to hold

---

[130] See further, 'Mechanism for Follow-up on Implementation of the Inter-American Convention Against Corruption'. Available at: OES/L. SerSG/MESICIC/ doc.201/0.

meetings on their own initiative without having the matters referred to them by the House of Representatives.

Unfortunately, no detailed analysis has been undertaken of the work of these departmentally related committees in either Guyana or Belize. However, it is reasonable to presume that their success will, ultimately, depend more or less on the same factors that affect the success or otherwise of departmentally related committees in other parliaments: the priority given to the work of the committees by their members and the extent to which the government actually heeds their recommendations.[131]

B. FINANCIAL SCRUTINY

The importance of their Parliament's role in supervising the public finances is reflected in the requirement to be found in all of the region's constitutions that all revenues raised by the government are paid into a Consolidated Fund, and the numerous detailed provisions regarding how money may be moved out of this fund.[132] The latter require the Minister of Finance (in most cases the same person as the Prime Minister) to prepare a budget showing the estimates of revenue and expenditure for each financial year, which is then tabled in the National Assembly (or the elected House in those countries with bicameral parliaments) for debate and approval. Inevitably, a government's majority in Parliament means that approval of its budget proposals is a foregone conclusion. However, two additional layers of ex post facto scrutiny of government expenditure are provided through the offices of the Auditor General and the Public Accounts Committee (PAC).

1. Auditors General

The Auditor General is appointed by the President or Governor General, as the case may be, acting in accordance with the recommendation of the Public Service Commission (PSC) after consultation

---

[131] See E Kaseke, 'Parliamentary Committees and Participatory Democracy in Belize' (2001) 26(1) and 26(2) *West Indies Law Journal* 115, 126.

[132] See, eg, Constitution of Antigua, Chapter VI.

with the Prime Minister.[133] Sometimes—as in Jamaica—if the Prime
Minister so requires the President or Governor General, as the case
may be, must refer the original recommendation and one subsequent
recommendation back to the PSC for 'reconsideration'.[134]

The Auditor General is responsible for auditing and reporting on
the public accounts of all government departments and is intended
to serve as a 'watchdog' on behalf of the public to guard against any
impropriety in the conduct of the public finances. The Auditor General
is also required to submit to the Minister of Finance (usually the Prime
Minister) every report they make, while the latter is required, 'not later
than seven days after Parliament first meets after he has received the
report', to lay the report before Parliament.

In recognition of their constitutional importance, Auditors General
enjoy a similar level of security to other senior public officers. Thus, an
Auditor General who has not reached the prescribed age may only be
removed for inability to exercise the functions of their office or for misbehaviour. In either case, the Auditor General can only be removed by the
President or Governor General, as the case may, be if the question of their
removal has been referred to a tribunal, appointed by the head of state, and
the tribunal has recommended their removal. In the performance of their
functions Auditors General are not subject to the direction or control of
any other person or authority, thus buttressing their independence from
the executive and guaranteeing their ability to perform the role assigned to
them without fear or favour.

Given the nature of their role, it is inevitable, however, that at some
point Auditors General will be brought into direct conflict with the government; especially with the ministers of the governing party responsible for accounting for the financial stewardship of the nation during
any period on which an Auditor General is reporting. This potential for
conflict can be most clearly seen in the case of the Auditor General of
Grenada, who was removed from office for a letter of rebuke which
she had written to the Prime Minister after she had discovered that the
report that she had sent him to lay before Parliament had been tam-
pered with. Although the Auditor General's challenge to her removal by
the tribunal was successful in proceedings before the High Court, it was
upheld by the Court of Appeal and, subsequently, by the JCPC.[135]

---

[133] Also known in Dominica, Grenada and St Kitts as the Director of Audit.

[134] s 120 (6) Constitution of Jamaica.

[135] *Julia Lawrence v AG Grenada* [2007] UKPC 18.

Elsewhere in the region, Auditors General have tended to be a good deal less proactive than this example would suggest. A report by Trevor Munroe, in 2001, thus noted that throughout the region there were serious deficiencies in the functioning of the Auditor General's office.[136] These included inadequate staffing and resources in many cases, and a general failure to file up-to-date reports.[137] This is most graphically illustrated by the facts of *Thomas v Harris* in which the High Court of Antigua noted that the audited accounts for 1985 to 1988 were not filed until 1999 and the accounts for 1989 were not filed until 2000.[138] As the Court also noted, notwithstanding the Auditor General's palpable dereliction of his constitutional duties, no action to remedy this default was taken by the Prime Minister. Indeed, as the Court observed, the inescapable conclusion was that this state of affairs actually suited the Government, which had been in power since Antigua had been granted independence in 1981. In the Court's view, the Government had, as a consequence of its longevity, 'perhaps grown complacent and unmindful of its public accountability to the citizens who had elected it in the first place'.

Even where the Auditor General does file up-to-date reports, however, there is no guarantee that they will be laid promptly before Parliament. One of the additional reasons for the letter of rebuke, referred to above, that was sent by the Auditor General of Grenada to the Prime Minister was the latter's inordinate delay in laying the report of the Auditor General before Parliament.

2. Public Accounts Committees (PACs)

PACs are tasked with scrutinising the accounts of government ministries and departments, as required by the Auditor General; reporting to Parliament in the case of any excess or unauthorised expenditure of public funds the reasons for such expenditure; and recommending any measures the PAC considers necessary in order to ensure that public funds are properly spent.[139] In those countries where the Constitution

---

[136] Munroe, *Transparency International Country Study Report: Caribbean Composite Study*, above (n 93).

[137] Ibid.

[138] *Thomas v Harris*, AG 2004 HC 18. Unreported. Available on file with the author.

[139] See, eg, s 98 Constitution of Antigua.

does not make express provision for the establishment of a PAC, PACs have been established by the Standing Orders of each parliament; save for Barbados where the PAC is a statutory body, established by the Public Accounts Committee Act 2003.

Whether they are established under the Constitution, or by way of Standing Order, there is very little detail about the precise composition of the PAC. There is, however, an expectation that the distribution of seats on the PAC, as on other Standing Committees, corresponds as much as possible to the distribution of seats in the whole Assembly.[140] This means that the governing party usually controls the majority of the seats on the PAC. To counterbalance this majority, it is usually provided that chairmanship of the PAC is given to a member of the opposition party. This is also supposed to serve an important symbolic function in so far as it indicates the willingness of both the Government and the Opposition to serve on the PAC in a bipartisan manner.[141]

Like other parliamentary committees, the PAC has the power to investigate and examine all issues referred to it by Parliament. In order to fulfill this role, however, the PAC is given additional and more specific powers, such as the power to examine public accounts and all the reports drafted by the office of the Auditor General.[142] The PAC also has the power to conduct investigations; receive all the documentation it considers necessary to adequately perform its functions; invite government members to attend PAC meetings and respond to questions; publicise the PAC's conclusions; report to Parliament; and to present the PAC's recommendations to government.

Notwithstanding their extensive powers of enquiry, the performance of PACs across the region has generally been perceived to be ineffectual. In many countries the PAC has met very infrequently, and in others it has not met at all. In Barbados, for example, the Constitution Review Commission noted that the PAC had only reported to Parliament twice in more than 30 years of existence.[143] In St Lucia, it was reported, in 2008, that the PAC had not been active in over 20 years. In St Kitts,

---

[140] See Trinidad, House of Representatives, Standing Order No 78.

[141] R Stapenhurst, R Pelizzo, DM Olson and LV Trapp (eds), *Legislative Oversight and Budgeting: A World Perspective* (World Bank, 2008).

[142] See s 119(4) Constitution of Trinidad and Tobago.

[143] *Report of the Barbados Constitution Review Commission* (Barbados, Government Printing Department, 1998).

the report of the Commission of Inquiry into financial mismanagement in that country noted that the PAC had not been functioning for many years.[144] In *Thomas v Harris*, the Court was informed that the PAC in Antigua had met only eight times between 1990 and 2003. Apparently, this was because three of its five members, who were appointed from the government side of the House, refused to attend meetings thereby making it impossible to establish a quorum. It is not always, however, the governing party, which is at fault. In Dominica, for example, it proved impossible to appoint a chair of the PAC for a period of two years, as the Opposition United Workers Party (UWP), had been boycotting Parliament since January 2010 in protest at the electoral victories of the Prime Minister and his Minister of Education, which the UWP were challenging on the ground of their alleged dual citizenship.[145]

Quite apart from the problems involved in convening meetings of the PAC, it has proved very difficult for PACs to establish the kind of bipartisan approach to their task which is necessary for an effective PAC.[146] This has meant that Opposition members have sought to use the PAC to create maximum embarrassment for the Government, while Government members have been disinclined critically to scrutinise Government expenditure since this would be likely to cause them trouble within their own party. Moreover, when a government changes hands, the new opposition may be reluctant to investigate matters which occurred when they were in power.

This is not to say that PACs everywhere have been wholly ineffectual. In some countries, such as Jamaica, the PAC has been able to highlight a number of instances of mismanagement and misappropriation of public funds.[147] One such example is Operation Pride, a government low-income housing programme, in which it was alleged that public contracts worth tens of millions of dollars had been corruptly awarded to contractors connected with the ruling PNP and that huge sums of money had been paid for work not done. The massive media coverage provoked by the PAC's report aroused public disquiet and led the Prime

---

[144] See Munroe, *Transparency International Country Study Report: Caribbean Composite Study*, above (n 93) 98.
[145] See 'Dominica PM slams Opposition Boycott' (26 October 2011). Available at: www.caribbean360.com.
[146] Stapenhurst et al, above (n 141).
[147] Ibid.

Minister to appoint a Commission of Inquiry. The report produced by
this Commission was so damning to Karl Blythe, the Minister of Water
and Housing, that he was forced to resign on 13 April 2002, a day after
the report had been handed over to the Prime Minister.[148] The transparency afforded by the publication of the PAC's reports thus, potentially
at least, provides a powerful deterrent to inappropriate activities.

However, this has not been seen as sufficient, ultimately, to com-
pensate for their lack of sanctioning powers. Though they can recommend corrective measures, very often no corrective action is taken by
the ministry concerned and, in those circumstances, the PAC has no
power to impose sanctions.[149] But without sanctioning systems that are
transparent, rooted in a visible regulatory framework and implemented,
it is difficult to envisage how PACs can deliver the level of financial
accountability necessary to deter and, ultimately, eradicate corruption
among public officials.

CONCLUSION

The factors which impinge upon the performance of Commonwealth
Caribbean parliaments, such as executive dominance, are, of course,
not unique to the region, but their impact has been magnified by a
number of factors. These have included the tendency of the FPTP
electoral system to produce very large majorities in some countries.
As we have seen, on a number of occasions post-independence, opposition parties have been effectively annihilated in terms of seats in
Parliament, leaving the winning party to govern entirely unopposed.
Additionally, the comparatively small size of the region's parliaments
and the absence of a cap on the number of ministers, means that they
are dominated to an extraordinary degree by members of the executive who are, in turn, bound by the doctrine of collective responsibility to toe the government line. This has made it virtually impossible
for a government to be dismissed on a parliamentary vote of no
confidence. Though the inclusion of a nominated element—either

[148] *The Angus Report on Operation PRIDE.* Excerpts available at: www.jamaica-
gleaner.com.
[149] T Munroe, *Transparency International Country Study Report: Jamaica* (Berlin,
Transparency International Secretariat, 2003).

within a single legislature or in the Upper House in those countries with bicameral parliaments—was intended to serve as something of a bulwark against executive dominance, the fact that the majority of senators are appointed and removed on the recommendation of the Prime Minister has more or less completely undermined this objective. Their small size has also meant that the region's parliaments have been unable to resource the kind of network of departmentally related committees which in other countries play a crucial role in scrutinising the executive.

However, the problems that bedevil Commonwealth Caribbean parliaments are not just a function of their small size; they are also a function of the region's history and its colonial legacy. With the exception of Barbados and the Bahamas, which were never subject to 'Crown Colony rule' and which retained a wholly elective House of Assembly throughout, it was only following the end of the Second World War that fully elected legislatures were finally established in the other countries in the region. Thus, by the time of independence, the region's parliaments had been afforded very little time to become acquainted with the traditions and conventions that underpinned the operation of the British Parliament upon which they were modelled, and which had been evolving over a number of centuries. As we have seen, while it is easy to replicate the offices and institutions of another parliament, there is no guarantee that they will be fully assimilated into the local political culture. To function effectively, these offices and institutions need to develop a strong ethic of bipartisanship, which has not, to date, always been evident in parliaments in the region. Too often, appointments to offices, such as Speaker and Deputy Speaker, have been used to try to secure a political advantage. Also, as we have seen from the example of Antigua, where a party has been in power for a prolonged period their relationship with the Auditor General may be too close to enable the latter meaningfully to act as the public's financial watchdog. Lack of cooperation between the main political parties has additionally meant that institutions, such as the PAC, have been unable to function effectively or, in some cases, function at all.

It is also significant that Commonwealth Caribbean parliaments have been obliged to function within a constitutional system where Parliament is no longer sovereign, but is 'subject to the provisions of the Constitution'. As we have seen with regard to the privileges of Parliament, the courts have interpreted the constitutional immunity afforded to MPs for statements made in Parliament very narrowly, and have treated the inherent powers of Parliament to punish its members for breach of privilege or contempt as extremely limited in scope. This has, arguably, diminished the authority of the region's parliaments, as has the establishment of extra-parliamentary Integrity Commissions across the region with power to monitor the conduct of and to punish MPs for failure to file statutory declarations and/or breaching the Code of Conduct for public officials. We have also seen in Belize the emergence of a 'basic structure' doctrine which would limit Parliament's power to amend the Constitution beyond the express constraints on Parliament's law-making powers as set out in the text of the Constitution.

The cumulative effect of the factors described above has been to alter the balance of power between the three branches of government to such an extent that it is reasonable to question whether Commonwealth Caribbean parliaments are still able effectively to discharge their constitutional functions. The answer is quite possibly not, and this is, and ought to be, of the utmost concern for all those who care about responsible and accountable government in the region. For, if a country's parliament is no longer seen as capable of performing its constitutional functions, there is a grave danger that those opposed to the government may be tempted to bypass that parliament altogether and seek to challenge the government by other non-parliamentary means, as demonstrated by the events in Dominica in 1978 and 1981, in Trinidad in 1970 and in Grenada in 1979, discussed in the introduction to this book.

FURTHER READING

A Bennett et al, *Dual Citizenship and Political Representation in Jamaica: Insights From Comparative Research* (Caribbean Policy Research Institute, 2008).

HA Ghany, 'The Commonwealth Caribbean: Legislatures and Democracy' in NDJ Baldwin (ed), *Legislatures of Small States: A Comparative Study* (Abingdon, Routledge, 2013).

P Laundy, *The Office of the Speaker in the Parliaments of the Commonwealth* (London, Quiller, 1984).

T Munroe, *Transparency International Country Study Report: Caribbean Composite Study* (Berlin, Transparency International Secretariat, 2004).

RAW Rhodes, J Wanna and P Weller (eds), *Comparing Westminster* (Oxford, Oxford University Press, 2011).

6

The Constitutional Role of the Courts

⟲

Background – Judicial Independence: National Courts and the Eastern Caribbean Supreme Court – The Caribbean Court of Justice – Constitutional Review – Conclusion

PART I: BACKGROUND

HAVING INHERITED THE common law from the British it is no surprise to learn that the court system of the Commonwealth Caribbean is modelled on that of England and Wales. There is thus, broadly speaking, a hierarchical, three-tier structure made up of inferior courts, superior courts and final appellate courts. Inferior courts include stipendiary magistrates (legally trained) and petty sessional courts (composed of lay persons assisted by a legally trained clerk). Their jurisdiction is defined by statute and, generally speaking, encompasses a summary criminal jurisdiction, as well as dealing with low monetary value civil matters and certain family proceedings. Superior courts comprise the High Court[1] and the Court of Appeal, which are collectively referred to as the Supreme Court. Unlike inferior courts, which owe their existence to statute, the Supreme Court is established by the Constitution, though its jurisdiction can be supplemented by ordinary legislation, such as the Supreme Court of Judicature Act to be found in each country. The jurisdiction of the Supreme Court cannot, however, be taken away other than by

---

[1] Confusingly, in some countries, eg, Belize and the Bahamas, the High Court is called the Supreme Court and there is an additional Court of Appeal. For a detailed discussion of the court system in the Commonwealth Caribbean, see RM Antoine, *Commonwealth Caribbean Law and Legal Systems*, 2nd edn (Oxford, Routledge-Cavendish, 2008).

the procedure prescribed for amendment to the Constitution,[2] and the powers of appeal of the Court of Appeal cannot be enlarged otherwise than by the procedure prescribed for amendments to the Constitution if such enlargement results in a limitation of the fundamental rights guaranteed by the Constitution.[3]

Broadly speaking, the High Court exercises both a civil and criminal jurisdiction, as well as an appellate jurisdiction in respect of the petty sessional courts and administrative tribunals on a point of law. Appeals from the magistrates' courts and the High Court go to the Court of Appeal. The eastern Caribbean islands—Antigua, Dominica, Grenada, St Lucia, St Kitts and St Vincent—share a common Supreme Court, the Eastern Caribbean Supreme Court (ECSC), established by the West Indies Associated States Supreme Court Order 1967, which is incorporated by reference in the Constitution of each of these countries. The ECSC comprises High Courts in each of the islands, staffed by a resident judge, and a single Court of Appeal. The Court of Appeal has its headquarters in St Lucia but it is an itinerant court, travelling from country to country within the region to hear appeals from the decisions of the High Court and magistrates' courts in civil and criminal matters. Any appeals from the courts of appeal throughout the region lie either to the Judicial Committee of the Privy Council (JCPC) or for those countries that have ratified its appellate jurisdiction—Barbados, Belize and Guyana—to the Caribbean Court of Justice (CCJ).

In this chapter I wish to focus on a single, but crucially important aspect of the superior courts' jurisdiction which concerns the role which they play in upholding the principle of constitutionalism. This requires that legislative and executive power be exercised within the limits fixed by the Constitution, which represents a fundamental or higher order law, and I will refer to the process by which the superior courts uphold this principle as 'constitutional review'. This is distinct from the inherent jurisdiction of the superior courts to review the acts and omissions of the executive in accordance with the traditional grounds of judicial review—illegality, irrationality and procedural impropriety[4]—which may be invoked, for example, where a public authority exceeds the powers conferred on it by Parliament, or has failed to observe a common

[2] *Re Niles (No 2)* (2003) 66 WIR 64.
[3] *The State v Boyce (Brad)* (2005) 65 WIR 283.
[4] *Council of Civil Service Unions v Minister for the Civil Service* [1985] AC 374.

law principle such as natural justice.[5] Though both powers of review are of fundamental importance in any political system which aspires to conform to the rule of law, and many of the issues discussed in this chapter are relevant to both, for reasons of space I will principally focus in this chapter on the courts' powers of constitutional review.[6]

In order for the judges to exercise their powers of review, both constitutional and judicial, effectively, it is imperative that they are independent. I will, therefore, begin, in part II, by examining the institutional arrangements in place at the national and sub-regional levels for securing judicial independence, in particular, by preventing executive interference in the appointment and removal of senior judges and in the determination of their salaries and their terms and conditions of service. I will, at the same time, consider the extent to which these institutional arrangements have been undermined by the wider political culture in the region, which has resulted in what many would regard as the undue 'politicisation' of relations between the executive and the judiciary.

Until recently, discussion of these issues would have been confined to the national and sub-regional appellate courts as local politicians held no sway over the composition of the final appellate court for the region, the JCPC. All that changed with the establishment, in 2005, of the CCJ, which, as noted above, is already the final court of appeal for Barbados, Belize and Guyana, and is intended ultimately to replace the JCPC as the final appellate court for the whole region. The process of replacing the JCPC has, however, proved to be highly contentious, not least because of concern that the politicisation of relations between the executive and judiciary will no longer be confined to the national and sub-regional level, but will extend to the region's highest appellate court. In part III, I will, therefore, consider how this and other related concerns have been addressed in the design of the CCJ's institutional structure.

Finally, in part IV, attention will turn to the legal framework within which the courts exercise their powers of constitutional review. Since the existence of a power to strike down legislation, in particular, represents a

---

[5] *Ridge v Baldwin* [1964] AC 40. In Barbados and Trinidad judicial review has been put on a statutory footing by the Administrative Justice Act of Barbados and the Judicial Review Act of Trinidad and Tobago.

[6] For a detailed discussion of the traditional grounds of judicial review in the context of the Commonwealth Caribbean, see A Fiadjoe, *Commonwealth Caribbean Public Law* (London, Cavendish, 2000). See also E Ventose, *Commonwealth Caribbean Administrative Law* (Abingdon, Routledge, 2013).

significant departure from the Diceyan notion of parliamentary supremacy[7] with which most Commonwealth Caribbean judges would have
been familiar as a result of their legal education and training, I will start
by exploring how the courts went about establishing the juridical basis
for this aspect of their constitutional review jurisdiction. I will then turn
to focus on what has proven to be one of the most controversial aspects
of the courts' constitutional review jurisdiction: namely, challenges to
legislative and executive action based on the Bills of Rights guaranteed
by each of the Commonwealth Caribbean constitutions. I will be concerned, in particular, to explore the principles of constitutional interpretation that have been developed by the courts when faced with such
challenges, always remembering that these have, in no small part, been
shaped by a final appellate court, the JCPC, which is both geographically
and culturally distant from the region.

PART II: JUDICIAL INDEPENDENCE: NATIONAL COURTS AND THE EASTERN CARIBBEAN SUPREME COURT (ECSC)

Judicial independence takes on a critical significance when one of the
parties to the proceedings is the government. If judges are to hold governments and legislatures to account when they transgress the limits
placed upon their actions by the Constitution it is, therefore, essential
that they are not predisposed to decide the outcome of the proceedings
in favour of the government because they have been subject to threats,
interference or manipulation by the latter. In order to achieve the kind
of political insularity required to prevent this, structural safeguards need
to be in place which provide significant checks and balances in the
appointment of senior judges, offer them security of tenure and protect their terms and conditions of service while in office. Beyond these
formal safeguards, judicial independence also requires a political culture
that respects the separation of the judicial and the executive spheres

---

[7] AV Dicey, *Introduction to the Study of the Law of the Constitution*, 10th edn (London, Macmillan, 1959) 39.

and the right of judges to determine when the latter has abused its legal powers or transgressed the limits laid down by the Constitution.[8]

A. APPOINTMENT OF JUDGES

All Commonwealth Caribbean constitutions include provisions for the appointment and removal of judges of the High Court and above, which are constitutionally entrenched to differing degrees across the region.

It is thus generally provided that the Chief Justice shall be appointed by the Prime Minister after consultation with the Leader of the Opposition.[9] Among the Member States of the Organisation of Eastern Caribbean States (OECS), which fall under the jurisdiction of the ECSC, the Chief Justice is formally appointed by the Queen, but the convention is that the Queen acts upon the recommendation of the President and Governors General of the OECS Member States.[10] Though the Prime Minister is required in many countries to consult the Leader of the Opposition, the Prime Minister is not, constitutionally, bound to accept the advice tendered by the latter and the consultation process is often no more than a formality; it can even happen, on occasion, that there is no Leader of the Opposition to consult. For example, in Trinidad, in 1972, the Opposition having boycotted the general elections, the Prime Minister bowed to pressure from the legal profession by appointing a new Chief Justice without having been able to consult the Leader of the Opposition. This appointment was particularly controversial because in choosing his new Chief Justice the Prime Minister bypassed both the acting Chief Justice and two other Appeal Court judges, each of whom, it was widely observed, had recently handed down judgments that had gone against the government.

Even in Belize, where the Constitution requires that the Leader of the Opposition must be given a 'genuine opportunity' to present their views before the decision about the Chief Justice's appointment

---

[8] See CM Larkins, 'Judicial Independence and Democratization: A Theoretical and Conceptual Analysis' (1996) 44(4) *American Journal of Comparative Law* 605.

[9] See, eg, s 98(1) Constitution of Jamaica.

[10] s 5 West Indian Associated States Supreme Court Order.

is taken,[11] we have seen this requirement ignored on at least one occasion when a meeting between the Prime Minister and the Leader of the Opposition to discuss the appointment of the Chief Justice was scheduled to take place after the appointment had, in fact, already been made by the Prime Minister (discussed in chapter four).[12] Guyana has, admittedly, gone somewhat further than any other country to ensure that the appointment of the Chief Justice has bipartisan support by amending its Constitution in 2001 to require the President to secure the agreement of the Leader of the Opposition before appointing both the Chancellor and the Chief justice.[13] However, prior to the elections in March 2001, President Jagdeo pressed ahead with the appointment of a new Chancellor and a new Chief Justice without awaiting the enactment of this constitutional amendment so that he could secure his choice of Chancellor and Chief Justice without needing to obtain the agreement of the Leader of the Opposition. It was further alleged that in order to make it possible for him to appoint his choice of new Chief Justice, the President ignored the advice of the Judicial and Legal Services Commission (JLSC), which he was constitutionally bound to follow,[14] when appointing a more senior High Court judge to the Court of Appeal. By this device the President was able to ensure that the more senior, and therefore the more eligible, judge was not available for selection as the new Chief Justice.[15]

Beyond the requirement of consultation, there are generally speaking few restrictions on who the Prime Minister can appoint as Chief Justice so long as the person chosen has the requisite legal qualifications.[16] A career in politics or even close association with members of the government is certainly not a constitutional disqualification, as demonstrated by the decision of Prime Minister Owen Arthur to appoint Sir David Simmons as Chief Justice of Barbados, the latter having been a senior Cabinet minister in Owen Arthur's Government from 1994

[11] s 129(2) Constitution of Belize.
[12] See *James Jam Mohammed v AG*, Supreme Court of Belize, Action 73 of 1999. Unreported. Available on file with the author.
[13] See now Art 127(1) Constitution of Guyana as amended in 2001.
[14] Art 128(1) Constitution of Guyana.
[15] See S Ryan, *The Judiciary and Governance in the Caribbean* (St Augustine, Trinidad, Sir Arthur Lewis Institute of Social and Economic Studies, University of the West Indies Press, 2001) 39.
[16] See, eg, s 98(3) Constitution of Jamaica.

until his appointment as Chief Justice in 2002. However, as Rose-Marie Antoine notes, in the small developing countries of the Commonwealth Caribbean, there is a relatively small pool of excellence upon which to draw and sometimes the qualities that mark a candidate out for high judicial office are the same as those that mark the candidate out for high political office.[17] As a consequence, the purity of the principle of separating the executive and the judiciary is sometimes compromised by the exigencies and realities of local conditions.[18]

Judges other than the Chief Justice are generally appointed by the President or Governor General, as the case may be, on the advice of the JLSC.[19] Here too, however, the Prime Minister's influence is evident in the composition of the JLSC, which usually includes the Chief Justice and the Chairman of the PSC (both of whom will themselves have been appointed by the Prime Minister) and one or more members recommended by the Prime Minister after consultation with the Leader of the Opposition.[20] This led the Task Force, which was commissioned by the ECSC to examine the structure and functioning of its JLSC, to conclude that it was widely seen as a 'legal fiction' and a 'rubber stamp', which invariably acted in accordance with the wishes of the Heads of Government of the OECS Member States.[21] As the Task Force reported, considerable dissatisfaction was expressed 'through the length and breadth of the region' with the fact that the political directorate had such an influential role in certain judicial appointments.[22]

The arrangements for the appointment of judges in Barbados and Belize do not conform to the above template, and are, if anything, even more susceptible to prime ministerial influence. Thus, in the case of Barbados, the Independence Constitution was amended in 1974 to provide that *all* judges, not just the Chief Justice, are appointed on

---

[17] Antoine, above (n 1).

[18] *Panton and Another v Minister of Finance and Another (No 2)* (2001) 59 WIR 418.

[19] See, eg, s 104(2) Constitution of Jamaica.

[20] See, eg, s 110 Constitution of Trinidad and Tobago and s 18 WIASSCO. The JLSC for OECS Member States is composed of the Chief Justice, who acts as the Chairperson; a Justice of Appeal or Puisne Judge appointed by the Chief Justice; a person, appointed by the Chief Justice with the concurrence of the Prime Ministers of not less than four of the Member States; and two members of the Public Service Commissions of the Member States, who are appointed in rotation for periods of three years.

[21] Cited by Ryan, above (n 14) 14.

[22] Ibid.

the recommendation of the Prime Minister after consultation with the Leader of the Opposition.[23] In the case of Belize, in addition to the Chief Justice,[24] the Justices of the Court of Appeal are appointed on the advice of the Prime Minister, albeit after consultation with the Leader of the Opposition.[25] In 2009, in exercise of the latter power the Prime Minister, Dean Barrow, appointed his brother, Denys Barrow, as a Justice of the Court of Appeal. Even though the appointment was supported by the Leader of the Opposition at the time, there was intense criticism of the appointment by members of the Bar Association who predicted that it would lead to conflicts of interest between Justice Barrow and members of the extended Barrow family, who occupied positions of influence within Belize.[26] The accuracy of this prediction was borne out within a year of Justice Barrow's appointment, when the Court of Appeal of Belize found that there had been an appearance of bias in his participation in the hearing of an appeal involving the Public Utilities Commission of which his son was a member. The Court of Appeal, accordingly, ordered the appeal to be reheard by a panel which did not include Justice Barrow,[27] and shortly thereafter he resigned.

Prime Ministers also have a role to play in a number of countries in the region—Barbados, Bahamas, Belize and the OECS Member States—in connection with extensions of a judge's appointment beyond the constitutionally prescribed retirement age.[28] In the case of the Chief Justice, the extension must have been recommended by the Prime Minister.[29] In recommending an extension the Prime Minister is usually required to consult the Leader of the Opposition, but failure to do so is not necessarily fatal; as in the case of the Bahamas, in 1988, when the Prime Minister apparently 'forgot' to consult the Leader of the Opposition before agreeing to the extension of the Chief Justice's tenure.[30] In such cases it is widely suspected that there is a strong political dimension to the decision whether or not to extend a judge's

---

[23]   s 81 Constitution of Barbados.
[24]   s 79(1) Constitution of Belize.
[25]   s 101(1) Constitution of Belize.
[26]   Belize Blog (26 January 2011). Available at: www.belizeblog.com.
[27]   *Belize Electricity Ltd v Public Utilities Commission*, Civil Appeal No 8 of 2009. Unreported. Available on file with the author.
[28]   See, eg, s 84(1A) Constitution of Barbados.
[29]   Ibid.
[30]   *Whitfield v AG*, BS 1989 SC 20. Unreported. Available on file with the author.

tenure. In Barbados, for example, the refusal of the Prime Minister to exercise his discretion to extend the tenure of the incumbent Chief Justice, Sir David Simmons, was a cause of much controversy, with the Chief Justice complaining that the decision was entirely 'political', and threatening to produce documents to prove this.[31] In the case of judges other than the Chief Justice, the extension must usually have been recommended by the JLSC.

Among the OECS Member States the power to extend a judge's term of office ostensibly lies with the JLSC. However, the JLSC can only act with the concurrence of the Heads of Government of all the Member States,[32] and in such a small region this can lead to unforeseen conflicts of interest. Thus, in one notorious case, two former Prime Ministers of St Lucia—Dr Vaughan Lewis and Sir John Compton—objected to the appointment of a retired judge as a chair of a Commission of Inquiry into certain land deals involving the two former Prime Ministers,[33] on the ground that the judge had been refused an extension of her term as a High Court judge at a time when Sir John Compton was the Prime Minister of St Lucia and Dr Vaughan Lewis was the Director of the OECS. Their refusal to extend the judge's tenure, they argued, gave rise to the risk of bias on the part of the chair of the Commission of Inquiry. Though their objection was ultimately upheld by the Eastern Caribbean Court of Appeal,[34] the incident dramatically highlights the difficulty in small island states of separating the judicial and executive spheres. The effect of this on the public's perception of the judiciary is encapsulated in the report of a Task Force headed by Reginald Dumas. Though the mandate of the report was to examine the structure and functioning of the JLSC in the OECS, there is no reason to suppose that the mood of the public that is noted the report is confined to the OECS Member States:

> The Task Force was in more than one jurisdiction of the court the recipient of allegations of relationships between executive and judiciary, high and

---

[31] T Slinger, 'Ex-CJ's vow', *Sunday Sun* (Barbados, 15 April 2012). Available at: www.nationnews.com/articles/view/ex-cjs-vow/.

[32] See s 5, West Indies Associated States Supreme Court Order.

[33] L Blom Cooper, Commission of Inquiry Report, *Standards in Public Life in St Lucia* (1998). Available at: www.slucia.com.

[34] *AG St Lucia et al v Lewis, AG St Lucia et al v Compton*, LC 1998 CA 4. Unreported. Available on file with the author.

low, which were seen as improper, unethical, and subversive of judicial independence, impartiality and integrity. The Task Force is also mindful of the considerable dissatisfaction expressed to it throughout the length and breadth of the region with the fact that under the [Supreme Court Order], the political directorate plays a key role in certain judicial appointments and in the extension (or not) of judges' tenure of office.[35]

B. REMOVAL OF JUDGES

As an additional safeguard against executive interference Commonwealth Caribbean constitutions usually provide for a three-stage process to be followed before a senior judge can be removed from office; the exceptions are Belize and Guyana, as explained below.

At the first stage of this process the Prime Minister, in the case of the Chief justice, and the JLSC in the case of other senior judges, must 'represent' to the President or Governor General, as the case may be, that the question of the judge's removal ought to be investigated by a tribunal; save in Belize where the question of a judge's removal must be investigated by the Belize Advisory Council.[36] The tribunal is usually composed of a chairman and two other members, selected by the President or Governor General, as the case may be, acting on the advice of the Prime Minister in the case of the Chief Justice, or the Prime Minister after consultation with the JLSC in the case of any other judges, from among judges who have held high judicial office.[37] In the case of the OECS Member States, the first stage is initiated by the Premier of one of the Member States in the case of the removal of the Chief Justice and the JLSC in the case of any other judge. The representation in both cases is made to the British Lord Chancellor, who appoints the tribunal.[38] At the same time as referring the question of the judge's removal to a tribunal, the President or Governor General, as the case may be, or the Lord Chancellor in the case of judges of the

---

[35] R Dumas, *Report of the Task Force Appointed by the Hon. Chief Justice to Enquire into the Structure and Functioning of the Judicial and Legal Services Commission* (2000). Quoted in Ryan, above (n 15) 15.

[36] s 98(4) Constitution of Belize.

[37] See, eg, s 100(6)(a) Constitution of Jamaica.

[38] s 8 WIASSCO.

ECSC, may suspend the judge from performing the functions of their office, pending the outcome of the tribunal's decision, or the decision of the JCPC if the tribunal recommends that the removal of the judge should be referred to that body.[39]

The second stage of the process comprises the investigation by the tribunal, following which the tribunal may 'recommend' that the question of the judge's removal be referred to the JCPC—in the case of Jamaica, Trinidad and the OECS Member States—or to the CCJ, in the case of Barbados.[40] The third and final stage of the process is review of the tribunal's recommendation by the JCPC or the CCJ respectively, following which advice is tendered to the President or Governor General, as the case may be, on whether the judge ought to be removed. The process is slightly different in Guyana under the 1980 Constitution. Here the Prime Minister makes the representation that the question of the Chief Justice's removal should be investigated by a tribunal, but in the case of the other judges the representation is made by the Judicial Services Commission. In all cases the recommendation of the tribunal has to be confirmed by the President.[41]

The inclusion of a three-stage process in the Independence Constitutions was intended to ensure that the recommendation to remove a judge could only be made following investigation by an independent tribunal, and even then the final decision on the judge's removal in the majority of cases lay with the JCPC. This, it was hoped, would cause the Prime Minister to give very serious consideration at the outset before representing to the head of state that the question of a judge's removal should be investigated by a tribunal, and would, furthermore, discourage the tribunal from making unmeritorious recommendations for the removal of a judge. As Ellis Clarke, Constitutional Adviser to the Cabinet on the draft Independence Constitution for Trinidad explained:

> Suppose they say there is a case to go to the Privy Council, then the case goes to the Privy Council and is heard by the Privy Council, and the Privy Council can say, and can say in clear and unmistakable terms that there was not a vestige of a case to come to them. They can criticize very strongly indeed the conduct either of the Prime Minister in initiating proceedings or

---

[39] See, eg, s 100(8) Constitution of Jamaica.
[40] s 84(4) Constitution of Barbados.
[41] Art 197(5) Constitution of Guyana.

the three judges if they think they are going to be weak and send the matter to the Privy Council that ought never to reach there.[42]

The advantages and disadvantages of this three-stage process were dramatically illustrated by events in Trinidad, in 2005, when the Chief Justice was alleged to have attempted to pervert the course of justice by trying to persuade the Chief Magistrate to dismiss charges brought against the former Prime Minister, Basdeo Panday, under the Integrity in Public Life Act. As a result of these allegations a tribunal, chaired by a senior British judge, Lord Mustill, was appointed by the President to investigate the question of whether or not the Chief Justice should be removed from office. In the meantime, the Chief Justice was suspended, pending the outcome of the tribunal's investigation. Although the tribunal eventually ruled that the Chief Justice should not be removed from office, considerable damage was nevertheless caused to the Chief Justice's reputation in the interim, and the tribunal was scathing about the events that had led to its appointment, which, in the tribunal's opinion, 'almost defied belief'. These included: a battle of press releases between the Chief Justice, the Chief Magistrate and the Attorney General; allegations against the Attorney General, who could have given evidence in rebuttal to the tribunal but did not; and the Chief Justice publicly arrested and later ushered three times into the dock in a criminal court to undergo a summary trial on charges based on allegations by the Chief Magistrate, only to be ushered out again on the final occasion in consequence of the refusal by the Chief Magistrate to give evidence against him. In the words of the tribunal:

> The air was full of rumour, innuendo and gossip, around and across deep political (and, we are forced to say, ethnic) divides. At least within this narrow field of view, the concept of the separation of powers seems to have been ignored. We need not go on. The picture is 'troubling' indeed, both for the Tribunal and for the peoples of Trinidad and Tobago.[43]

---

[42] United Kingdom National Archives, CO 1031/3226, Explanatory Memorandum by the Constitutional Adviser to the Cabinet on the Draft Independence Constitution for Trinidad and Tobago, 16th April, 1962, 10–11. Cited by HA Ghany, *Changing our Constitution: A Comparison of the Existing Constitution of Trinidad and Tobago and the Working Document on Constitutional Reform for Public Consultation* (2009) 11. Available at: www.reformtheconstitution.com.

[43] See summary. Available at: www.ukscblog.com.

In other cases the procedure followed at the first and second stages of the process has not always complied with the principles of natural justice and the courts have been obliged to give detailed guidance on what is expected in terms of fairness at both of these stages. Thus, it is has been held that at the first stage of the process, when the JLSC convenes to consider whether or not to recommend the appointment of a tribunal to investigate whether a judge should be removed from office, fairness requires that the judge concerned should know what is alleged against them so that if they have an answer they can give it.[44] Fairness may also require that the judge be allowed to appear before the JLSC to be informed of or to answer the allegations of misbehaviour.[45] In Belize, where the three-stage process common elsewhere in the region is modified to the extent that in the first instance it is the Governor General who considers whether the question of the removal of the judge ought to be investigated and the final recommendation is made by the Belize Advisory Council (BAC) rather than the JCPC or CCJ,[46] fairness still requires that before the Governor General refers the question to the BAC for investigation the Governor General should hear what, if anything, the particular judge may have to say, on the material or complaint.[47] The JCPC has, however, also made it clear that there is no constitutional requirement that the hearing before the BAC should be in public and that the rule against bias is not breached by the fact that the Chairman of the BAC may also be a member of the Bar Association, even if the complaint against the judge being investigated originates from the Bar Association or one of its members.[48]

In Guyana, an additional layer has been added to the process for the removal of senior judges by the Time Limit for Judicial Decisions Act 2009 (the Act). This Act fleshes out the constitutional provision that a judge may be removed from office for persistently failing to give written or oral decisions and reasons for the decisions by expressly prescribing the time limits for decisions in civil and appeal cases: 120 days and 30 days respectively.[49] Where a judge fails to comply with these time limits

[44] *Rees v Crane* [1994] 2 AC 173.
[45] *Barnwell v AG Guyana* (1993) 49 WIR 88.
[46] s 98(5) Constitution of Belize.
[47] *Meerabux v AG Belize* (Action No 65 of 2001) Supreme Court of Belize. Unreported. Available on file with the author.
[48] *Meerabux v AG Belize* [2005] 2 AC 513, 529.
[49] ss 4 and 5 Time Limit for Judicial Decisions Act 2009.

the Chancellor must ask the Registrar of Courts to notify the judge that if the judge persists in their default action may be taken to remove the judge from office. In addition, the Act requires the Registrar of Courts to submit to the Speaker of the National Assembly an annual report for the preceding year, identifying each case of non-compliance with the prescribed time limits and any notices served by the Registrar upon a defaulting judge.[50] The report must then be laid by the Speaker before the National Assembly, though the Bill expressly precludes the National Assembly from debating the conduct of any judge mentioned in the report.[51]

C. TERMS AND CONDITIONS OF SERVICE

Because of the judiciary's dependence on the other branches of government for its financial and material support it has been described variously as a 'vulnerable institution' and a 'fragile bastion'.[52] It is for this reason that most Commonwealth Caribbean constitutions provide that judicial salaries are a charge on the Consolidated Fund and that judges' salaries shall not be altered to their disadvantage after their appointment.[53] Even so there is always the risk that the value of the judges' salaries and other allowances may be eroded during the judges' term of office. Thus, for example, in the Bahamas, where the Government is under a statutory obligation[54] to appoint a commission to review the salaries of judges every three years, the Government failed on two occasions, in 2003 and in 2006, to appoint a commission, resulting in no review of judges' salaries taking place for more than six years. This led not only to a heated public debate about judicial salaries, but also to a series of challenges to the independence of judges presiding over cases, pending the appointment of a commission to review judicial salaries.[55]

---

[50]   Ibid, s 7.

[51]   Ibid, s 11(3).

[52]   See N Stephen, 'Judicial Independence' in S Shetreet and J Deschenes (eds), *Judicial Independence: The Contemporary Debate* (Dordrecht, Martinus Nijhoff, 1985) ch 49.

[53]   See, eg, s 101(1) Constitution of Jamaica and s 136(6) Constitution of Trinidad and Tobago.

[54]   Pursuant to s 4 Judges Remuneration and Pensions Act 2008.

[55]   *R v Jones*, BS 2007 SC 9; *Neymour v AG*, BS 2006 SC 43; and *A v B et al*, BS 2007 SC 19. All unreported. Available on file with the author.

Commonwealth Caribbean constitutions also usually provide that the judges' other terms and conditions of service shall not be altered to their disadvantage during their term of office. As a result, in 2007, the Government of Trinidad's attempt to enact legislation which would have required senior judges to comply with the requirements of the Integrity in Public Life Act with regard to the annual disclosure of their assets and to comply with a Code of Ethics was struck down by the High Court on the grounds, inter alia, that it constituted an alteration of the terms of service of judges appointed prior to the amendment to the Constitution to their disadvantage.[56]

There are however, other, less direct means by which governments can make a judge's working life more or less tolerable. As Keith Patchett has commented:

> It calls for a man of exceptional character, particularly in a small society, to withstand the sustained pressure of public and private criticism, of the wilful ignoring of his requests for executive attention to his official claims on Government, of the cumulation of petty frustration of his legitimate personal requirements which in such matters as housing, leave, tax and allowances he must constantly refer to Government, of the apparent preferment of other person of less ability and so-on.[57]

The other side of this coin is the offer of inducements to judges to toe the political line of the party in government. Nowhere has this been more blatant than during the Burnham era in Guyana, when all sorts of special privileges and perks were made available to compliant judges, including, 'chauffeur cars, free gasoline and utilities, generous housing and duty allowances, equally generous leave packages, and access to foreign exchange when this resource was scarce'.[58] In addition, customs officials were instructed not to search judges on their return to the country and judges were promised that they would be considered for diplomatic and other high profile postings on retirement.[59] According to James and Lutchman, the price paid for this largesse was 'judicial obsequity' and the opening up of a gap between the Constitution on paper and the Constitution in action, with judges finding ever more

---

[56] *Integrity Commission v AG Trinidad*, TT 2007 HC 201. Unreported. Available on file with the author.
[57] Quoted in Ryan, above (n 15) 17.
[58] Ibid, 30.
[59] Ibid.

ingenious ways of excusing flagrant infringements of the Constitution
by the executive.[60]

D. POLITICAL CULTURE

While the institutional arrangements described above are important they
are not the only safeguard of judicial independence; it is also important
that the judiciary is respected by the other branches of government as a
separate and autonomous entity. Unfortunately, however, the perceived
level of political interference in the judiciary is high.[61] While this is, of
course, difficult to prove, the following two examples may help to illustrate the kinds of political pressures faced by judges in the region.

The first example is Guyana during the Burnham era when the
President openly referred to members of the judiciary as, 'my judges
who do my bidding'. Under President Burnham, the ruling PNC was
declared to be 'paramount' to all other agencies of government, and
it was made clear to the judges that whenever the meaning of a particular law was unclear or ambiguous they were expected to give an
interpretation which was consistent with the national goal of creating a
new socialist order.[62] This message was reinforced in an address to the
judges by the Chancellor of the Judiciary in 1981 in which he informed
them that 'socialist democracy is now an inseparable and organic part
of our nationalist ethos'.[63] The consequences of failing to promote
the nationalist ethos were also made clear as Burnham was fond of
boasting: 'I am not God. God forgives!'[64] Guyanese judges were thus
required to function in an environment that was insecure and that
actively discouraged judicial independence.[65]

[60] R James and H Lutchman, *Law and the Political Environment in Guyana*
(Georgetown, Guyana, Institute of Development Studies, University of Guyana,
1984) quoted in Ryan, above (n 15) 25.
[61] C Barrow-Giles, *Regional Trends in Constitutional Developments in the Commonwealth
Caribbean* (Conflict Prevention and Peace Forum paper, 2010). Available at: www. agora-
parl.org/search-resources-results?combine=trends%20in%20constitutional%20
development%20in%20the%20commonwealth%20caribbean.
[62] Ibid, 26.
[63] Quoted in Ryan, above (n 15) 27.
[64] Ibid, 29.
[65] Ibid, 30.

The second example is Trinidad, between 1995 and 2001, which witnessed two very tense encounters between the Chief Justice and the Attorney General that were widely perceived as attempts by the Government to assert its authority over the judiciary. The first concerned a Bill, which the Attorney General sought to introduce and which, if implemented, would have made the JLSC subject to review by a Joint Select Committee of Parliament. From the Chief Justice's point of view, the most objectionable feature of the Bill was that the Chief Justice, as Chairman of the JLSC, could be compelled by the Joint Select Committee to testify and be subject to cross-examination by MPs. In turn, this would give a disgruntled person who was dissatisfied with a decision of the JLSC not to appoint them as a judge, or not to extend their tenure as a judge beyond the age of retirement, the opportunity to lobby members of the Joint Select Committee and get them to embarrass and harass members of the JLSC by a hostile cross-examination carried out in public, or by making and publishing an adverse report on the decisions of the JLSC. Notwithstanding the Chief Justice's objections, the Government was able to use its majority to secure the Bill's passage through the House of Representatives and it was only in the Senate, at the insistence of the Independent members, that the Bill was ultimately amended to exclude the JLSC from the Joint Select Committee's remit.[66]

The second encounter concerned a dispute about who should have responsibility for the administration of justice in Trinidad—the Attorney General or the Chief Justice—and whether the latter was responsible to the former for the administration of the courts. This dispute was remarkable not only for its very public nature, being conducted in an exchange of letters published in the national newspapers, but also for the degree of hostility between the Government and the judiciary which it generated, leading at one point to a threat by Trinidad's judges, all but one of whom supported the Chief Justice, either to strike or join in a mass resignation. In order to avoid this catastrophe, and to bring about a rapprochement between the Chief Justice and the Attorney General, the Law Association of Trinidad appointed a former Court of Appeal judge, Justice Georges, to investigate the causes of the dispute

[66] Ibid, 53.

and attempt to mediate the differences between the Chief justice and Attorney General.[67]

Unfortunately, however, Justice George's report, which came down largely in favour of the Chief Justice, did not achieve this objective. Instead, it was rejected by the Government which proceeded immediately to establish a Commission of Inquiry (the Commission), to enquire into the management and administration of justice in Trinidad with reference, inter alia, to 'allegations that the Executive has attempted to undermine the independence of the Judiciary'. The establishment of the Commission was highly controversial, not least because it was composed of three foreigners and led by a former British Lord Chancellor, Lord McKay, who had a reputation for 'bringing the judiciary under a tight leash'.[68] Many among the legal community considered that the Government's real reason in establishing the Commission was to discredit or humiliate the Chief Justice who it was widely believed had embarrassed the Government by exposing their plan to bring the judiciary under closer executive control. Indeed, for a long time the President resisted the Prime Minister's advice to appoint the members of the Commission while he sought legal advice on whether it was constitutional for him to do so if there was a risk that the enquiry by the Commission would violate the principle of the separation of powers. In the event, the President only finally agreed to appoint the Commission in order to avoid a constitutional crisis.[69]

The issues addressed in the Commission's report were wide ranging, including the judicial appointments process, the mechanisms for dealing with complaints against judges, whether there should be a Chancellor and who should be the medium through which communications should flow between the executive and the judiciary, but its principal focus was on the relationship between the Chief Justice and the Attorney General. While the Commission was careful in its conclusion to make it clear that it considered that it would be unhelpful to rake over what had happened between these two and to apportion blame, it did note that the responsibility of the Attorney General included communication

[67] Ibid, 69.
[68] P Richards, 'Trinidad & Tobago: Commission Clears Government of Interference in Judiciary Charge', *Inter Press Service News Agency* (13 October 2000). Available at: www.ipsnews2.wpengine.com.
[69] Quoted in Ryan, above (n 15) 73.

between the executive government and the judiciary and that the former was entitled to full information from the judiciary, not on the basis that it was accountable to him, but on the basis that Parliament and the public are entitled to full information about the standards attained by the administration of justice. Predictably, the report was seized upon by the Prime Minister as vindication of his Attorney General's position in the dispute with the Chief Justice and, within a year of the publication of the Commission's report, the Chief Justice retired.

PART III: THE CARIBBEAN COURT OF JUSTICE (CCJ)

Against the backdrop described above, it is perhaps no surprise that concern about the excessive politicisation of relations between the executive and the judiciary featured prominently in the debate which raged across the region about the desirability of replacing the JCPC with the CCJ as the region's final appellate court. Previously, the fact that local politicians had no influence over the composition of the JCPC offered a promise of neutrality which it was feared would be compromised if it were replaced by a regional court, the composition of which could be influenced by local politicians. In this section I will begin by exploring the contours of that debate before turning to examine the mechanisms that have been put in place to address these concerns and to secure the independence of the CCJ and its judges.

A. THE DEBATE ABOUT THE CCJ's APPELLATE JURISDICTION

Though it is possible to trace the idea of a regional appellate court as far back as 1901, the idea really began to gain momentum in 1987 when the Caribbean Community and Common Market (CARICOM) Heads of Government Conference agreed to consider a proposal by Trinidad for the establishment of a Caribbean Court of Appeal.[70] At around

---

[70] See D Simmons, 'The Caribbean Court of Justice: A Unique Institution of Caribbean Creativity' (2004–05) 31 *Commonwealth Law Bulletin* 1, 72–73.

the same time, CARICOM was investigating ways of strengthening the regional economic integration movement. These two ideas subsequently coincided in the Report of the West Indian Commission (WIC), *Time for Action*, in 1992, which concluded that the need for a regional court with both an *appellate* jurisdiction and an *original* jurisdiction to give effect to the economic integration objectives of CARICOM was now 'overwhelming' and 'fundamental to the process of integration itself'.[71] The response to the WIC's recommendations was, however, to say the least, divided. While the proposal for a regional court with an original jurisdiction in matters involving CARICOM met with more or less complete agreement across the region, the proposal for a regional court with an appellate jurisdiction proved to be far more controversial. The arguments on both sides of the debate about a regional appellate court can be briefly summarised as follows.

Those in favour argued, first, that having a regional appellate court would improve access to justice for citizens of the region. Though there was a steady flow of appeals from the region to the JCPC, the vast majority were appeals against convictions for murder and appeals raising constitutional issues arising out of the imposition of the death penalty, where the defendants were very often represented on a pro bono basis by British lawyers. The number of appeals in civil cases was, by comparison, relatively few.[72] Second, it was argued that it was inconsistent with the post-independence status of Commonwealth Caribbean countries to have ultimate legal sovereignty vested in a foreign court. As Sir David Simmons remarked, this may have been in part an emotional argument, but such 'psychological considerations are important and the symbolism is not to be discounted'.[73] This sentiment was echoed by Rex Nettleford, a member of the WIC:

> It is thought that the [JCPC], however, flawed, remains to many better than anything we can design for ourselves ... A West Indian Court of Appeal is

[71] Report of the West Indian Commission, *Time for Action*, 2nd edn (Kingston, University of the West Indies Press, 1993) 11.

[72] See D Simmons, 'The Caribbean Court of Justice' (2005) 29 *Nova Law Review* 169–98, 177.

[73] Quoted in S McIntosh, *Caribbean Constitutional Reform: Rethinking the West Indian Polity* (Kingston, Jamaica, Caribbean Law Publishing Company, 2002) 266.

therefore a necessary institutional manifestation of our will to self-respect and self-esteem.[74]

Third, it was argued that a regional appellate court would be able to develop a distinctively Caribbean jurisprudence. As the Honourable Michael de la Bastide, who was to be appointed the first President of the CCJ, explained: 'It is very important that the judges who make the decisions which create our jurisprudence have a close and very intimate connection with our societies'.[75]

These are each, individually, strong arguments, and together they make a compelling case for the establishment of a regional appellate court. They were not, however, enough to dispel the concern of some of the CCJ's opponents that there was a hidden agenda at work. In particular, it was feared that the Heads of Governments' enthusiasm for establishing a regional appellate court was principally motivated by a series of judgments delivered by the JCPC: beginning, in 1993, with its landmark judgment in *Pratt and Morgan v AG Jamaica*,[76] which cumulatively had the effect of seriously curtailing the right of the region's governments to implement the death penalty. This, in turn, gave rise to the fear that the Heads of Government intended to establish a regional appellate court that would be composed of local judges who, unlike the judges of the JCPC, would respect their desire to continue to implement the death penalty; in other words, 'a hanging court'.

Quite apart from the complicating factor of the death penalty, the CCJ's opponents were also concerned about a cluster of issues affecting its institutional structure. Would the CCJ be adequately funded? Would its judges be insulated from political interference? Would it be sufficiently entrenched within the Constitution of each country to ensure that a government could not amend the Constitution to restrict or eliminate their citizens' rights of appeal to the CCJ by a simple majority vote? I will now turn to explore how the Heads of Government collectively sought to respond to each of these concerns.

[74] Also quoted in McIntosh, ibid, 272.
[75] M de la Bastide, 'The Case for a Caribbean Court of Appeal' (1995) 5 *Caribbean Law Review* 401, 429.
[76] *Pratt and Morgan v AG Jamaica* [1994] 2 AC 1.

1. Funding of the CCJ

The Commonwealth Caribbean includes some of the poorest countries in the Western hemisphere.[77] How then to secure the funding necessary to guarantee the CCJ's independence and to ensure that it functioned at a level appropriate to a final appellate court for the entire region? The record of a number of governments in the region in meeting their financial obligations in respect of regional institutions was poor and fears that the same governments might be equally neglectful in meeting their contributions to the funding of the CCJ were compounded by the failure of successive national governments across the region to invest in the infrastructure of their civil and criminal justice systems.[78] In response to these concerns, the Heads of Government agreed that the CCJ would be financed through the mechanism of a trust fund of US$100 million. This was intended to cover the running costs of the Court, the salaries of the judges and the expenses of the Regional and Judicial Legal Services Commissions (RJLSC) (discussed further below).[79] The trust fund was raised on the international money markets by the Caribbean Development Bank (CDB) on behalf of the national governments, and the latter undertook to repay their respective share of the loan to the CDB.[80] To prevent a national government from breaching this undertaking, the loans were charged by law on the Consolidated Fund or public revenues of each country.[81]

In order to guard against political interference, provision was made for the trust fund to be administered by a board of trustees, the members of which are drawn primarily from the private sector and civil society.[82] While it was anticipated that the original sum invested in the trust fund would be sufficient to guarantee the funding of the CCJ in perpetuity, provision was also made for the adequacy of the fund to

---

[77] See Index Mundi. Available at: www.indexmundi.com.

[78] PK Menon, 'Regional Integration: A Case Study of the Caribbean Community (CARICOM)' (1995) 5 *Caribbean Law Review* 85.

[79] See K Malleson, 'Promoting Judicial Independence in the International Courts: Lessons from the Caribbean' (2009) 58 *International & Comparative Law Quarterly* 671, 678.

[80] Ibid.

[81] Art XXVIII, Agreement Establishing the Caribbean Court of Justice Trust Fund (Trust Fund Agreement).

[82] Trust Fund Agreement, Art VI.

be reviewed from time to time and for the national governments to be required to make additional contributions to the fund if its resources should be found to be inadequate.[83]

2. Appointment and Removal of the CCJ's Judges

Because of the widespread concern that had been expressed across the region about the role of the executive in the judicial appointments process, it was accepted by the Heads of Government that it was crucial to insulate the appointment of judges to the CCJ, as far as possible, from political interference. Accordingly, responsibility for the selection and appointment of judges of the CCJ, with the exception of the President, is vested in the RJLSC.[84] This is a very unusual arrangement for an international court—where the normal procedure is for judges to be appointed by governmental nomination and/or election—but is a system with which the Heads of Government were familiar from their experience of the appointment of judges to their own national courts and to the ECSC. If political interference was to be avoided, however, the independence of the RJLSC was also crucial. Therefore, it was agreed by the Heads of Government that membership of the RJLSC should not be dominated by politicians or lawyers, but would include other sections of the wider community. As a result, the RJLSC is composed of 11 members, including: the President of the CCJ as chair; two lawyers; two lay people; two academics; two representatives of the regional Bar; and two chairs of the Public Service Commissions and JLSCs of the Member States (appointed by rotation in alphabetical order).[85]

With the exception of the President, appointments of the CCJ's judges by the RJLSC are made by a majority of votes of all members.[86] Once appointed, a judge may sit until they reach the age of 72.[87] Originally, there was no provision for extending a judge's tenure beyond this age—presumably to avoid the incentive that the prospect of such

---

[83] Ibid, Art VII.
[84] Art V, Agreement Establishing the CCJ (Agreement).
[85] Agreement, Art I.
[86] Ibid, Art IV, para 7.
[87] Ibid, Art IX, paras 1 and 3.

an extension might offer to judges to hand down judgments that favour national governments. However, as a result of a recent Protocol to the Agreement, during the CCJ's 'evolutionary phase', which will end when the maximum number of judges prescribed by the Agreement have been appointed, a judge's tenure may be extended until the judge reaches the age of 75.[88] A judge of the CCJ may only be removed from office for inability to perform the functions of their office, whether arising from illness or any other cause, or for misbehaviour,[89] and only then after a majority vote of all members of the RJLSC, having first been referred to a tribunal, consisting of a chairman and not less than two other members selected by the RJLSC from among persons who have held a senior judicial appointment.[90]

Separate provision has been made with regard to the President who is appointed by a qualified majority vote of three-quarters of the Heads of Government.[91] This would appear to offer more scope for interference by the Heads of Government, but this is limited by the requirement that the Heads of Government must appoint as president someone recommended by the RJLSC.[92] The President holds office for a non-renewable term of seven years or until the President reaches the age of 72, whichever is earlier.[93] The President may be removed from office by a qualified majority vote of three-quarters of the Heads of Government.[94] However, as with their appointment, the President's removal is subject to the recommendation of the RJLSC, which itself must act on the advice of a tribunal that can only be appointed if at least three of the Heads of Government represent to the others that the question of the President's removal ought to be investigated.[95] In such a case, the members of the tribunal are selected by the Heads of Government.[96]

---

[88] Art II, para 1(b), Protocol to the Agreement Establishing the Caribbean Court of Justice Relating to the Tenure of Office of Judges of the Court.

[89] Agreement, Art IX, para 4.

[90] Ibid, para 6(a).

[91] Agreement, Art IV, para 6.

[92] Ibid.

[93] Agreement, Art IX, para 2. This may be extended until the age of 75 or the date on which he completes seven years in office, whichever is first.

[94] Agreement, Art IX, para 6(b).

[95] Ibid.

[96] Ibid.

3. Constitutional Entrenchment of the CCJ

The right of appeal to the JCPC was included in all but one of the Independence Constitutions and was expressly entrenched at varying levels across the region. For example, under the Constitution of Barbados, which has now ratified the appellate jurisdiction of the CCJ, the abolition of the right of appeal to the JCPC required the support of at least two-thirds of both Houses of Parliament.[97] In Trinidad, currently, it requires the support of three-quarters of the membership of the House of Representatives.[98] All the former Associated States of the Eastern Caribbean require, in addition to various majorities in Parliament, approval by referendum.[99] The exception to the above is Jamaica, where the right of appeal to the JCPC is included in the Independence Constitution, but is not constitutionally entrenched.[100] This omission is significant because it led the People's National Party (PNP) while in government, to assume that it could introduce legislation to amend the Constitution and replace the right of appeal to the JCPC with a right of appeal to the CCJ by means of ordinary legislation; ie, by a simple majority vote. The advantage from the PNP perspective was that this meant that the Constitution could be amended without the support of the opposition Jamaica Labour Party (JLP), which they knew they could not secure. This assumption was, however, challenged in the case of *Independent Jamaican Council of Human Rights (1998) Ltd v AG Jamaica*.[101]

In bringing this challenge, the appellants were concerned that the effect of the legislation proposed by the PNP would have been to establish a court of superior jurisdiction which could overturn decisions of both the Jamaican Supreme Court and the Jamaican Court of Appeal, but which enjoyed none of the entrenched protection afforded by Chapter VII of the Constitution to these courts. This included the provisions designed to guarantee the security of tenure of the judges of both courts as well as the judges' terms and conditions of service, which could only altered by a Bill which had secured the support of not

---

[97] s 49(2)(e) Constitution of Barbados.
[98] s 54(3)(b) Constitution of Trinidad and Tobago.
[99] See, eg, s 47(5) Constitution of Antigua and Barbuda.
[100] Part III, Constitution of Jamaica.
[101] *Independent Jamaican Council of Human Rights (1998) Ltd v AG Jamaica* [2005] 2 AC 356.

less than two-thirds of all members of both Houses of Parliament. As counsel for the appellants, Dr Lloyd Barnett explained, 'It would make a mockery of the Constitution if the safeguards entrenched to ensure the integrity of the legal process in Jamaica could be circumvented by creating a superior court enjoying no such constitutional protection'.[102]

Though the Agreement Establishing the CCJ (the Agreement), also contained a number of provisions designed to protect the security of tenure of the CCJ's judges and their terms and conditions of service, which were arguably equal to if not stronger than the protection afforded to judges by Chapter VII of the Jamaican Constitution, the problem, as the appellants explained, was that the Agreement could be amended by the Heads of Government and would then require only an affirmative resolution of the Jamaican Parliament to take effect in the domestic law of Jamaica. This was a strong argument, but the fact remained that the right of appeal to the JCPC was not constitutionally entrenched. According to the appellants, however, 'it was the substance of the law that must be regarded not the form'. The question to be answered was thus whether a power to review the decisions of the higher courts of Jamaica could properly be entrusted to a new court which, whatever its other merits, did not enjoy the protection afforded to the higher judiciary of Jamaica, without adopting the procedure mandated by the Constitution for the amendment of an entrenched provision. In answering this question, the JCPC decided that the test was not whether the protection provided by the Agreement was stronger or weaker than that which existed before, but whether, in substance, it was different; for if it was different the effect of the legislation would be to alter the regime established by Chapter VII of the Jamaican Constitution. In the JCPC's view it was, indeed, different and, accordingly, it was necessary to follow the procedure appropriate for the amendment of an entrenched provision.

Notwithstanding the decision of the JCPC in this case there still remains some disagreement in Jamaica about the procedure to be followed for substituting the CCJ in place of the JCPC. For their part, the JLP have consistently stated that they would not be prepared to support any Bill to replace the JCPC with the CCJ, which had not also been approved by a majority of Jamaica's citizens in a referendum. This argument is based on the presumption that the amendment section of the Constitution (section 49) would itself have to be amended in order to afford the CCJ the same level of protection afforded to the Supreme Court and the Court of Appeal, and section 49 can only be amended by way of referendum. In practice, whether the JLP's interpretation is correct matters not because, as a matter of *realpolitick*, so long as the JLP sticks to its guns, a referendum will be required before the PNP is able to secure the two-thirds majority necessary to secure the legislation's passage through Parliament.

B. THE PROSPECTS FOR THE CCJ's APPELLATE JURISDICTION

Notwithstanding the measures put in place by the Heads of Government to allay the concerns of those opposed to the CCJ, only three countries currently subscribe to its appellate jurisdiction—Guyana, Barbados and Belize. This makes it increasingly difficult for its supporters to justify the sums invested in its creation. However, the recent announcement by the Prime Minister of Jamaica that she wishes to see her country ratifying the CCJ's appellate jurisdiction,[103] and the declaration by Trinidad's Prime Minister that she intends to ratify the CCJ's criminal appellate jurisdiction,[104] gives reason for some cautious optimism about the CCJ's future. Of course, there is no guarantee that either will be able to secure the special majorities necessary to amend their respective Constitutions to give effect to the CCJ's appellate jurisdiction, but in both cases the Opposition appears to be prepared to support such an amendment. In addition, there have been calls by the Prime Minister of Dominica for the OECS Member States collectively to ratify the CCJ's appellate jurisdiction.[105]

---

[103] O Bowcott, 'Jamaica's colonial-era ties to the UK legal system continue to fray', *The Guardian* (London, 6 January 2012). Available at: www.theguardian.com/world/2012/jan/06/jamaica-ties-uk-legal-system.

[104] 'T&T to embrace CCJ as its final Court of Appeal', *Trinidad Express Newspapers* (26 April 2012). Available at: www.trinidadexpress.com/news/TT-to-embrace-CCJ-as-its-final-Court-of-Appeal-148968175.html.

[105] 'Dominica to join CCJ', *NationNews.Com* (28 March 2012). Available at: www.nationnews.com/articles/view/dominica-to-join-ccj.

The CCJ's decision in *AG (Barbados) v Joseph and Boyce*[106] may also have helped to allay the concerns of its opponents that it would be 'a hanging court'. In this case the CCJ not only upheld the justiciability of the prerogative of mercy, but also affirmed the right of condemned prisoners to await the outcome of their petition to international human rights bodies before they are executed. It is true the CCJ also confirmed that 'the death penalty falls within internationally acceptable conduct on the part of civilised states' and was willing to extend the time limit for execution of the death sentence beyond the five years laid down by the JCPC in *Pratt and Morgan*, but the rationale for granting this extension was to take account of delays in the processing of petitions by international human rights bodies and it will, as a consequence, have the advantage of allowing the Government of Barbados to fulfil its international obligations without incurring the risk of falling foul of the *Pratt and Morgan* deadline.

Thus, the CCJ has not only answered local demands for 'autochthony', in the sense that it is truly a home-grown court, and for the severance of the link with the former imperial power which is embodied in the JCPC, but has also demonstrated that it is a final appellate court which takes account of the values of the societies over which it exercises jurisdiction.

PART IV: CONSTITUTIONAL REVIEW

By the time the first countries in the region were attaining their independence it was already a well established principle of the JCPC's jurisprudence that 'a legislature has no power to ignore the conditions of law-making that are imposed by the instrument which itself regulates its power to make law'.[107]

However, this body of jurisprudence was concerned with the law-making powers of colonial legislatures. Post-independence the question was: how would the courts of these newly independent countries respond when asked to review the constitutionality of legislation enacted

---

[106] *AG (Barbados) v Joseph and Boyce*, CCJ Appeal No CV2 of 2005.
[107] *Bribery Commission v Ranasinghe* [1964] PC 172, 197G.

by their 'sovereign' parliaments? For Commonwealth Caribbean judges, no less than the judges of the JCPC, the power to strike down legislation that is inconsistent with the Constitution still represented a significant departure from the Diceyan notion of the legislative supremacy of Parliament with which they were familiar. One of their first tasks in the post-independence era was, therefore, to locate the juridical basis for the exercise of this jurisdiction.

A. LOCATING THE JURIDICAL BASIS FOR CONSTITUTIONAL REVIEW

None of the Commonwealth Caribbean constitutions expressly provide for a power of constitutional review of legislation. But could such a power be derived by way of necessary implication from the text of these constitutions? This was the question which confronted the Court of Appeal of Trinidad in *Collymore and Abraham v Attorney General*,[108] which has been described by some commentators as the Commonwealth Caribbean's equivalent of *Marbury v Madison*.[109] In this case the Court of Appeal of Trinidad was asked to review the constitutionality of the Industrial Stabilisation Act 1965, which, it was alleged, infringed the right of free collective bargaining and the right to strike implied by the constitutionally guaranteed right of freedom of association. Before dealing with these issues, however, the Court decided that it was necessary to deal with the logically prior question of whether it was empowered by the Constitution to strike down Acts of Parliament in the absence of an express constitutional power to do so. This question was especially relevant in the context of Trinidad's 1962 Independence Constitution because, unlike other Commonwealth Caribbean constitutions, it did not contain a supreme law clause, declaring that laws which are inconsistent with the Constitution are, to the extent of that inconsistency, void.[110]

Trinidad's Independence Constitution did, however, contain a network of provisions which the Court regarded as relevant to establishing its power to review the constitutionality of legislation

---

[108] *Collymore and Abraham v Attorney General* (1968) 12 WIR 5 CA (Trinidad and Tobago).
[109] *Marbury v Madison*, 5 US 137.
[110] See, eg, s 2 Constitution of Antigua and Barbuda.

enacted by the Trinidadian Parliament. First, pursuant to section 36, Parliament's power to make laws was expressly 'subject to the provision of this Constitution'. Second, section 2 provided that 'no law shall abrogate, abridge or infringe or authorise the abrogation, abridgement or infringement of any of the rights and freedoms guaranteed by the Constitution'.[111] Third, pursuant to section 6, if any person alleged that their fundamental rights as guaranteed by the Constitution were being or were likely to be violated they could apply to the High Court for redress. On the basis of these provisions Chief Justice Wooding was moved to declare that:

> I am accordingly in no doubt that our Supreme Court has been constituted, and is, *the guardian of the Constitution*, so it is not only within its competence but also its right and duty to make binding declarations, if and whenever warranted, that an enactment passed by Parliament is *ultra vires* and therefore void and of no effect because it abrogates, abridges or infringes ... one or more of the rights and freedoms recognized and declared by [Chapter 1] (emphasis added).[112]

Justice Phillips, concurring, argued that once it was accepted that any law which offended against the prohibitions contained in section 2 of the Constitution was invalid, it was obvious that 'even without express provision' a power of constitutional review of legislation must reside in the Supreme Court. Any lingering doubts about this were, according to Justice Phillips, comprehensively erased by the express terms of section 6.[113]

It is to be noted that in *Collymore*, the Court was concerned with the courts' power to review legislation which contravened the fundamental rights guaranteed by the Constitution. Moreover, the enforcement provision contained in section 6, to which the Court attached considerable weight, was concerned with the right to apply to the High Court for redress in respect of violations of the fundamental rights guaranteed by the Constitution. What then about legislation which is alleged to infringe the other provisions of the Constitution, ie, the non-Bill of Rights provisions, for example, a statutory provision which sought to empower a body other than the Governor General acting on the advice of the Public Service Commission to make appointments to public

---

[111] Subject to the provisions of ss 3, 4 and 5 Constitution of Trinidad and Tobago.
[112] At 9A-8.
[113] At 21I and 22B.

offices? There are two possibilities. First, a number of Commonwealth Caribbean constitutions—Antigua, Dominica, Grenada, Guyana, St Kitts, and St Vincent—contain an identical enforcement provision in respect of violations of the non-Bill of Rights provisions of the Constitution.[114] Arguing by analogy with *Collymore*, such an enforcement provision, combined with a supreme law clause, would empower the courts to review the constitutionality of legislation that violates the non-Bill of Rights provisions of the Constitution on exactly the same basis as the courts are empowered to review violations of the Bills of Rights provisions.

The second possibility is relevant to those constitutions, such as the Jamaican Constitution, that do not contain an express enforcement provision for the non-Bill of Rights provisions of the Constitution. In the case of these constitutions it may be argued that a power of constitutional review is necessarily implied by the limits placed on Parliament's law-making powers by its constituent nature. This is essentially the approach that the JCPC adopted in *Hinds v The Queen*,[115] in which the JCPC struck down certain provisions of Jamaica's Gun Court Act, which purported to confer on the Full Court Division of the Gun Court, which was composed of persons qualified and appointed as resident magistrates, a jurisdiction which under the provisions of Chapter VII of the Constitution could only be exercised by a person qualified and appointed as a judge of the Supreme Court. *Hinds* is of particular significance because it was the first piece of legislation enacted by a post-independence Parliament in the Commonwealth Caribbean to be struck down by the JCPC.

More recently, the courts' power to review the constitutionality of legislation has even been extended, in some countries, by statute to permit the Attorney General on behalf of the Cabinet to refer to the Court of Appeal questions concerning, inter alia, the interpretation of the Constitution and the constitutionality or interpretation of any legislation enacted by Parliament.[116] Thus, in *Attorney General's Reference*

---

[114] See, eg, s 119 Constitution of Antigua and Barbuda.

[115] *Hinds v The Queen* [1977] AC 175.

[116] See, eg, Antigua—The Attorney General's Reference (Constitutional Questions) Act 2009.

(Constitutional Questions), Re:[117] the Court of Appeal of St Lucia was asked to answer a series of questions regarding the Eastern Caribbean Supreme Court (Rates of Pension) Judges (Act) and the constitutional entitlement to a pension of a judge who has retired from office before the constitutionally mandated retirement age.

B. BILLS OF RIGHTS AND CONSTITUTIONAL REVIEW

Having located the juridical basis for their power of constitutional review the next task for Commonwealth Caribbean judges was to develop principles of constitutional interpretation which would allow them to discharge their role as 'guardian[s] of the Constitution' while at the same time respecting the democratic mandates vested in the executive and the legislature respectively. This would require a fine balance to be struck, especially in cases involving constitutional challenges based on the Bill of Rights guaranteed by each of the Independence Constitutions.

As noted in chapter one, the Bills of Rights to be found in the region's Independence Constitutions were modelled on the European Convention on Human Rights (ECHR), with the exception of Trinidad. Here, the Bill of Rights was broadly modelled on the Canadian Declaration of Rights, but with the addition of certain rights, such as the right to equal treatment by a public authority and freedom of movement. Commonwealth Caribbean Bills of Rights thus seek to protect the so-called 'first generation' rights: that is civil and political rights that take the form of negative protection against the actions of the government. Though there are minor differences between the region's Bills of Rights, they each typically include the following: the right to life; the right to liberty; freedom of movement; protection from arbitrary arrest or detention; protection from inhuman treatment; protection from slavery or forced labour; freedom from deprivation of property; freedom of religion and conscience; freedom of expression; freedom of assembly and association; and protection from discrimination on the grounds of race, place of origin, political affiliations, race, creed or sex. Though the Bills of Rights contained

---

[117] *Attorney General's Reference (Constitutional Questions), Re*, LC 2010 CA 8. Unreported. Available on file with the author.

in the Constitutions of Trinidad and Guyana were amended when they became a republic and a 'Socialist Cooperative' respectively, they did not diverge fundamentally from their predecessors, save that in the case of Guyana, there were several extensions to the 'limitation' sub-clause in respect of the right to property.[118]

Notwithstanding their origins in the ECHR, the inclusion of a Bill of Rights in the Independence Constitutions of former British colonies was a relatively recent phenomenon,[119] and Commonwealth Caribbean judges, therefore, had little to draw upon by way of precedent when interpreting these Bills of Rights. Their task was made all the harder by two additional factors: first, by the inclusion in the Independence Constitutions of saving clauses which preserved certain pre-independence laws and forms of lawful punishment, such as the death penalty, from constitutional scrutiny even if they were in conflict with one or more provisions of the Bill of Rights; and second, by the fact that the judges of the final appellate court, the JCPC, were being asked to adjudicate on issues that affected societies whose values they did not necessarily share and about which they knew relatively little. Both of these factors will need to be bone in mind as we explore the presumptions and principles of interpretation that were developed to guide Commonwealth Caribbean judges when exercising their powers of constitutional review.

1. The Presumption of Constitutionality

When discussing the presumption of constitutionality as it is applied in the context of the Commonwealth Caribbean,[120] it is important to distinguish between two different applications of the presumption. The first, which is relatively unproblematic, is as a canon of construction. Applied in this way the presumption requires a court, if it is possible, to read the language of a

---

[118] M De Merieux, *Fundamental Rights in the Commonwealth Caribbean* (University of the West Indies, Faculty of Law Library, 1992) 38.

[119] B Simpson, *Human Rights and the End of Empire: Britain and the Genesis of the European Convention* (Oxford, Oxford University Press, 2001) 870.

[120] The operation of such a presumption is not, of course, unique to the Commonwealth Caribbean and has been applied by US courts for over a century. See the landmark article of J Thayer, 'The Origins and Scope of the American Doctrine of Constitutional Law' (1893) 7 *Harvard Law Review* 129.

statute as subject to an implied term which avoids conflict with any constitutional limitations.[121] As Lord Cooke has explained, this application of the presumption requires courts to 'read down' legislation, if sufficiently precise implications may be articulated, so as to make it conform to the Constitution.[122] Thus, in the Jamaican case of *R v Boxx*,[123] the amended Offences Against the Person Act 1992, which provides for a mandatory death sentence for any murder committed in the course or furtherance of a robbery, was *presumed* to be subject to an implied judicial discretion to impose a death sentence in order to be compatible with an accused's rights under sections 17(1) and 20(1) of the Jamaican Constitution. It may not, however, always be possible to read down legislation in this way. Thus, in *Leonard Hector v AG Antigua*,[124] the JCPC refused to construe section 33B of the Public Order (Amendment) Act 1976, which criminalised statements likely to undermine public confidence in the conduct of public affairs, as if this were immediately followed by the words 'in a manner which tends to disturb public order'. The offending provision was, accordingly, adjudged to violate the constitutionally guaranteed right to free expression.

The second application of the presumption is more controversial as it involves the court in presuming that a statute is constitutional unless it has been shown to be unconstitutional and the burden on the party seeking to prove that a statute is unconstitutional is a heavy one.[125] The reason for this was explained by the Court of Appeal in *Faultin v AG Trinidad*[126] by reference to a statement by Isaacs J of the High Court of Australia:

> Nullification of enactments and confusion of public business are not lightly to be introduced. Unless, therefore, it becomes clear beyond reasonable doubt that the legislation in question transgresses the limits laid down by the organic law of the Constitution, it must be allowed to stand as the true expression of the national will.[127]

This second application of the presumption most often comes into play in cases where a question arises whether legislation that is alleged

[121]   *AG v Momodou Jobe* [1984] AC 689.
[122]   *Observer Publications Ltd v Matthew* [2001] UKPC 11 [49].
[123]   *R v Boxx*, JM 2002 CA 52. Unreported. Available on file with author.
[124]   *Leonard Hector v AG Antigua* [1990] 2 AC 312.
[125]   *Mootoo v AG Trinidad* (1979) 30 WIR 411, 415.
[126]   *Faultin v AG Trinidad* (1978) 30 WIR 351.
[127]   *Federal Commissioner of Taxation v Munro* (1926) 38 CLR 180.

to interfere with one or more provisions of the Bill of Rights can be justified as necessary in the public interest or to protect the rights and freedoms of others. For example, in *AG v Antigua Times Ltd*,[128] the JCPC was asked to consider whether legislation, which required the publishers of newspapers to pay an annual licence fee and to deposit a sum of $10,000 with the Accountant General to satisfy any judgment of the Supreme Court for libel, was necessary for any of the purposes permitted by section 10 of the Constitution. These included, inter alia, defence, public safety, public order, public morality or public health, or for the purpose of protecting the reputations, rights and freedoms of other persons. In the JCPC's view, the proper approach to this question was to presume, until the contrary appears or is shown, that all Acts passed by the Parliament of Antigua were necessary for the purposes permitted by section 10 of the Constitution.

A similar approach was taken by the JCPC in *Hinds* when considering the constitutionality of certain provisions of the Gun Court Act, which allowed for hearings *in camera*, in alleged breach of section 20(3) of the Constitution, which provided that all proceedings of every court shall be held in public. As Lord Diplock noted, by section 20(4) of the Constitution, persons other than the parties and their legal representatives could be excluded from proceedings 'in the interests of defence, public safety, public order, public morality ... or the protection of the private lives of persons concerned in the proceedings'. In deciding whether or not the provisions of the Gun Court Act were saved by this provision Lord Diplock declared:

> By s 48(1) of the Constitution the power to make laws for the peace, order and good government of Jamaica is vested in Parliament; and prima facie it is for Parliament to decide what is or is not reasonably required in the interests of public safety or public order. Such a decision involves considerations of public policy which lie outside the field of the judicial power.[129]

This meant that a court should start with the presumption that the circumstances existing in Jamaica were such that hearings *in camera* were reasonably required in the interests of public safety or public order. Such a presumption could be rebutted, but only if the Court was satisfied that 'Parliament was either acting in bad faith, or had misinterpreted the

---

[128] *AG v Antigua Times Ltd* [1976] AC 16.
[129] [1976] 1 All ER 353, 369.

provision of the Constitution under which it purported to act'.[130] Since no evidence had been adduced to rebut the presumption and since, unlike the judges of the Court of Appeal of Jamaica, the judges of the JCPC had no personal knowledge of the circumstances in Jamaica that gave rise to the Gun Court Act, Lord Diplock was not satisfied that the presumption had been rebutted in this case.

It may be argued that Lord Diplock's reasoning reflects the uneasiness felt generally by judges of the JCPC in imposing their view of what may be reasonably required to protect the interests of the citizens of countries from which they are both geographically and culturally remote. As Lord Hoffmann subsequently observed:

> Although the [JCPC] has done its best to serve the Caribbean ... our remoteness from the community has been a handicap. We have been necessarily cautious in doing anything which might be seen as inappropriate in local conditions and although this caution may have occasionally saved us from doing the wrong thing, I am sure it has also sometimes inhibited us from doing the right thing.[131]

However, remoteness, whether cultural or geographic, does not account for the widespread acceptance of this application of the presumption by local judges when deferring to their respective parliaments, as reflected in the remarks of Chief Justice Hyatali in *AG Trinidad v Mootoo*:

> Legislators, as well as judges, are bound to obey and support the Constitution and it is to be understood that they have weighed the constitutional validity of every Act they pass. Hence the presumption is always in favour of the constitutionality of a statute, not against it; and the Courts will not adjudge it invalid unless its violation of the Constitution is, in their judgment, clear, complete and unmistakable.[132]

Instead, it would seem that when invoked by the local courts this second application of the presumption of constitutionality is based on a traditional Diceyan view of the respective constitutional and institutional competences of the courts and the legislature, which is coming to seem increasingly anachronistic when compared with the *'culture of*

---

[130] Ibid.

[131] Speech at the Annual Dinner of the Law Association of Trinidad and Tobago (10 October 2003).

[132] *AG Trinidad v Mootoo*, TT 1976 CA 23. Unreported. Available on file with author.

justification' predominant elsewhere in the Commonwealth. The latter shifts the burden away from the applicant and onto the State to provide a substantive justification for any interference with fundamental rights.[133] To date, however, the only successful invocation of this latter approach has been in the case of *Observer Publications Ltd v Matthew* in which Lord Cooke held that the Government of Antigua had failed to show that their refusal to grant a broadcasting licence to the appellants was justified on any of the extensive grounds authorised in section 12(4) of the Constitution. Moreover, the impact of the *Observer Publications* case is limited by the fact that the JCPC was concerned in that case with the constitutionality of the decision of the Government to refuse to grant a broadcasting licence, rather than with the constitutionality of the telecommunications legislation of Antigua. The JCPC has yet to declare that it is for the Government in the first instance to justify legislative interference with a constitutional right.

2. Saving Clauses and the '*Nasralla* Presumption'

Quite apart from the restrictions imposed by the presumption of constitutionality, the courts' power of constitutional review is also heavily circumscribed by the inclusion in the Independence Constitutions of saving clauses for pre-independence laws and forms of punishment that were lawful prior to independence. These saving clauses are of two types. The first, which may be categorised as a *partial* savings clause, preserves all forms of punishment that were lawful prior to independence. Thus, while section 17(1) of the Constitution of Jamaica offers a guarantee against inhuman or degrading treatment or punishment, section 17(2) provides that:

> Nothing ... done under the authority of any law shall be held to be ... in contravention of this section to the extent that the law in question authorises the infliction of any description of punishment which was lawful in Jamaica immediately before [the date of Independence].

Such partial savings clauses can be found in all the early Commonwealth Caribbean constitutions, and it was not until the Constitutions of Saint

---

[133] See M Cohen-Eliya and I Porat, 'Proportionality and the Culture of Justification' (2010) 59(2) *American Journal of Comparative Law* 463–90.

Vincent and Dominica were enacted in 1978 that the drafters finally saw fit to dispense with such a clause. The second type of saving laws clause, which may be categorised as a *general* savings clause, is even more extensive and affords immunity from constitutional challenge to all laws that were in force at the time of independence. Thus, section 26(8) of the Constitution of Jamaica provides that:

> Nothing contained in any law in force immediately before the appointed day shall be held to be inconsistent with any of the provisions of this Chapter, and nothing done under the authority of any such law shall be held to be done in contravention of any of these provisions.

Identical clauses can be found in the Constitutions of Trinidad, Barbados, the Bahamas and Belize; though, in the case of Belize, the clause was for a fixed term only and expired five years after independence.[134]

Clearly, the inclusion of a partial savings clause anticipated a potential inconsistency between forms of punishment, such as the death penalty and judicial flogging, which were still widely enforced across the region, and the constitutional right not to be subjected to torture or to inhuman or degrading punishment or other treatment. General saving clauses, on the other hand, were intended to afford a measure of stability in the period of transition from colonial rule to independence. Governments in the region needed to be sure that they had some laws in place upon which they could rely as they embarked upon independence. As one of the members of the Joint Select Committee charged with the drafting of Jamaica's Bill of Rights observed: if a saving clause for existing laws were not included, 'our first months of independence (might) … be spent ransacking the body of our existing statutes to determine which have survived and which have not'.[135] The Bills of Rights contained in the Commonwealth Caribbean constitutions were thus intended to guard against the dangers that lay in the future: to prevent the governments of these newly independent countries from infringing the rights that had been enjoyed by their citizens prior to independence. It was not countenanced at the time of independence that their citizens' rights might also be infringed by existing laws or existing forms of punishment.

---

[134] See s 21 Constitution of Belize.

[135] Joint Constitution Committee, *Report of the Sub-Committee on Human Rights* (unpublished) 8. Cited by T Munroe, *The Politics of Constitutional Decolonization: Jamaica 1944–1962* (Mona, Jamaica, Institute of Social and Economic Research, University of the West Indies, 1972) 159.

For the first two decades after independence the leading case on the effect of these savings clauses upon constitutional interpretation was *DPP v Nasralla*.[136] The principal issue in this case was whether the provision on *autrefois acquit* to be found in section 20(8) of the Jamaican Constitution was simply declaratory of the common law or whether it expressed the rule on *autrefois acquit* differently from the common law, and, if so, whether it is the rule as it is expressed in section 20(8) rather than under the common law which should prevail. In the JCPC's view, the answer to this question was to be found in the text of the Constitution itself and, in particular, the inclusion of a general savings clause for existing laws:

> Whereas the general rule, as is to be expected in a Constitution and as is here embodied in section 2 [the supreme law clause], is that the provisions of the Constitution should prevail over other law, an exception is made in Chapter III [the Bill of Rights]. *This Chapter ... proceeds on the presumption that the fundamental rights which it covers are already secured to the people of Jamaica by existing law.* The laws in force are not to be subjected to scrutiny to see whether or not they conform to the precise terms of the protective provisions. The object of these provisions is to ensure that no future enactment shall in any matter which the chapter covers derogate from the rights which at the coming into force of the Constitution, the individual enjoyed (emphasis added).[137]

The effect of the general saving laws clause in the JCPC's view was thus twofold. First, it barred any attempt to challenge the validity of an existing law on the ground that it violated one of the fundamental rights guaranteed by the Constitution. Second, it prevented the court from drawing any distinction between the rights guaranteed by the Constitution and the rights that were guaranteed by the laws in force immediately before independence. The courts were thus required to presume (the '*Nasralla* presumption') that the rights guaranteed by the Constitution were the same as those that were already secured by existing laws. To presume otherwise would mean that pre-independence laws could be adjudged incompatible with the rights guaranteed by the Constitution, and this could lead to the type of legal instability that the inclusion of a general saving laws clause was intended to prevent.

---

[136] *DPP v Nasralla* [1967] 2 AC 238.
[137] Ibid, 24G.

Taken to its logical conclusion, such a presumption results in what has been described in another context as a 'frozen concepts' approach to the interpretation of the Bill of Rights,[138] and for at least the first two decades after independence the *Nasralla* presumption had a profoundly inhibiting effect upon the development of the fundamental rights guarantees of the Independence Constitutions, as the courts insisted that they were merely declaratory of existing common law rights.[139] The high water mark of this approach was the JCPC's decision in *Riley v AG Jamaica*.[140] In this case the JCPC was asked to consider whether a period of prolonged delay in carrying out the execution of a prisoner sentenced to death amounted to a cruel and unusual punishment contrary to section 17(1) of the Jamaican Constitution. The majority considered that the discussion of this issue was effectively precluded by the partial savings clause in section 17(2) of the Constitution. This meant that the appellant could not invoke the protection of section 17(1) unless he could show that the legality of a delayed execution could have been challenged before independence: 'If the like description of punishment had been inflicted in like circumstances before independence, would this have been authorised by the law?'[141] Since the appellant was unable to demonstrate that a delayed execution would have been unlawful prior to independence his appeal failed.

As the dissenting judgment in *Riley* made clear, however, such an approach to the constitutionality of delay in the execution of the death penalty was entirely at odds with the developing jurisprudence of the Supreme Courts of a number of other Commonwealth countries.[142] It was also at odds with the developing jurisprudence of international human rights bodies, such as the European Court of Human Rights (ECtHR), which advocated a 'purposive approach' towards the interpretation of fundamental rights guarantees.[143] As we shall discover, however, it was not long before this purposive approach began to influence the JCPC's approach towards constitutional interpretation.

---

[138]   With reference to s 1 Canadian Bill of Rights 1960. See J Jaconelli, *Enacting a Bill of Rights* (Oxford, Clarendon Press, 1980) 47, 127.

[139]   See, eg, *Hope et Al v New Guyana Co Ltd*, GY 1979 CA 1 (unreported) and *Banton et al v Alcoa Minerals Ltd* (1971) 17 WIR 304.

[140]   *Riley v AG Jamaica* [1983] AC 719.

[141]   Ibid, 726F.

[142]   Eg, *Rajendra Prasad v State of Uttar Pradesh* [1979] 3 SCR 78, 130.

[143]   *Soering v UK* (1989) 11 EHRR 439.

3. The 'Purposive Approach'

The 'purposive approach' requires judges to seek the interpretation that is most appropriate in order to achieve the objective of affording protection of fundamental rights. It also requires judges to interpret fundamental rights guarantees in the light of present day conditions and with regard to developments and commonly accepted standards in other countries. As members of the JCPC became increasingly familiar with the human rights jurisprudence of other courts and of international human rights bodies such as the ECtHR, which favoured a purposive approach, it was inevitable that this would begin to inform their approach towards the interpretation of Commonwealth Caribbean Bills of Rights.

The first appearance of the purposive approach in a Commonwealth Caribbean context (broadly defined) can be traced to Lord Wilberforce's judgment in *Minister of Home Affairs v Fisher*.[144] As Lord Wilberforce explained, the broad and ample style in which the Bills of Rights to be found in Independence Constitutions of the type common in the Commonwealth Caribbean are drafted, laying down principles of width and generality, called for, 'a generous interpretation avoiding what has been called "the austerity of tabulated legalism"', suitable to give individuals the full measure of the fundamental rights and freedoms referred to'.[145] While judges must continue 'to pay respect to the language which has been used and to the traditions and usages which have given meaning to that language and take account of the rules of interpretation where they may apply', they must ultimately 'be guided by the principle of giving full recognition and effect to those fundamental rights and freedoms with a statement of which the Constitution commences'.[146]

4. Tensions between the 'Purposive Approach' and the '*Nasralla* Presumption'

Though it was clearly in accord with developments in human rights jurisprudence elsewhere, the application of the purposive approach in

---

[144] *Minister of Home Affairs v Fisher* [1980] AC 319.
[145] Ibid, 328F–H.
[146] Ibid, 329E–F.

the context of the Commonwealth Caribbean did not sit well with the *Nasralla* presumption. As a result, in the years following *Minister of Home Affairs v Fisher* the tension between the two resulted in the JCPC over-ruling itself on no less than three occasions within the space of a decade; a remarkable record for a final appellate court. On each occasion the central issue was the operation of death penalty regime in the region.

On the first occasion, in *Pratt and Morgan v AG Jamaica*, the JCPC over-ruled its majority judgment in *Riley* by adopting a purposive approach towards the interpretation of the partial saving clause in section 17(2) of the Jamaican Constitution. This meant that section 17(2) was confined to authorising the descriptions of punishment for which a court may pass sentence, and should not, therefore, prevent the court from taking into account prolonged delay in the execution of the sentence in decid-ing whether or not this violated the constitutional guarantee against inhuman or degrading treatment or punishment.

On the second occasion, in *Lewis v AG Jamaica*,[147] the JCPC over-ruled its earlier decisions on no less than three issues. First, it over-ruled its judgments in both *De Freitas v Benny*[148] and *Reckley v Minister of Public Safety and Immigration (No 2)*[149] by holding that a decision about whether or not to exercise the prerogative of mercy was, indeed, justi-ciable. Second, it overruled its earlier judgments in both *Fisher (No 2) v Minister of Public Safety and Immigration*[150] and *Higgs v Minister of National Security*,[151] wherein it had been held that a condemned prisoner did not have a constitutional right to await the outcome of their petition to an international human rights body before they were executed. Adopting a purposive approach to the interpretation of the right to the protection of the law guaranteed by section 13 of the Jamaican Constitution, the JCPC held that this was comprehensive enough to include the right of a condemned prisoner to complete their petition to international human rights bodies before the decision whether the prisoner was to be executed was taken. Third, it overruled its earlier judgment in *Thomas v Baptiste*,[152] by holding that a purposive approach towards the interpretation

---

[147] *Lewis v AG Jamaica* [2000] 3 WLR 1785.
[148] *De Freitas v Benny* [1976] AC 239.
[149] *Reckley v Minister of Public Safety and Immigration (No 2)* [1996] AC 527.
[150] *Fisher (No 2) v Minister of Public Safety and Immigration* [2000] 1 AC 434.
[151] *Higgs v Minister of National Security* [2000] 2 AC 228.
[152] *Thomas v Baptiste* [2000] 2 AC 1.

of the right not to be subject to inhuman or degrading treatment or punishment meant that the conditions in which a condemned prisoner was being held could be taken into account in deciding whether or not to commute the death sentence.

The third and most recent occasion on which the JCPC overruled itself was in *Boyce and Joseph v AG Barbados*.[153] In this case an enlarged panel of seven members of the JCPC overruled, by the narrowest of majorities, its judgment in *Roodal v The State*,[154] delivered only six months earlier, by holding that the mandatory death penalty for murder, being an existing law, was saved from constitutional challenge by the general savings clause in the Constitution of Barbados.

The impact of this body of jurisprudence on the operation of the death penalty in the region cannot be overestimated.[155] As a result of the decision in *Pratt and Morgan* alone, Jamaica was obliged to commute the sentences of 105 prisoners who had already been on death row for five years, while Trinidad commuted the sentences of 53 death row prisoners and Barbados commuted nine death sentences.[156] Furthermore, fearing that the delay in processing appeals to international human rights bodies made it impossible to abide by the five-year deadline laid down in *Pratt and Morgan*, and would require them to commute the sentences of even more prisoners, a number of governments in the region denounced the right of appeal to such bodies in death penalty cases. The Government of Jamaica was the first to denounce the right of appeal in 1997, followed shortly afterwards by the Government of Trinidad in 1998. Indeed, the Government of Trinidad went a stage further by denouncing the Inter-American Convention on Human Rights in its entirety and withdrawing from the Protocol to the International Covenant on Civil and Political Rights allowing petitions to the Human Rights Committee.[157]

---

[153] *Boyce and Joseph v AG Barbados* [2004] UKPC 32.

[154] *Roodal v The State* [2003] UKPC 78.

[155] See LR Helfer, 'Overlegalizing Human Rights: International Relations Theory and the Commonwealth Caribbean Backlash against Human Rights Regimes' (2002) 102 *Columbia Law Review* 1832.

[156] D Simmons, 'Judicial Legislation for the Commonwealth Caribbean: The Death Penalty, Delay and the Judicial Committee of the Privy Council' (1998) 3 *Caribbean Law Bulletin* 1, 6.

[157] See G McGrory, 'Reservations of Virtue? Lessons from Trinidad and Tobago's Reservation to the First Optional Protocol' (2001) 23(3) *Human Rights Quarterly* 769–826.

5. Whither Savings Clauses?

In *Lambert Watson v R*,[158] in which the JCPC considered the constitutionality of Jamaica's mandatory death penalty legislation, Lord Hope chastised a number of his colleagues for seeking to devise ever more formalistic and ingenious ways of transcending the effect of the saving clauses to be found in Commonwealth Caribbean constitutions in order to promote a purposive approach to constitutional interpretation. In Lord Hope's view, the solution to the jurisprudential difficulties presented by the savings clauses lay not with the courts, but with the region's parliaments, which have the power to amend their constitutions to remove them, if they so wish.[159] However, if Lord Hope thought that the region's governments might be prompted by his remarks to take action to remove the savings clause from their constitutions he was, sadly, mistaken. On the contrary, a number of governments in the region, provoked by the JCPC's jurisprudence in cases such as *Pratt and Morgan* and *Lewis*, have instead sought to circumvent the restrictions imposed by the JCPC on the operation of the death penalty by amending their constitutions to reinforce the effect of the savings clauses.

Thus, in 2002, the Constitution of Barbados was amended to ensure that those prisoners who had been sentenced to a mandatory death penalty and who had suffered delay in the carrying out of their execution, or who had been held in inhuman or degrading prison conditions, would not be able to mount a constitutional challenge on the ground that their right not to be subject to torture or inhuman or degrading treatment or punishment had been violated.[160] Jamaica followed suit, and in 2011 amended its Constitution along similar lines.[161] The Government of Trinidad also sought and narrowly failed to secure an amendment to its Constitution,[162] which would have gone even further by additionally precluding a constitutional challenge on the ground that the warrant for the execution of the sentence of death had been read to the condemned man on more than one occasion.

[158] *Lambert Watson v R* [2004] UKPC 32.
[159] Ibid, [54].
[160] Constitution (Amendment) Act 2002.
[161] Charter of Fundamental Rights and Freedoms (Constitutional Amendment) Act 2010.
[162] Trinidad Constitution (Amendment) (Capital Offences) Bill 2011.

The inclusion of general saving clauses in the original Independence Constitutions may arguably have been justified by the need for legal stability during the transition from colonial rule to independence. However, the more recent efforts of the region's governments to amend their constitutions to reinforce the effect of these savings clauses clearly has nothing to do with legal stability and everything to do with their determination to place the laws surrounding the death penalty absolutely beyond the reach of constitutional review. Moreover, this profoundly anti-constitutional tendency is not limited to the laws surrounding the death penalty. Jamaica's new Charter of Fundamental Rights and Freedoms (the Charter), for example, which replaces the original Bill of Rights in its entirety, also contains saving clauses for laws relating to obscene publications, abortion and sexual offences. The last-mentioned reflects the widespread condemnation of homosexuality both in Jamaica and the wider Caribbean,[163] and is clearly intended to ensure that the laws criminalising homosexuality cannot be challenged on the grounds that they interfere with any of the rights contained in the Charter.

CONCLUSION

The principle of constitutionalism requires judges to play a crucial role in ensuring that the executive and the legislature do not exceed the limits imposed upon them by the Constitution. In order to defend against the temptation for politicians to subvert this principle for partisan political gains, Commonwealth Caribbean constitutions contain a number of 'prophylactic devices'[164] designed to minimise the scope for political influence in the appointment and removal of judges, and in the determination of their terms and conditions of service. We have seen, however, that despite the inclusion of these prophylactic devices there is widespread concern, at both the national and sub-regional levels, about the scope for interference by the executive both in the appointments process and in decisions about whether or not to extend a judge's

---

[163] See O Bowcott and M Wolfe-Robinson, 'Gay Jamaicans launch legal action over island's homophobic laws', *The Guardian* (London, 26 October 2012).

[164] A term coined by Ryan, above (n 15) 11.

tenure when he or she reaches retirement age. Though there may be less scope for interference in the removal of senior judges, which in most cases still needs to be approved by the JCPC, we have seen how in the case of the attempt to remove the Chief Justice of Trinidad even this safeguard was not sufficient to prevent the process from being contaminated by the political and ethnic divisions within that country.

We have also seen that there are numerous ways in which the executive can seek indirectly to influence the judiciary: for example, the offer or denial of privileges that lie outside their standard terms and conditions of service; the excessive oversight of judicial administration, as is alleged to have occurred in Trinidad under the United National Congress administration; and the blatant disregard for the principle of the separation of powers between the executive and judiciary, as occurred in Guyana during the Burnham era. In contrast to the above, every effort has been made when establishing the CCJ to secure its financial independence by means of a trust fund and to insulate its appointments process as far as possible from political influence, by assigning responsibility for the appointment of all its judges, apart from the President, to the RJLSC from which politicians are entirely excluded.

Notwithstanding the various encroachments upon the independence of the judiciary that we have considered in this chapter, we have also seen how the judges, for their part, have sought to develop principles of constitutional review which respect the requirements of inter-institutional comity between the respective branches of government. In the context of the Commonwealth Caribbean this process has, however, been complicated by two linked factors. The first is having its final appellate court located outwith the region and populated by judges with no real connection to the countries over which they are exercising jurisdiction. The second is the inclusion in most constitutions of partial or general saving clauses and the presumption implicit in such clauses—the *Nasralla* presumption—which is entirely at odds with the purposive approach to constitutional interpretation favoured by many of the judges of the JCPC. From a human rights perspective the purposive approach has, undoubtedly, had a beneficial effect in so far as it has more or less brought to a halt the implementation of the death penalty in the region. However, an unintended consequence of the purposive approach, which is much less beneficial from a human rights perspective, has been the denunciation by the governments of a number of countries of their obligations under various international human rights treaties and the amendment of a number of constitutions in order to curtail the courts' powers of constitutional review. The end result of the purposive approach has thus been, somewhat ironically, the gradual undermining in certain countries in the region of two of the basic tents of constitutionalism: the supremacy of the Constitution and the protection afforded by the courts against abuse of power by the State.

FURTHER READING

RM Antoine, *Commonwealth Caribbean Law and Legal Systems*, 2nd edn (Oxford, Routledge-Cavendish, 2008).

M De Merieux, *Fundamental Rights in the Commonwealth Caribbean* (University of the West Indies, Faculty of Law Library, 1992).

LR Helfer, 'Overlegalizing Human Rights: International Relations Theory and the Commonwealth Caribbean Backlash against Human Rights Regimes (2002) 102 *Columbia Law Review* 1832.

R James and H Lutchman, *Law and the Political Environment in Guyana* (Georgetown, Guyana, Institute of Development Studies, University of Guyana, 1984).

K Malleson, 'Promoting Judicial Independence in the International Courts: Lessons from the Caribbean' (2009) 58 *International & Comparative Law Quarterly* 671.

S McIntosh, *Caribbean Constitutional Reform: Rethinking the West Indian Polity* (Kingston, Jamaica, Caribbean Law Publishing Company, 2002).

DE Pollard, *The Caribbean Court of Justice: Closing the Circle of Independence* (Kingston, Jamaica, Caribbean Law Publishing Company, 2004).

S Ryan, *The Judiciary and Governance in the Caribbean* (St Augustine, Trinidad, Sir Arthur Lewis Institute of Social and Economic Studies, University of the West Indies, 2001).

Report of the West Indian Commission, *Time for Action*, 2nd edn (Kingston, University of the West Indies Press, 1993).

7

The Constitutional Implications of Regional Economic Integration

---

Background – Institutional Structure of CARICOM, Mode of Governance and the 'Original' Jurisdiction of the Caribbean Court of Justice (CCJ) – The Organisation of Eastern Caribbean States (OECS) – Conclusion

PART I: BACKGROUND

IT IS DIFFICULT at this distance of time to fully appreciate the immense sense of shock and disappointment that accompanied the collapse of the West Indies Federation (WIF) in 1962. Sir Grantley Adams, the former Premier of the WIF, described it as 'a shattering blow ... fatal to the idea of West Indian Unity';[1] while the noted Caribbean economist, Norman Girvan, then an undergraduate at the University of the West Indies, spoke of 'the feeling that a whole world had collapsed'.[2] Certainly, with the dismantling of the WIF in 1962, the idea of establishing some form of *political* union between Britain's Caribbean territories was effectively dead in the water. The idea of proceeding with some form of *economic* union, however, had already been hinted at in the announcement by Eric Williams that Trinidad's withdrawal from the WIF was 'without prejudice to the future establishment of a Common Economic Community embracing the entire Caribbean area'.[3] Though Williams's vision of establishing a pan-Caribbean

---

[1] *Sunday Guardian* (Barbados, 3 June 1962) quoted by E Wallace, *The British Caribbean: From the Decline of Colonialism to the End of Federation* (Toronto, University of Toronto Press, 1977) 21.

[2] N Girvan, 'West Indian Unity', *New World Fortnightly* No 45 (8 August 1966) 11.

[3] E Williams, *The Nation*, vol 4(16) (15 January 1962).

Economic Community—embracing not only the British Caribbean territories but also the French and Dutch colonies in the region—was ultimately never realised, the seeds which he had sown were shortly to bear fruit, in July 1965, when the Governments of Barbados and British Guiana (now Guyana) announced their intention to create a free trade area by establishing a Caribbean Free Trade Association (CARIFTA). They were joined soon thereafter by Trinidad and the remaining British territories (with the exception of the Bahamas): Antigua, British Honduras (now Belize), Dominica, Grenada, Jamaica, Montserrat, St Kitts, St Lucia and St Vincent.

Eight years later, in 1973, the Caribbean Community and Common Market (CARICOM) was established by the Treaty of Chaguaramas (ToC) with the aim, inter alia, of creating a common market regime and the strengthening, coordination and regulation of trade and economic relations between the Member States.[4] Parallel to the birth of CARICOM was the creation by the eastern Caribbean islands of the Eastern Caribbean Common Market (ECCM), established by the West Indies Associated States Council of Ministers, in 1968, and subsequently transformed by the West Indies Associated States (WISA) in 1981, into the Organisation of Eastern Caribbean States (OECS) under the Treaty of Basseterre (ToB), with aims very similar to those of CARICOM. The OECS Member States are comprised of Antigua, Dominica, Grenada, Montserrat, St Kitts, St Lucia and St Vincent.

While there were a number of factors which contributed to the emergence of the economic integration movement in the region in the 1960s, one of the most potent was the continuing reliance by countries in the region, even after independence, upon the preferential treatment afforded to their exports by Britain and the threat posed by the latter's accession to the European Community. If successful, this could have meant that they would have had to compete on equal terms with the other Member States of the European Community (now the European Union (EU)) for access to the British market. In the face of this threat it was believed that it was only by forming an economic community and negotiating as a unified bloc that Commonwealth Caribbean countries could obtain the best terms for their exports to Britain and to other European Community countries. The birth of CARICOM was, however, not only a reaction to the challenges presented by Britain's

---

[4] Art 4, Treaty of Chaguaramas (ToC).

accession to the European Community, it was also a product of the perceived success of the latter which, it was hoped, could be replicated by the countries of the Commonwealth Caribbean by the creation of a common market for their goods, services and capital.

In this chapter I wish to consider the constitutional implications of the creation of both these regional integration organisations—CARICOM and the OECS—and the impact that membership of these organisations has had on the legal orders of their Member States. For the reasons which I explore in part II, membership of CARICOM has, up until now, had nothing like the degree of impact that membership of the EU has had on the legal orders of its Member States. However, this may be about to change following the decision of the Heads of Government to move to the next level of economic integration with the introduction of the Caribbean Single Market and Economy (CSME), in 2006, under the Revised Treaty of Chaguaramas (RTC), and the vesting of the Caribbean Court of Justice (CCJ) with an original jurisdiction to interpret and apply the RTC. This is separate and distinct from the CCJ's appellate jurisdiction to hear civil and criminal appeals and appeals on constitutional matters, which was discussed in chapter six. In part III, I will seek to compare and contrast the position of the Member States of CARICOM with that of the Member States of the OECS, which were in many respects already in a more advanced state of economic integration than CARICOM, but which in 2010 went even further down the path towards integration by establishing an Economic Union under the Revised Treaty of Basseterre (RTB).[5]

PART II: INSTITUTIONAL STRUCTURE OF CARICOM, MODE OF GOVERNANCE AND THE 'ORIGINAL' JURISDICTION OF THE CARIBBEAN COURT OF JUSTICE (CCJ)

The distinctive nature of the institutional structure established by the ToC has to be viewed in the context of the political environment out of which the economic integration movement emerged after the collapse of the WIF (discussed in chapter one). While the federal experience had arguably paved the way for economic integration in so far as

---

[5] Ratified on 18 June 2010.

it had encouraged the region's political leaders to meet regularly, had acquainted them at least, with the idea of a customs union, and had been accompanied by functional cooperation in a number of key areas,[6] it had also left them highly sceptical about any form of *political* union. They had briefly experienced the effects of political union as a result of their membership of the WIF, and two of its leading members, Jamaica and Trinidad, had made it abundantly clear that they wanted no further part in it. The struggle for independence and self-government, which had coincided with the establishment of the WIF, had also left the region's political leaders with 'an intense concern for constitutional form and the exact location of authority';[7] island self-government had become 'the kernel of the political culture of the region'.[8] This was reflected in the determination of the Heads of Government that cooperation in the pursuit of economic integration and the creation of a common market should not in any way encroach upon or limit their recently acquired, sovereign decision-making powers. The Heads of Government thus rejected the supranational tendencies of the European Community, as it then was, in favour of an institutional model based firmly on the principle of intergovernmentalism, ie, one that would involve no delegation of power or 'pooling' of sovereignty. This is manifest in the institutional structure and mode of governance laid down by the ToC, which, subject to the largely cosmetic revisions and modifications introduced subsequently by the RTC, continues to provide the basic organisational framework for CARICOM to this day.

A. ORGANS OF THE COMMUNITY

CARICOM is dominated by two principal organs: the Conference of Heads of Government (the Conference) and the Community Council of Ministers (the Community Council).[9] The Conference is charged with primary responsibility for determining the policy of the Community and can

---

[6] JH Proctor, 'The Functional Approach to Political Union: Lessons from the Effort to Federate the British Caribbean Territories (1956) 10(1) *International Organization* 35.

[7] A Payne, *The Political History of CARICOM* (Kingston, Jamaica, Ian Randle Publishers, 2008) 234.

[8] Ibid, 235.

[9] Art 13, Revised Treaty of Chaguaramas (RTC).

issue policy directives to the other organs and bodies of the Community concerning the policies to be pursued for the achievement of the objectives of the Community.[10] It is also responsible for taking 'Decisions' (for the legal status of such Decisions see below) for the purpose of establishing the necessary financial arrangements for meeting the expenses of the Community,[11] is the final authority in Decisions affecting the Community's external relations, and can consider and resolve disputes between Member States.[12] To assist the Conference a CARICOM Bureau has been established, consisting of the current chairman and the immediately outgoing and incoming chairmen of the Conference. The Bureau has responsibility for initiating proposals for development and approval by the Ministerial Councils (see below), and facilitating implementation of Community Council Decisions, both at regional and national levels.[13]

The Community Council, which is composed of 'Ministers responsible for Community Affairs and any other Minister designated by the Member States in their absolute discretion',[14] has primary responsibility for the development of Community strategic planning and coordination in the areas of economic integration, functional cooperation and external relations.[15] It also has responsibility for promoting and monitoring the implementation of Community Council Decisions in Member States as well as receiving and considering allegations of breaches of obligations arising under the RTC.[16]

These two organs are assisted by four Ministerial Councils: the Council for Finance and Planning (COFAP); the Council for Trade and Economic Development (COTED); the Council for Foreign and Community Relations (COFCOR); and the Council for Human and Social Development (COHSOD).[17] Each Ministerial Council is composed of ministers, or alternates designated by each Member State, and is supervised by the Community Council which can approve or amend proposals generated by these bodies.[18]

---

[10] Art 12, paras 1 and 7 RTC.
[11] Ibid, para 4 RTC.
[12] Ibid, para 8 RTC.
[13] Ibid, para 11 RTC.
[14] Art 13, para 1 RTC.
[15] Ibid, para 2 RTC.
[16] Ibid, para 4(d) RTC.
[17] Arts 14, 15, 16 and 17 respectively.
[18] Art 13, para 3(a) RTC.

The main administrative organ of the Community is the Community Secretariat, which is headed by a Secretary General,[19] who is assisted by 'such other staff as the Community may require'.[20] The Secretary General, who is appointed by the Conference, on the recommendation of the Community Council, has a variety of tasks including, inter alia, 'developing, as mandated, Decisions of the competent organs of the Community into implementable proposals',[21] and 'monitoring and reporting on, as mandated, the implementation of Community Decisions'.[22] The Secretariat is responsible, inter alia, for the following: servicing the meetings of the Conference, the Council and the Ministerial Committees; taking appropriate follow-up action on Decisions at such meetings; initiating and carrying out studies related to the objectives of CARICOM; providing services to Member States at their request in respect of matters relating to the achievement of the objectives of the Community; and undertaking any other duties assigned to it by the Conference and other organs and institutions of the Community.[23]

The institutional structure established by the ToC, as revised by the RTC, thus lacks any of the element of supranationality that is such a distinctive feature of the EU. Executive power is located more or less exclusively in the Conference of the Heads of Government, which is the ultimate policy-making body and which can issue directions to the Community Council as to the policy to be pursued. The latter is in turn, a much less powerful institution than the Council of Ministers within the EU, and enjoys none of the legislative and executive powers exercised by that body. Moreover, there is no equivalent within CARICOM of the European Commission. Without wishing to underestimate the important role played by the Secretariat at various times in CARICOM's history,[24] it does not enjoy anything like the resources of the European Commission; nor is it a body independent of the Member States, which can act as a decisive force in the integration process. The Secretariat cannot initiate policy, and while it is responsible for monitoring the implementation of Decisions (see below) of the

---

[19] Appointed by the Conference on the recommendation of the Council of Ministers. Art 24, para 1 RTC.

[20] Art 23, para 2 RTC.

[21] Art 24, para 2(b) RTC.

[22] Ibid, para 2(f) RTC.

[23] Art 25 RTC.

[24] Payne, above (n 7) 206.

competent organs, it cannot take action against Member States which fail to implement such Decisions.[25]

B. MODE OF GOVERNANCE

1. Decision-Making and Voting Procedures

The lack of *supranationality* in the institutional structure of CARICOM is equally absent from its decision-making procedures. Thus, while *Decisions* of the Community Council and the Ministerial Councils may be taken by a qualified majority vote, being not less than three-quarters of the Member States,[26] and *Recommendations* of Community Organs may be made by a majority of two-thirds of the Member States,[27] the latter have no binding force[28] and any Member State may opt out of obligations arising out of the former,[29] subject to the agreement of the Conference and provided that the fundamental objectives of the Treaty are not thereby prejudiced. The RTC does not make it clear who should decide whether the fundamental objectives of the RTC have been prejudiced, but presumably it must be the Conference, since the Conference's agreement is required before a Member State can opt out of its obligations. Article 29 of the RTC further provides that where an issue has been determined by a two-thirds majority of the Member States to be of critical importance to the national well-being of a Member State, Decisions of the Community Council and Ministerial Councils have to be reached by an affirmative vote of all the Member States. Unanimity is also required for Decisions of the highest Community organ—the Conference.[30]

---

[25] For the main functions of the European Commission, see Art 17(1) Treaty on the Functioning of the European Union (TFEU).

[26] Art 29, para 2, RTC.

[27] Art 27, para 6 RTC.

[28] Ibid.

[29] Art 27, para 4, RTC.

[30] Art 28, para 1, RTC.

2. Sources of Law

The RTC is the primary source of CARICOM law. By Article 211 of the RTC Member States and individuals (subject to certain pre-conditions) can bring proceedings before the CCJ against any Member State which is in violation of its obligations under the RTC.

A secondary source of CARICOM law is Decisions of the Conference and it is now clear, following the CCJ's judgment in *Shanique Myrie v Barbados*,[31] that individuals may also bring proceedings before the CCJ against a Member State which is in violation of its obligations arising out of a Decision of the Conference.

In this case the claimant, a Jamaican national, brought proceedings against the Government of Barbados for denying her the right of entry to Barbados pursuant to a Decision of the Heads of Government taken at their 2007 Conference which permitted all CARICOM nationals a right of entry and an automatic six month stay in another Member State. Lawyers for the Government of Barbados had sought to argue that the claimant could not seek to enforce a Decision of the Conference because Article 240(1) RTC provides that Decisions of the Conference and other organs do not create legally binding rights and obligations for the nationals of a Member State unless and until they have been transposed into the municipal law of that Member State.[32] In the CCJ's view, however, this argument was mistaken because it was based on the orthodox dualist approach to international law, which requires the provisions of an international treaty to be incorporated into the domestic law of a State before the treaty can be enforced under the national law of that State. Here, however, the question was not whether the Decision was enforceable at the *domestic* level, but rather whether it was enforceable at the *Community* level. Article 240(1) RTC was concerned exclusively with the creation of rights and obligations at the *domestic* level and their enforceability in *domestic* law. This is why, according to the CCJ, Article 240(2) requires Member States to act expeditiously to give effect to Decisions of the competent Organs and Bodies of the Community in their municipal law. This is reinforced by Article 9, which requires Member States 'to take all appropriate measures, whether general

---

[31] *Shanique Myrie v Barbados.* Unreported. CCJ Application No OA 2 of 2012.
[32] Art 240, para 1 RTC.

or particular, to ensure the carrying out of obligations arising out of the [RTC] or *resulting from Decisions taken by the Organs and Bodies of the Community*' (emphasis added).

To accept the submissions of the Government of Barbados on this issue would, in the CCJ's view, have been a retrograde step and would have meant, effectively, that the States had not progressed beyond the voluntary system that had been in force prior to the CSME. It would also prejudice the attainment of the aims and objectives of the CSME if binding regional Decisions could be invalidated at the Community level by the failure on the part of a particular State to incorporate those Decisions locally. If domestic incorporation were a condition precedent to the creation of Community rights, an anomalous situation could be created in which some Member States had incorporated the decision and others had not. In the CCJ's view:

> This would be untenable as it would destroy the uniformity, certainty and predictability of Community law.

Together, the provisions of the RTC and Decisions of the Conference are an important source of rights for the individuals of Member States. Many of the obligations which the RTC imposes upon Member States are very open-textured, such as the obligation not to discriminate on the grounds of nationality,[33] and to abstain from any measures which could jeopardise the attainment of the objectives of the CSME.[34] There are also wide-ranging prohibitions against imposing restrictions on the right of establishment,[35] the provision of services,[36] and the movement of capital[37] and skilled CARICOM nationals.[38] Moreover, these rights can, as we have seen in the case of *Myrie*, be supplemented by Decisions of the Conference of Heads of Government. There is, therefore, considerable scope for the judges of the CCJ to flesh out and breathe life into these provisions in the exercise of the Court's original jurisdiction, but as the experience of legal integration within the European Union (EU) demonstrates much will depend upon how the CCJ treats the relationship between the RTC and national law.

[33] Art 7 RTC.
[34] Art 9 RTC.
[35] Art 30 RTC.
[36] Art 36 RTC.
[37] Art 41 RTC.
[38] Art 46 RTC.

In the case of the EU, the relationship between the law of the EU and national law was shaped, and ultimately defined, by the European Court of Justice (ECJ) through the development of the twin doctrines of the 'supremacy' of Community (now EU) law and of 'direct effect', both of which proved to be crucial to legal integration within the EU. The doctrine of 'supremacy' meant that wherever there was an inconsistency between EU law and national law the former prevailed. As the ECJ declared in *Costa v ENEL,* this was because

> The executive force of Community law cannot vary from one State to another in deference to subsequent domestic laws, without jeopardizing the attainment of the objectives of the Treaty.[39]

The doctrine of supremacy has been declared to be 'the most important constitutional issue of the community legal order',[40] but it is interdependent on the doctrine of direct effect, which provides that, independently of the legislation of Member States, 'directly effective' EU law confers upon individuals rights which they can enforce before their national courts.[41] It would be difficult to exaggerate the importance of the contribution that the doctrine of direct effect has made to legal integration within the EU. Not only did it shift a great deal of the responsibility for applying EU law to national courts and, to this extent, converted national courts into 'Community courts',[42] but it also offered a positive incentive to individuals to hold the governments of Member States to account for violations of EU law.[43] Moreover, as a result of the preliminary request procedure, which allows a national court to request the ECJ to give a preliminary ruling on the interpretation of the Treaties of the EU where it 'considers that a decision on the question is necessary to enable it to give judgment',[44] the ECJ was provided with a steady supply of cases requiring clarification of important questions of EU law and this, in turn, afforded the ECJ numerous opportunities to expand the scope and reach of EU law. With the benefit of hindsight, it can fairly be said that absent the doctrines of supremacy and *direct* effect it

---

[39]   Case 6/64 [1964] ECR 585.

[40]   P Eleftheriadis, 'Aspects of European Constitutionalism' (1996) 21 *European Law Review,* 34–5.

[41]   Case 26/62 *Van Gend en Loos* [1963] ECR 1, 12.

[42]   Eleftheriadis above n 40.

[43]   A Burley and W Mattli, 'Europe Before the Court: A Political Theory of Legal Integration,' (1993) 47 *International Organization*, 1.

[44]   Art 267 TFEU.

is extremely doubtful that EU law would ever have achieved the degree of penetration into the national legal orders of its Member States which so distinguishes the EU from other international organisations.

For reasons which I will explore in the next section it is unlikely, however, that the RTC will achieve anything like the same degree of penetration into the legal orders of the Member States of CARICOM.

C. ORIGINAL JURISDICTION OF THE CARIBBEAN COURT OF JUSTICE (CCJ)

By virtue of Article 211 of the RTC, the CCJ can hear and determine disputes, including: (a) disputes between Member States; (b) disputes between Member States and the Community; (c) referrals from national courts or tribunals of Member States; and (d) applications by individuals with special leave of the Court. This would appear to correspond in broad terms with the jurisdiction of the ECJ. Thus, Member States can refer a dispute with another Member State to the CCJ. Member States may also refer a dispute with the organs of the Community to the CCJ. In addition, a national court or tribunal can make a referral to the CCJ. The neatness of the identification of the jurisdiction of the CCJ with that of the ECJ is, however, somewhat misleading. On closer inspection it can be seen that the correspondence is not exact and that there are, at least, two important differences which have a bearing on the question of the relationship between the RTC and national law. The first is the entitlement of individuals, with leave of the CCJ, to bring proceedings against a Member State which is in violation of its obligations under the RTC. The second concerns the circumstances in which a national court is required to refer a dispute to the CCJ.

1. Proceedings by Individuals

The importance of individuals to the EU has been emphasised by the ECJ on many occasions, but while it is true that individuals have always been able to challenge acts of EU institutions by bringing proceedings before the ECJ[45] there has, however, been no corresponding right for an individual to bring proceedings directly against a Member State before the ECJ. Instead,

---

[45] Art 263 TFEU.

individuals who wish to complain about breaches of EU law by a Member State have to refer their complaint to the European Commission, which must first try to resolve the complaint by agreement with the Member State concerned and has an absolute discretion whether or not to refer the complaint to the ECJ.[46] Alternatively, as a result of the doctrine of direct effect an individual can seek to enforce those rights which are 'directly effective' under EU law in proceedings before national courts.

By contrast with the position within the EU, under paragraph (d) of Article 211 of the RTC individuals can bring proceedings against Member States directly before the CCJ; subject to the requirement that they must first obtain special leave of the CCJ, which can only be granted if the conditions specified in Article 222 of the RTC are met. These are as follows: first, that the RTC intended that the right or benefit which the applicant is seeking to enforce should 'enure to the benefit' of individuals; second, that the applicant has been prejudiced in respect of the enjoyment of that right; third, that the Member State entitled to espouse the claim in proceedings before the Court has either omitted or declined to espouse the claim, or else has expressly agreed that the applicant may espouse the claim in lieu of the Member State so entitled; and, fourth, that it is in the interests of justice for the applicant to be allowed to espouse the claim.

Fortunately, some light has been shed on these somewhat Byzantine provisions by the CCJ's decision in the case of *Trinidad Cement Ltd and TCL Guyana Incorporated v The Co-operative Republic of Guyana*,[47] which was the first case to be determined by the CCJ in the exercise of its original jurisdiction. In this case, the Government of Guyana sought to oppose the grant of special leave to the applicants to bring proceedings against the Government of Guyana for its alleged failure to maintain a Common External Tariff (CET) in respect of the importation of cement from third countries, pursuant to Article 82 of the RTC. Their opposition to the grant of special leave was based on two grounds. First, it was argued that it was important that the right to bring proceedings under the RTC should be restricted to Member States because:

> The bringing of proceedings by one State against another under the Treaty may have serious political implications for the continuation and future of the Community because the Treaty intends that the Contracting Parties operate as joint partners in the Caribbean Community and [CSME]. Only in

[46] Art 258 TFEU.
[47] *Trinidad Cement Ltd and TCL Guyana Incorporated v The Co-operative Republic of Guyana* [2008] CCJ 1 (OJ). Available at: www.caribbeancourtofjustice.org.

the event of a breach of Community obligations of the greatest magnitude is it foreseeable that such proceedings would be contemplated by one State against another.[48]

The CCJ, however, rejected this argument, in a passage that is highly evocative of the ECJ's reference in *Van Gend en Loos* to the Preamble to the EU's founding Treaty—the Treaty of Rome:

> From ... the Preamble one deduces that, in an age of liberalisation and globalisation, the Contracting Parties are intent on transforming the CARICOM sub-region into a viable collectivity of States for the sustainable economic and social development of their peoples: that the CSME is regarded as an appropriate framework or vehicle for achieving this end and that *private entities .... are to play a major role in fulfilling the object and goals of the RTC*. The CSME is intended to be private sector driven (emphasis added).

Since it was clear from the Preamble that the Member States envisaged that private entities would have an important role to play in achieving the objectives of the RTC, it followed that they should be entitled in their own right to enforce the benefits conferred on them by the RTC.

Second, it was argued by the Guyanese Government that as a result of being registered for business in Guyana the applicants were disqualified from bringing proceedings against the Government of Guyana as their 'state of nationality'. This argument was based on the requirement under paragraph (c) of Article 222 of the RTC that the Member State entitled to espouse the claim in proceedings before the Court must have either omitted or declined to espouse the claim, or else have expressly agreed that the applicant may espouse the claim in lieu of the Member State so entitled. The purpose of this provision, it was submitted, was to protect the right of each Member State always to have the option of itself bringing any proceedings that a private entity might wish to bring; a right which would be defeated if a Member State could be named as a defendant to proceedings brought by a private entity against its state of nationality. In the CCJ's view, however, it had never been the intention of the Heads of Government to prohibit a private entity from bringing proceedings against its own 'state of nationality.' Such a prohibition would inhibit the achievement of the goals of the RTC by impacting on companies who chose to incorporate in an allegedly delinquent Member State. Indeed, the latter could be encouraged to violate the RTC with impunity in circumstances where such persons were the only ones who suffered prejudice.

---

[48] Ibid, [17].

Furthermore, the interpretation of paragraph (c) of Article 222 of the RTC contended for by the Guyanese Government would offend the non-discrimination clause in Article 7 of the RTC, which provides that, 'Within the scope of application of this Treaty and without prejudice to any special provision contained therein, any discrimination on grounds of nationality only shall be prohibited'. If a private entity could not bring proceedings against its state of nationality then they could suffer a severe disadvantage 'on grounds of nationality only'.

The CCJ's judgment in *Trinidad Cement Ltd* sends the clearest possible signal that that the CCJ intends to support the right of individuals to bring proceedings against a Member State, including their own, by adopting a generous and purposive approach to the interpretation of the conditions prescribed by Article 222 of the RTC for the grant of special leave. This was subsequently affirmed by the grant of special leave to the claimant in the *Myrie* case (discussed above) to bring proceedings against the Government of Barbados for the denial of her right to entry to Barbados pursuant to a Decision of the Heads of Government at their 2007 Conference.[49]

The willingness of the CCJ to grant special leave to individuals and businesses to bring proceedings against Member States will undoubtedly have important constitutional implications to the extent that the citizens of Member States can now hold to account the governments of Member States, including their own, for violations of their obligations under the RTC by bringing proceedings before the CCJ. The judgment does not, however, deal with the question of the relationship between the RTC and national law, or the doctrine of direct effect, both of which, we have seen, were crucial to legal integration within the EU. To gain an insight into how the CCJ is likely to approach these questions it is necessary to consider what the judges of the CCJ have said extra-curially about the reference procedure under Article 214 of the RTC.

2. The Reference of Disputes by a National Court under Article 214 of the Revised Treaty of Chaguaramas (RTC)

The circumstances in which a national court may refer questions of interpretation of the RTC to the CCJ are set out in Article 214 of the RTC:

> Where a national court or tribunal which is seised of an issue whose resolution involves a question concerning the interpretation or application of this

---

[49] *Shanique Myrie v Barbados.* Unreported. CCJ Application No OA 2 of 2012.

Treaty the court or tribunal concerned *shall*, if it considers that a decision on the question is necessary to enable it to deliver judgment, refer the question to the [CCJ] before delivering judgment (emphasis added).

While there has, as yet, been no case in which the issue has been argued before the CCJ, it is clear from a number of extra-curial statements which the judges have made since taking office that they do not regard the existence of the referral procedure under Article 214 of the RTC as a good or sufficient reason for following the lead of the ECJ in *Van Gend en Loos* in affirming the direct effect of the RTC. Thus, Justice Nelson has declared, extra-judicially, that:

> Unlike the position in Europe, the direct effect of the [RTC] in conferring rights on Community nationals does not result in Community rights being invoked or enforced in national courts … *National courts have no jurisdiction* (emphasis added).[50]

This is because, the judges have argued, the jurisdiction conferred upon the CCJ by Article 211 of the RTC is 'exclusive'. The use of the word 'shall' in Article 214 of the RTC, accordingly, implies that a referral to the CCJ is obligatory whenever a national court is faced with a question that involves the interpretation or application of the RTC. This, at least, is the gloss that has been put upon Article 214 by Justice de la Bastide (former President of the CCJ):

> An important reinforcement of the *exclusivity* of the Court's jurisdiction is the requirement for referral by the national courts of member states to the CCJ of any question or issue arising in proceedings before these courts which involve interpretation or application of the Treaty. The wording of [Article 214] would seem to make it mandatory for the national court (a) to make the referral in the specified circumstances and (b) to accept and act on the answer which the CCJ provides to the question referred to it (emphasis added).[51]

Thus, one of the principal justifications relied upon by the ECJ in *Van Gend en Loos* for upholding the direct effect of the EC Treaty, namely the existence of a preliminary reference procedure from national courts, appears to carry no weight with the judges of the CCJ. This was perhaps

---

[50] 'The Caribbean Court of Justice and the CARICOM Single Market and Economy' (1 September 2005). Available at: www.caribbeancourtofjustice.org.

[51] 'The Role of the Caribbean Court of Justice in the CARICOM Single Market and Economy', annual dinner of the Georgetown Rotary Club, Georgetown, Guyana (24 February 2007).

predictable given the legal traditions of the majority of the Member States of CARICOM, which subscribe to the dualist principle that rights conferred by international treaties are not enforceable under municipal law unless and until they have been incorporated into municipal law. Objections to the direct effect of the RTC based on the dualist principle ought, however, to disappear now that the majority of Member States have enacted legislation incorporating the RTC into their domestic law; but, as we shall see, this has not occurred.

3. Incorporation of the Revised Treaty of Chaguaramas (RTC)

While the legislation incorporating the RTC in each Member State is not identical in all respects, it does in each case, without exception, provide that the RTC, which is appended as a schedule, 'shall have the force of law'.[52] Furthermore, in the cases of Guyana, Jamaica, St Lucia, St Vincent and Trinidad, the legislation also provides that 'in the event of any inconsistencies between the provisions of this Act and the operation of any other law, the provisions of this Act shall prevail to the extent of the inconsistency'.[53] This would suggest that within the legal orders of these Member States the RTC is *supreme* law and resembles the status of EU law within Britain, following the enactment of the European Communities Act, in 1972, when Britain became a member of the European Community. As Lord Denning observed in *McCarthy's Ltd v Smith*, commenting on the priority given to Community (now EU) law under English law:

> It is given by the European Communities Act 1972. Community law is now part of our law; and wherever there is any inconsistency, Community law has priority. *It is not supplanting English law. It is part of our law* (emphasis added).[54]

It would appear, however, that the CCJ's judges are determined to maintain their *exclusive* jurisdiction over the RTC, even if this means denying individuals the right to invoke the RTC in proceedings before a national court. According to Justice Hayton, the primary purpose of incorporating the RTC into domestic law was not to empower national

---

[52] See, eg, s 3 Caribbean Community Act 2005, Trinidad.
[53] See, eg, s 8 Caribbean Community Act 2005, Trinidad.
[54] *McCarthy's Ltd v Smith* [1979] 3 All ER 325.

courts to give domestic effect to the RTC, but rather to allow them to refer questions of interpretation and application of the RTC to the CCJ, in accordance with Article 214 of the RTC.[55] In Justice Hayton's view, as a result of the *compulsory* and *exclusive* nature of the jurisdiction conferred upon the CCJ by Article 211 of the RTC, there is simply no possibility of national courts being allowed to give domestic effect to the RTC.[56]

The curious effect of this line of reasoning is that even though the RTC has 'the force of law' in the legal systems of those Member States which have enacted the RTC, and has indeed been effectively declared to be the supreme law of Guyana, Jamaica, St Lucia, St Vincent and Trinidad, national courts of these countries are still unable to give effect to the RTC because to do so would be inconsistent with the *exclusive* jurisdiction of the CCJ under Article 211 of the RTC. Furthermore, individuals are unable to invoke, let alone enforce, the RTC before their national courts because Article 214 of the RTC imposes an *obligation* upon national courts to refer questions of interpretation or application of the RTC to the CCJ. I will return in my conclusion to reflect upon how this approach is likely to impact upon legal integration within CARICOM, but first I wish to examine the relationship between OECS law and national law within the Member States of the OECS, which offers an interesting counterpoint to the position within CARICOM.

PART III: THE ORGANISATION OF EASTERN CARIBBEAN STATES (OECS)

Following the withdrawal of Jamaica and Trinidad from the WIF, the remaining territories, which were promptly dubbed the 'Little Eight', informed the Colonial Secretary that they wanted to form a new federation, an Eastern Caribbean Federation (ECF), with a capital in Barbados, and to become independent by January 1963. These islands had shared a long history of administrative and other links as a result of colonial rule and the sense of a distinctive eastern Caribbean identity

---

[55] 'The Role of the Caribbean Court of Justice: An Overview', Conference of Society of Trusts & Estates, Barbados (3 February 2006). Available at: www.caribbeancourtofjustice.org.

[56] Ibid.

had been reinforced by their experience within the WIF. Unfortunately, however, the imbalance in population and wealth among these territories, which had caused many of the WIF's problems, had not disappeared upon its dissolution. There remained important differences of opinion within each of the eastern Caribbean islands about the desirability of federation and, as successive local governments announced their decision not to join the ECF, the British authorities accepted that they would have to find some alternative solution for these remaining territories. Thus, a new form of association between Britain and these territories—'Associated Statehood'—was established under the West Indies Act (WIA) 1967,[57] which was to last until each of the islands attained independence.

It was during this period that a number of the key institutions that would come to underpin the OECS were established. These included: the Eastern Caribbean Currency Authority which, in 1965, replaced the British Currency Board and was vested with responsibility for issuing and regulating the eastern Caribbean Dollar, eventually being transformed into the Eastern Caribbean Central Bank; and the West Indies Associated States Supreme Court, which was established, in 1967, under provisions contained in the WIA 1967, as the superior court of record for all of the islands with Associated State status together with the Crown colonies of Montserrat and the British Virgin Islands,[58] and which eventually became the Eastern Caribbean Supreme Court (ECSC), the name by which it is currently known. Indeed, even before the enactment of the WIA 1967, the Heads of Government had entered into an informal association known as the West Indies Associated States (WISA) Council of Ministers, the most significant achievement of which was the ratification of the Agreement establishing the ECCM in 1968. Ostensibly, the ECCM had broadly the same objectives as CARIFTA—namely, the elimination of trade barriers between Member States and the development of common policies in targeted areas such as agriculture and industry—but its real purpose was to strengthen the negotiating hand of the eastern Caribbean islands (which had been granted formal recognition under CARIFTA as less

---

[57] See further M Broderick, 'Associated Statehood—A New Form of Decolonisation' (1968) 17(2) *International & Comparative Law Quarterly* 368.

[58] Provision was also made for Montserrat and the Virgin Islands to come under its jurisdiction.

developed countries) in order to wring more concessions out of the more developed countries within CARIFTA—Jamaica, Trinidad and Barbados. Membership of the ECCM was the same as that of the WISA Council of Ministers, but the two organisations continued to operate as separate entities, each with their own Secretariat. However, the ToB, which was ratified in 1981, rationalised this structure.

A. THE TREATY OF BASSETERRE (TOB)

Incorporating the Agreement establishing the ECCM, the ToB created a single organisation, bringing together areas of economic cooperation already occurring under the ECCM and cooperation in foreign affairs, which was already occurring, though in a rather limited way, through the WISA Council of Ministers. The main innovation in the ToB was the added emphasis given to the need to harmonise foreign policy and the introduction of mutual defence and security as an additional area of cooperation.[59]

While the ToB expressly recognised the need for closer cooperation between Member States in a number of areas, the institutional structure and mode of governance which it established was, like that of CARICOM, exclusively intergovernmental: there was to be no surrender by the Member States of their sovereign decision-making powers. Executive power was vested in the Authority, comprising the Heads of Government of the Member States, which was the supreme policy-making institution, responsible for the general direction and control of the OECS. Immediately below the Authority were three committees, comprising the ministers responsible for the relevant areas in the governments of the Member States: the Foreign Affairs Committee, which was responsible for the progressive development of OECS foreign policy; the Defence and Security Committee, which was responsible for coordinating the efforts of Member States for collective defence and for the development of close ties among the Member States in matters of external defence and security; and the Economic Affairs Committee, which was responsible for discharging those functions previously undertaken by the Economic Affairs Committee of the ECCM, such as trade and

---

[59] P Lewis, *Surviving Small Size: Regional Integration in Caribbean Ministates* (Barbados, University of the West Indies Press, 2002).

development. The fifth and final institution was the Central Secretariat, which was responsible for the general administration of the OECS.

In keeping with the principle of intergovernmentalism, Decisions of the Authority and other competent institutions required the unanimous approval of all Member States. Furthermore, Decisions of the Authority and other institutions of the OECS were only binding on Member States to the extent that the latter gave a general undertaking to take all appropriate measures to ensure the carrying out of obligations arising under or resulting from Decisions taken by the institutions of the OECS by securing the enactment of such legislation as was necessary to give effect to such Decisions.[60] Within the OECS, there existed no body or mechanism capable of enforcing this undertaking and, as a result, many of the Decisions of the Authority and other institutions were not implemented. This failure to establish an enforcement mechanism under the ToB came in time to be identified as one of the chief obstacles to greater economic integration within the region,[61] and when the decision was taken to establish an Economic Union and a Single Financial and Economic Space it was, accordingly, agreed by the Heads of Government that the institutional structure and mode of governance of OECS should be revised in order to address this 'implementation gap' within OECS Member States.

B. THE REVISED TREATY OF BASSETERRE (RTB)

The single most significant change introduced by the RTB is thus a system for generating secondary OECS law in the areas of 'legislative competence' of the organs of OECS. This is set out in Article 5, paragraph 3, which provides that:

Without prejudice to the generality of the foregoing—

(a)   a full Member State which is independent undertakes to enact the legislation necessary to:

    (i)   delegate to the [OECS] the said Member State's authority to legislate in the areas of competence of the [OECS]; or

---

[60] Art 4, Treaty of Basseterre (ToB).

[61] E Huntley, *The Treaty of Basseterre & OECS Economic Union* at 6. Available at: www.oecs.org.

(ii) receive Acts of the [OECS] made by the OECS Authority, and Regulations and Orders made by the Council of Ministers, from the [OECS] in the areas of competence of the [OECS]

with the intention that the Acts, Regulations and Orders have *direct effect* (author's own emphasis) in the laws of the Member States.

There are, under Article 14, paragraph 1, five main areas of legislative competence: the common market and customs union; monetary policy; trade policy; maritime jurisdiction; and civil aviation. In these areas a Member State is not required to take steps to repeal its existing laws in relation to such matters provided that they are otherwise compatible with the RTB, but must refrain from the date of the RTB from enacting any new legislation in relation to such matters save with the prior approval of the Authority. There are, under Article 14, paragraph 2 an additional three further areas of legislative competence: common commercial policy; environmental policy; and immigration policy, and in these areas Member States reserve their right to legislate 'in relation to those matters within aspects of such policy not pre-empted by any Act of the Organisation'.

In so far as it requires Member States to delegate to the OECS their authority to legislate in the areas of competence outlined above, the RTB has introduced a significant element of supranationality into what was previously an essentially intergovernmental organisation. However, the RTB continues to respect the dualist nature of the legal systems of the Member States by recognising that the Acts, Regulations and Orders generated by the OECS will only have direct effect in the laws of the Member States upon the enactment of a municipal Act to this effect. At present, a draft Bill 'which will implement the [RTB] into the domestic law of the Member States' has been prepared by the OECS Chief Parliamentary Counsel, but is yet to be enacted by all Member States.[62]

The RTB further seeks to define the constitutional relationship between the institutions of the OECS, on the one hand, and the Member States, on the other, by reference to two principles, which are designed to constrain the legislative powers of the Organs of the OECS. In the parlance of the EU these are commonly known as the principles

---

[62] See Communique, 54th Meeting of OECS Authority (23–24 January 2012). Available at: www.oecs.org.

of *subsidiarity* and of *proportionality*. Thus, with regard to the areas of legislative competence listed under Article 14, paragraph 2, the OECS can only enact Acts of the Organisation if and in so far as the objectives of the proposed action cannot, in the opinion of the Authority, be sufficiently achieved by the Member States and can, therefore, by reason of the scale or effects of the proposed action, be better achieved by enacting an Act of the Organisation.

In conjunction with the introduction of a system for generating secondary OECS law four new organs, each involved in different ways with the generation of secondary OECS law, have been introduced into the institutional structure of the OECS by the RTB. First, there is the Council of Ministers, which comprises ministers from each Member State nominated by their Head of Government, which is responsible for considering and reporting to the Authority on recommendations of the Commission (see below) for the making of Acts of the OECS as well as considering and enacting into law 'Regulations' to give effect to Acts of the OECS.[63] Second, alongside the Council of Ministers there is the Economic Affairs Council (EAC), which comprises ministers nominated by the Heads of Government of Member States. The EAC is the principal organ of the Economic Union and is responsible for supervising the application of the Protocol on Economic Union.[64] Third, there is the Assembly, which comprises members elected by representative of the legislatures of the Member States (each full Member State can elect five of its members to the Assembly, representing as nearly as possible the proportion of government and opposition members in the electing parliament). The Assembly is responsible for considering and reporting to the Authority and Council of Ministers on Community law to be enacted by the latter and any other matter referred to the Assembly by the Authority.[65] The first inaugural session of the Assembly took place in August 2012. Finally, there is the Commission, which replaces the Secretariat and is the principal organ responsible for the administration of the OECS. Though its main functions are of an administrative nature, it is also responsible for making recommendations to the Authority on

---

[63] Art 9 RTB.
[64] Art 11 RTB.
[65] Art 10 RTB.

the making of OECS law and providing drafts to be considered before enactment, as well as monitoring the implementation of OECS law.[66]

None of the above bodies, however, have any responsibility for enforcing secondary OECS law or for ensuring that the general undertaking contained in Article 5 paragraphs 1 and 2 is complied with by the Member States. So far as the latter is concerned it would appear that it is up to the Member States themselves to monitor each others' compliance with the RTB and with Decisions of the OECS organs. Thus, by Article 18, where a dispute arises 'regarding the interpretation and application of the [RTB] ', which presumably includes a situation where a Member State is failing to comply with its obligations under the RTB, an eligible party, which term includes both full and associate Member States but not individuals or businesses, can invoke the dispute settlement procedures under the Annex on Settlement of Disputes. If a dispute has not been settled by any of the available dispute settlement procedures listed in the Annex, which include good offices, consultation, conciliation and arbitration, any eligible party can request adjudication of the dispute by the Eastern Caribbean Court of Appeal (ECCA) and a decision of the ECCA is binding upon the parties to the case.[67] This is known as the 'treaty jurisdiction' of the ECCA and is additional to its jurisdiction as the High Court and Court of Appeal of the Member States of the OECS. This is, undoubtedly, a significant advance on the dispute settlement procedure under the ToB, which relied on a Conciliation Commission, empowered to prepare a report for the Director-General of the Central Secretariat containing its conclusions 'regarding the facts or questions of law', which was binding upon the parties. There is, however, a danger in relying exclusively upon the Member States to police each other's compliance with their obligations under the RTB. Considerations of *realpolitik* mean that the governments of Member States are likely to fear the unpleasantness that might follow the referral of a violation by another Member State to the ECCA. Such fears are encapsulated in the submissions of counsel for the Government of Guyana in the *TCL* case referred to above, where it was argued that the bringing of proceedings by one Member State against another under the RTC could have serious political implications for the continuation and future of CARICOM.

---

[66] Art 12 RTB.
[67] Annex on Settlement of Disputes, para 6.3.

So far as secondary OECS law is concerned, the presumption appears to be that once this has been incorporated into the national law of Member States individuals will be able to bring proceedings before the ECSC against any Member State which is alleged to be in breach of secondary OECS law. This has some of the advantages of the EU doctrine of direct effect in the sense that it provides an incentive for individuals or businesses to bring proceedings to enforce secondary OECS law in national courts and converts the latter into 'OECS courts'. However, it also begs the question of how to ensure the uniform and consistent application of secondary OECS law since the RTB lacks an express 'preliminary reference procedure' comparable to Article 222 of the RTC. It is arguable that an express preliminary reference procedure was unnecessary since the ECCA is part of the ECSC, but a decision of the ECSC regarding the interpretation and application of legislation enacted by the competent organs does not appear to fall within the treaty jurisdiction of the ECCA, which is confined to hearing disputes between Member States regarding the interpretation and application of the RTB itself. This means that the ECCA will have to operate a dual jurisdiction: one in respect of the interpretation and application of the RTB (its treaty jurisdiction), and another in respect of cases involving secondary OECS law (its ordinary appellate jurisdiction). It would have been much less confusing if the ECCA's treaty jurisdiction embraced both.

CONCLUSION

As we have seen, economic integration within the EU necessarily entailed a profound impact on the legal orders of its Member States, which were required to accept the supremacy of EU law and to permit individuals to invoke and enforce EU law in proceedings before their national courts even where it was incompatible with national law.

Until recently, the two major economic integration organisations within the region, CARICOM and the OECS, have managed entirely to avoid impinging upon the legal orders of their respective Member States by cleaving to an exclusively intergovernmental model of regional integration. This allowed Member States to cooperate with each other while preserving their autonomy and respected the dualist nature of their legal systems by ensuring that Decisions of the principal organs of their respective regional organisations were not binding under municipal law, unless and until they had been transposed by enactment into the municipal law of the Member States. The reasons for pursuing this model of regional integration are deeply embedded in the region's colonial history, in particular, the ill-fated WIF and the struggle to achieve island self-government. However, this model of regional integration has not been successful in achieving the aims or objectives of either of these integration organisations. They have, accordingly, been obliged more recently to revise their institutional structures and to adopt a more supranational mode of governance, which more closely approximates to the EU model of regional integration.

Within CARICOM this is reflected in the vesting of the CCJ with an original jurisdiction to interpret and apply the RTC as well as the enactment of the RTC into the domestic law of the majority of its Member States. It is doubtful, however, whether this will have anything like the transformative effect upon legal integration within CARICOM that has been attributed to the doctrines of supremacy and direct effect within the EU. For the CCJ to function as an effective vehicle for legal integration it needs to be supplied with a steady flow of applications, which will afford it the opportunities that it needs to expand the reach and scope of the RTC. This is unlikely to occur for three reasons. First, there is no independent body within CARICOM, which is empowered to bring proceedings against delinquent Member States. Second, Member States are unlikely to bring proceedings against each other because of the political fallout that would be likely to ensue from such proceedings. And third, if individuals and businesses are unable to enforce or invoke the RTC in proceedings before their national courts, they may be unwilling to bring a claim before a regional court, the judges and procedures of which are unfamiliar both to them and their lawyers.[68] Underlying all this is the danger that if the governments of Member States do not regard themselves as under the constant threat of enforcement proceedings they will continue to ignore their obligations under the RTC.

The OECS has sought to bridge its own implementation gap by conferring law-making powers upon its principal organs in the designated areas of legislative competence and to provide that laws so enacted by

---

[68] See further, D O'Brien and S Morano-Foadi, 'The Caribbean Court of Justice and Legal Integration within CARICOM: Some Lessons from the European Community' (2009) 8 *Law and Practice of International Courts and Tribunals* 399.

the principal organs will have direct effect in the municipal laws of the Member States. This means that individuals and businesses will be able to enforce secondary OECS law in proceedings before the ECSC and is in addition to the ability of Member States to bring proceedings before the ECCA in connection with any dispute with another Member State regarding the interpretation and application of the RTB itself. However, it remains to be seen whether together these initiatives will be enough to bridge the implementation gap. The experience of other international organisations,[69] including CARICOM, suggests that the occasions on which Member States will be prepared to invoke the treaty jurisdiction of the ECSC against another Member State will be rare. Member States cannot, therefore, be relied upon to serve as effective 'guardians' of the RTB. Nor can individuals and businesses since they only have the right to bring proceedings to enforce secondary OECS law before the ECSC. Thus the implementation gap, at least so far as the RTB is concerned, may remain as difficult to bridge as ever.

FURTHER READING

A Burley and W Mattli, 'Europe before the Court: A Political Theory of Legal Integration' (1993) 47 *International Organization* 1.

P Lewis, *Surviving Small Size: Regional Integration in Caribbean Ministates* (Barbados, University of the West Indies Press, 2002).

D Lowenthal (ed), *The West Indies Federation: Perspectives on a New Nation* (Westport, Connecticut, Greenwood Press, 1976).

D O'Brien and S Morano-Foadi, 'The Caribbean Court of Justice and Legal Integration within CARICOM: Some Lessons from the European Community' (2009) 8 *Law and Practice of International Courts and Tribunals* 399.

A Payne, *The Political History of CARICOM* (Kingston, Jamaica, Ian Randle Publishers, 2008).

---

[69] Eg, the European Community. See R Dehousse, *The European Court of Justice: the Politics of Judicial Integration* (Basingstoke, Macmillan, 1998) 20.

8

Post-Independence Constitutional Reform

Introduction – The Case for Constitutional Reform – Obstacles to Constitutional Reform – The Jamaica Charter of Rights and Freedoms – Conclusion

PART I: INTRODUCTION

TO THE EXTENT that their Independence Constitutions were not 'autochthonous' it was predicted that Britain's former colonies would take steps quite soon after independence to embody their constitutions and to proclaim their independence by means of an Act of their own sovereign legislatures.[1] It is now, however, almost 50 years since Jamaica and Trinidad and Tobago became the first countries in the Commonwealth Caribbean to achieve independence, and 30 years since St Kitts became the last country to do so, yet in this time only two countries, Trinidad and Guyana, have enacted new constitutions under the authority of their own respective legislatures. This is all the more remarkable when one considers that, by the year 2000, the majority of the 91 countries that emerged into statehood from Western colonial rule in the second half of the twentieth century had rewritten their original constitutions, and in many cases more than once.[2]

This does not mean, however, that there has been a lack of interest in constitutional reform in the Commonwealth Caribbean during this period. Over the last two decades constitutional review commissions have been established in almost every country and a conference

---

[1] K Wheare, *The Constitutional Structure of the Commonwealth* (Oxford, Clarendon Press, 1960) 113.

[2] J Go, 'A Globalizing Constitutionalism? Views from the Postcolony, 1945–2000' (2003) 18 *International Sociology* 71, 71.

on constitutional reform in the region was held in Barbados in 2002, under the auspices of the Organization of American States and the United Nations Development Programme. Yet, for all this activity and rhetoric, there has been relatively little to show in terms of tangible constitutional reforms. Very few of the recommendations of these various constitutional review commissions have been acted upon and those that have been implemented have generally been at the margins of the constitutional text.[3]

In this concluding chapter I will, first, set out the case for constitutional reform. I will then discuss the obstacles, both political and legal, that have tended to inhibit constitutional reform. Finally, I will use the example of the recent introduction of the Jamaican Charter of Rights and Freedoms to illustrate the complex nature of constitutional reform in the region.

PART II: THE CASE FOR CONSTITUTIONAL REFORM

The arguments for constitutional reform within the region tend to fall under two related headings: democratic governance and the legacy of colonial rule.

A. DEMOCRATIC GOVERNANCE

The arguments that fall under this first heading are very much concerned with the need to combat corruption, to stem the tide of apathy which is said to be reflected in the low turn out of voters in elections, to engage citizens more actively in the political process and generally to strengthen and revitalise democracy within the region. As noted in the introduction to this book, there is a widespread perception that the so-called 'Westminster model,' which was inherited upon independence, has failed the region in a number of important respects.[4] As we saw in

---

[3] Z Elkins and T Ginsburg, 'Constitutional Reform in the English-Speaking Caribbean: Challenges and Prospects' (2011) 16. Available at: www.agora-parl.org.

[4] See, eg, C Barrow-Giles, *Regional Trends in Constitutional Developments in the Commonwealth Caribbean* (2010). Available at: www.agora-parl.org/search-resources-

chapter three, it is believed that the 'first past the post' system which, with the exception of Guyana, is the electoral system of choice across the region, has encouraged a 'winner takes all' political culture and that this, in turn, has led to the corruption of public life in general and the emergence of 'clientilism'[5] in a number of countries. We saw too, in chapter four how the tendency of the Westminster model to concentrate power in the executive and, within the executive, in the office of the Prime Minister, has been exacerbated by the very extensive powers of appointment vested in the Prime Minister by the Independence Constitutions, and by the Prime Minister's power to request a dissolution of Parliament at their convenience. This has led, in different countries and at different times, to a highly autocratic style of government. Finally, we saw in chapter five how the small size of local legislatures and their dominance by government ministers means that they are often weak and ineffectual, being unable to provide the check upon executive power that is—in theory at least—such a crucial element of the Westminster model.

In response to these criticisms, the constitutional review commissions that have been established across the region in the last two decades have made a number of far-reaching recommendations for reform of the Westminster model. While it is difficult to generalise about these, certain common themes do emerge. The first is a call to limit the Prime Minister's powers of political patronage when appointing the most senior public officials, including judges. The second is the enhancement of the role of local parliaments in scrutinising the executive by creating parliamentary Select Committees,[6] placing a cap on the number of ministers in the legislature,[7] changing the composition of the Senate by limiting the number of senators whom the Prime Minister can

results?combine=trends%20in%20constitutional%20development%20in%20 the%20commonwealth%20caribbean and the report prepared by T Munroe, *Transparency International Country Study Report: Caribbean Composite Study 2004.* Available at: www.transparency.org.

[5] S Ryan, *Winner Takes All: The Westminster Experience in the Caribbean* (Trinidad, University of the West Indies, ISER, 1999) 317.

[6] See, eg, *Report of the Barbados Constitution Review Commission* (Barbados, Government Printing Department, 1998) 49.

[7] See, eg, *Final Report of the Political Reform Commission of Belize* (2000), para 8.12. Available at: www.ambergriscaye.com.

appoint and, in some cases, even abolishing the Senate altogether.[8] The third is the reform of the electoral process through the introduction of a mixed electoral system, which would include a significant element of proportional representation.

B. THE LEGACY OF COLONIAL RULE

Linked to the need to revitalise democratic governance have been demands to sever the remaining links with the region's colonial past. The arguments that fall under this heading have tended to focus on three areas. The first involves replacing the Queen as head of state. The second involves replacing the Judical Committee of the Privy Council (JCPC) with a regional final court of appeal—the Caribbean Court of Justice (CCJ). The third involves an even more fundamental issue—the demand for the 'patriation' of the Independence Constitutions themselves. This alludes not only to their lack of autochthony, but also to the perception that they were drafted exclusively by British civil servants in Whitehall and then imposed upon Britain's colonies in the region as a condition of being granted independence.[9] Though it could be argued that the process of decolonisation was actually a good deal more consensual than this account would suggest,[10] as we saw in chapter one the circumstances in which a number of the Independence Constitutions were drafted were not always ideal. Trevor Munroe, for example, who has written extensively about the drafting of Jamaica's Independence Constitution, argues that the process was fatally compromised by the haste with which the draft Constitution was prepared, by the very limited public consultation which took place and by the eagerness of those responsible for drafting the Independence Constitution to replicate the model of government inherited from the former colonial power, rather than seizing upon independence as an opportunity to mark a

---

[8] See, ibid, para 9.3.

[9] Barrow-Giles, above (n 4).

[10] H Johnson, 'The British Caribbean from Demobilization to Constitutional Decolonization' in WR Louis and J Brown (eds), *Oxford History of the British Empire Vol 4* (Oxford, Oxford University Press, 2001) 620.

definite break with the past by rejecting the symbols and institutions of colonialism.[11]

As a result, a compelling narrative has subsequently emerged in which the Independence Constitutions have been presented as the product of an oligarchic, elitist exercise, rather than the 'collective self'; as 'received instruments from former colonial masters',[12] imposed from without and, therefore, lacking legitimacy. Hence, the pressing need for the Independence Constitutions to be 'patriated'. As the report of the Constitution Review Commission of Barbados explains:

> The patriation of the Barbados Constitution is both an emotional and a legal issue. In relation to the first issue, the people of Barbados in their submission to us made clear their deep feeling that our Supreme Law has to be, in every sense of the word indigenous and autonomous. There is undoubted consensus that the Constitution should be a product of the Barbados Parliament and completely Barbadian. This would rid our Supreme and basic Law of any trace of the colonial format, remove any possible judicial or theoretical doubt about the power of the British Parliament to legislate further in relation to the Barbados Constitution and clearly signal that we are in all respects 'firm craftsmen of our fate'.[13]

PART III: OBSTACLES TO CONSTITUTIONAL REFORM

While the recommendations of the various constitutional review commissions have led to some important reforms they have tended to be of a somewhat piecemeal nature: such as, limiting the number of terms a Prime Minister can remain in office;[14] providing that if a member of the House of Representatives crosses the floor their seat shall be declared vacant;[15] or reforming the composition of the Electoral Commission.[16] There has thus been no 'root and branch' reform of the Westminster

---

[11] Munroe, above (n 4).

[12] S McIntosh, *Caribbean Constitutional Reform, Rethinking the West Indian Polity* (Kingston, Jamaica, Caribbean Law Publishing Company, 2002).

[13] *Report of the Barbados Constitution Review Commission*, above (n 6) para 2.3.

[14] Eg, Belize Constitution (Sixth Amendment) Act 2008.

[15] Eg, Belize Constitution (Second Amendment) Act 2001.

[16] Antigua Representation of the People (Amendment) Act 2001.

model. For example, there has, as yet, been no switch to unicameralism in those countries with upper and lower Houses of Parliament, and the first past the post electoral system continues to be the system of choice across the region.

More progress has been made in eradicating the surviving symbols of colonial rule, but even this has been somewhat uneven. Thus, we have seen that since being granted independence only two countries in the region have amended their Constitutions to become republics: Guyana, in 1970 and Trinidad, in 1976; Dominica having been a republic from the outset. To date, no other country in the region has managed to amend its Constitution to become a republic, though such has been the recommendation of every constitutional review commission that has taken place in the region within the last two decades, with one exception. The exception is the Political Reform Commission of Belize, which reported in 2000, and which was unable to arrive at a majority recommendation on the issue, but this can, in large part, be explained by reference to concerns about the security of Belize in relation to Guatemala's claims over Belize and the fear that replacing the British monarch as head of state might decrease Britain's willingness to come to the aid of Belize in the event of an invasion from Guatemala. Trinidad and Guyana also continue to remain the only countries in the region to have patriated their Constitutions since becoming independent. But most surprisingly of all, in view of the support that the CCJ received from all but one of the Heads of Government in the region at the time of its establishment, only two countries—Barbados and Belize—have replaced the JCPC with the CCJ as their final court of appeal, Guyana having abolished the right of appeal to the JCPC when it became a republic in 1970.

There are several possible explanations for this relative constitutional inertia. First and foremost is, as we have seen, that all the reforms outlined above would, at the very least, require a special majority in one or both Houses of Parliament to bring about the necessary amendments to the Constitution. In most cases, a majority of votes in a referendum would also be required. When Guyana amended its Constitution to become a republic in 1970 it was able to do so by means of a simple majority as a result of the inclusion of a clause allowing for this in its Independence Constitution.[17] Elsewhere, however, special majorities

---

[17] Art 73(5) Constitution of Guyana.

have been difficult to achieve, especially when the issue of constitutional reform has been exploited for political point-scoring between rival political parties. The classic example of this has been the uneven progress that has been made in replacing the JCPC with the CCJ. The requirement of a special majority has allowed opposition parties, even if they were in favour of the CCJ when in government, to block any proposal to amend the Constitution to provide for a right of appeal to the CCJ as a way of frustrating the political programme of the governing party.[18] On other occasions, proposals for constitutional reform have been reduced to a form of horse-trading between political parties. Thus, in Trinidad, in 2009, the opposition United National Congress made it clear that they would only support the governing People's National Movement's (PNM) proposal to abandon the Westminster model in favour of an executive presidency in return for the introduction of an electoral system based on proportional representation.

A second reason for this relative constitutional inertia has been a general lack of appetite for constitutional reform outside the political class. While the various constitutional review commissions have been careful not to make the same mistake as those that drafted the Independence Constitutions and have consulted as widely as possible, the public have not always been persuaded of the need for constitutional reform, as vividly demonstrated by the citizens of St Vincent when asked to vote in the referendum on constitutional reform in November 2009.

This referendum was the culmination of a process which had been initiated by the Unity Labour Party Government led by Prime Minister, Ralph Gonsalves, and which began in 2003 with the appointment of a Constitutional Review Commission (CRC). The CRC was composed of 25 people from a cross-section of the political, social and legal community (including the diaspora) and was part funded by both the Organization of American States and the United Nations Development Programme. The process of consultation was a thorough one, with various publications being produced along the way, outlining the options available along with the level of progress achieved, and thus encouraging a significant input from across Vincentian society and the wider diaspora. The final report was published in 2005 and again in revised

---

[18]   As has occurred in Trinidad. See MA Lilla, 'Promoting the Caribbean Court of Justice as the Final Court of Appeal for States of the Caribbean Community' (2008). Available at: www.ncsc.org.

form in 2006. It was comprehensive and recommended a number of major reforms to the country's Constitution and political system, including: removal of the British monarch as head of state; reform of the legislature and the electoral system; reform of the executive and its relationship with the bureaucracy; and a host of other measures related to combating corruption. Once the draft Constitution was finalised 15,000 copies of it were printed and distributed cheaply to ensure that most people in the country—of approximately 30,000 households—would have access to it. This was accompanied by numerous town hall meetings where the Drafting Committee, along with members of the Constitutional Reform Steering Committee—a slimmed-down version of the CRC—and Government, discussed the process with the wider population, all then broadcast live on national radio, continuing the pattern of television and radio coverage that had accompanied many of the parliamentary debates on the subject.[19] In the end, however, all this deliberation and consultation with the citizens of St Vincent ultimately came to nothing as it failed to persuade a sufficient majority of them of the need for constitutional reform, and the Constitutional Reform Bill was, ultimately, rejected by 55 per cent of voters in the referendum.

A third possible reason for this relative constituional inertia is the absence of a necessary catalyst, such as a major political crisis, which would galvanise politicians into action. Thus, for example, it is arguable that the 1976 reforms to the Constitution of Trinidad were in direct response to the emergence of the black power movement in the late 1960s and early 1970s and the threat that it posed to the PNM's hegemony.[20] Elsewhere in the region the post-independence period has generally been characterised by its relative political stability, which has made it correspondingly harder to persuade the region's politicians to discard, or to undertake major reform of, a model which for all its manifest deficiencies has secured this political stability. Certainly, the two examples of countries in the region that have rejected the Westminster

---

[19] For a more detailed account of the events leading up to the referendum, see ML Bishop, 'Slaying the "Westmonster" in the Caribbean? Constitutional Reform in St Vincent and the Grenadines' (2011) 13 *British Journal of Politics and International Relations* 420–37.

[20] Constitution Commission of Trinidad and Tobago, *Report of the Constitution Commission* (Port of Spain, 1974). Available at: www.ttparliament.org.

model—Guyana and Grenada (albeit temporarily)—have not inspired their neighbours to follow suit.

PART IV: THE JAMAICA CHARTER OF RIGHTS AND FREEDOMS

Against this backdrop the Jamaica Charter of Rights and Freedoms (the Charter) represents something of an anomaly. Even if did take some twenty odd years, two Joint Select Committees, and a Constitution Commission to produce, the Charter is an example of constitutional reform that was not precipitated by a major political crisis, and yet was successful in managing to attract the necessary political consensus to achieve the special majority required for its enactment.

The Charter is, however, a rather curious example of constitutional reform. On the one hand, it contains a number of what might be broadly described as 'progressive' features. For example, it increases the number of protected rights, which now include the right to vote, the right to a healthy and productive environment, the right of every child to free education (at least through to primary level), the right to fair, humane and equal treatment and the right to a passport. It also improves the protection of a number of the existing rights, such as freedom of the person, the right to due process and property rights, while at the same time extending *locus standi*, and removing the immunity from constitutional challenge for Acts of Parliament which have achieved a special majority. On the other hand, it contains a cluster of provisions relating to the death penalty, equality and laws criminalising homosexuality and abortion, which are profoundly reactionary, not only maintaining the status quo, but actively entrenching it. Thus, for example, section 13(8) of the Charter provides that neither inordinate delay nor the conditions in which a condemned man is detained, no matter how inhumane, will be sufficient grounds to challenge the constitutionality of the execution of a death sentence. Moreover, by virtue of section 13(12) existing laws relating to the sexual offences, including those which criminalise homosexuality and abortion, are rendered immune from constituional challenge, while the equality provisions contained in section 13(3) have been drafted in such a way as to exclude any possibility of sexual orientation being a prohibited ground of discrimination.

It is, at the least, arguable, that it is these more reactionary provisions that contributed to the Charter's success in attracting support across the political spectrum in Jamaica. Because the Charter reflected popular attitudes towards key issues, such as the death penalty, abortion and homosexuality,[21] support for the Charter entailed little political risk for either of the main parties—the Jamaica Labour Party and the People's National Party—who were well aware during the passage of the Bill through Parliament of the concerns of their constituents regarding these issues. By cordoning off the death penalty from judicial scrutiny the Charter also ensures that the Jamaican Parliament and not the judges of the JCPC have the final say about how the death penalty will operate. Thus, at one and the same time, the Charter manages to weaken one of the links with colonial rule, while at the same time avoiding the outright abolition of appeals to the JCPC; an issue which, as we saw in chapter six, has previously proven to be politically toxic. In these circumstances, failure to support the amendments to the Independence Constitution introduced by the Charter carried with it the risk that its opponents could be characterised as being 'soft' on violent crime, or of having neocolonial tendencies, preferring a system of rights protection bequeathed by the former imperial power to something rooted in Jamaican soil and reflecting Jamaican values.

Though it is by far the most successful example, Jamaica, is not the only country to seek to reform its Bill of Rights. As we saw in chapter six, the Constitution of Barbados was amended in 2002 to ensure that those prisoners who had been sentenced to a mandatory death penalty, but who had suffered delay in the carrying out of their execution, or who were held in inhuman or degrading prison conditions, could not mount a constitutional challenge on the grounds that their right not be subject to torture or inhuman or degrading treatment or punishment had been violated.[22] In 2011, the Government of Trinidad sought

---

[21] Jamaican popular culture is imbued with denunciations of same-sex sexuality, as is evidenced by popular dancehall songs advocating violence against gay men, and there are regular reports in the press of members of the gay community being assaulted or killed. See C Nelson, 'Lyrical Assault: Dancehall Versus the Cultural Imperialism of the North-West' (2008) 17 *Southern California Interdisciplinary Law Journal* 231; Human Rights Watch, *Hated to Death: Homophobia, Violence, and Jamaica's HIV/Aids Epidemic* (New York, Human Rights Watch B, 2004).

[22] Barbados Constitution (Amendment) Act 2002.

and narrowly failed to secure an amendment to its Constitution[23] which would have gone even further than this by additionally precluding a constitutional challenge on the ground that the warrant for the execution of the sentence of death had been read to the condemned man on more than one occasion. We also saw in chapter five that the Government of Belize has, albeit unsuccessfully, sought to amend its Constitution to remove the protection of the right to property, under section 17 of the Constitution, to the owners of certain interests in land, and to disapply the 'supreme law' clause of the Constitution to 'a law to alter any of the provisions of this Constitution which is passed by the National Assembly in conformity with s 69 of the Constitution'.

CONCLUSION

All the Commonwealth Caribbean countries, with the exception of Guyana, have remained remarkably faithful to the Westminster model of government. Almost as enduring as the Westminster model have been those two most visible symbols of colonial rule: the Queen as head of state and the JCPC as the final court of appeal. This relative lack of constitutional reform, which marks the region out from the rest of the postcolonial world where rapid constitutional reform has been taking place, is open to a number of possible interpretations.

On the one hand, it could be argued that it reflects a certain conservatism, a refusal to face up to the challenge of reforming a model of government inherited from the former imperial power that is, in a number of important respects, unsuited to these small developing countries which lack the institutional and economic resources to support such a model. A cynical view might even be that the political elite lack the willpower to reform this system of government because of the extent to which they benefit from the 'winner takes all culture' which it has produced.[24] This has motivated some politicians in their desire to win to 'rig' elections, to seek to evade the courts' jurisdiction to review

[23] Trinidad Constitution (Amendment) (Capital Offences) Bill 2011.
[24] JI Dominguez, 'The Caribbean Question: Why has Liberal Democracy (Surprisingly) Flourished?' in JI Dominguez et al (eds), *Democracy in the Caribbean* (Baltimore, John Hopkins University Press, 1993) 57.

decisions of their Constituency Boundaries Commissions and, in one case, unlawfully to remove the chairman of an Electoral Commission which had invalidated the election results in certain constituencies which had been won by members of the governing party. It has also encouraged Prime Ministers in some countries to make appointments to the most senior public offices based entirely on political loyalty and to undermine the neutrality of their Public Service Commissions. As a result, a number of the institutions that have been established with a view to holding the government to account, such as Integrity Commissions, Auditors General, Public Accounts Committee, have been not capable of discharging their functions effectively.

A more positive interpretation would be that the absence of radical constitutional reform reflects a determination on the part of the region's politicians and its peoples to remain loyal to a set of constitutional principles—the separation of powers, two-party politics, accountable and responsible government, free and fair elections, an independent judiciary and the rule of law—which, for all its manifest deficiencies, are embodied in the Westminster model. This determination is demonstrated in a number of different ways. First, by the efforts to establish Electoral Management Bodies to supervise the conduct of elections and Integrity Commissions which are intended to combat corruption in public life. Second, by the role assigned to the official Opposition which remains enshrined in each of the region's constitutions, even if there have been several instances of the governing party winning all the seats available in an election. Third, the conventions of individual and collective ministerial responsibility are still recognised, in principle, and even if local parliaments are not always able to hold ministers to account there is in most countries a free press which does not shirk from performing this task. Fourth, the privileges of Parliament are still respected by the courts and, whatever the misgivings about the independence of the latter, courts across the region have proved themselves sufficiently independent on numerous occasions to hold both their parliaments and their governments to account if either exceeds the limits imposed upon them by the Constitution. In many ways this apparent determination to remain true to this set of constitutional principles makes it all the more disappointing when governments in the region seek to subvert the tenets of constitutionalism by placing their actions and the laws enacted by local parliaments beyond the reach of constitutional review.

Ultimately, however, whatever interpretation one places on post-independence constitutionalism and, however justified the criticisms of the operation of the Westminster model in the region, the one incontrovertible fact is that successive governments across the region have respected the outcome of elections, notwithstanding the efforts of some politicians to rig those elections.[25] The region has, to this extent at least, passed the 'two-turnover' test identified by Huntington as a measure of consolidated democracy.[26] This is in marked contrast to the postcolonial scene in other regions, Africa for example, where by the end of the 1980s not a single head of state in three decades had allowed themselves to be voted out of office, and where out of a list of 50 countries almost all were one-party states or military dictatorships.[27] Though elections may be only one test of the vitality of a democracy this is no small achievement in a region the constitutional history of which has been disfigured by slavery and its baleful legacy. It also suggests that whatever the challenges that lie ahead for the region as a result of the forces of globalisation and economic pressures, the people's right of self-determination, which is after all at the core of democratic politics, will endure.

FURTHER READING

Z Elkins and T Ginsburg, 'Constitutional Reform in the English-Speaking Caribbean: Challenges and Prospects' (2011) 16.
S McIntosh, *Caribbean Constitutional Reform, Rethinking the West Indian Polity* (Kingston, Jamaica, Caribbean Law Publishing Company, 2002).
S Ryan, *Winner Takes All: The Westminster Experience in the Caribbean* (Trinidad, University of the West Indies, ISER 1999).

---

[25] See HA Ghany, 'The Commonwealth Caribbean: Legislatures and Democracy in NDJ Baldwin (ed), *Legislatures of Small States: A Comparative Study* (Abingdon, Routledge, 2013).

[26] S Huntington, *The Third Wave: Democratization in the Late Twentieth Century* (Norman, University of Oklahoma Press, 1991).

[27] M Meredith, *The State of Africa: A History of Fifty Years of Independence* (London, Free Press, 2005) 378–85.

Index